MW01046104

Land Tenure, Ge~d~ ~ and ~ ~ 'isation

Land Tenure, Gender and Globalisation
Research and Analysis from
Africa, Asia and Latin America

Edited by
Dzodzi Tsikata & Pamela Golah

An imprint of Kali for Women

International Development Research Centre
Ottawa . Cairo . Dakar . Montevideo . Nairobi . New Delhi . Singapore

Land Tenure, Gender and Globalisation
Research and Analysis from Africa, Asia and Latin America
Edited by Dzodzi Tsikata and Pamela Golah

Jointly published (2010) by
ZUBAAN
an imprint of Kali for Women
128 B Shahpur Jat, 1st floor
NEW DELHI 110 049
Email: zubaan@gmail.com and zubaanwbooks@vsnl.net
Website: www.zubaanbooks.com
ISBN 978 81 89884 72 7

and
International Development Research Centre
PO Box 8500, Ottawa, ON KIG 3H9
Canada
info@idrc.ca / www.idrc.ca
ISBN 978-1-55250-463-5 (e-book)

© International Development Research Centre

10 9 8 7 6 5 4 3 2 1

Zubaan is an independent feminist publishing house based in New Delhi with a strong academic and general list. It was set up as an imprint of India's first feminist publishing house, Kali for Women, and carries forward Kali's tradition of publishing world quality books to high editorial and production standards. *Zubaan* means tongue, voice, language, speech in Hindustani. Zubaan is a non-profit publisher, working in the areas of the humanities, social sciences, as well as in fiction, general non-fiction, and books children and for young adults under its Young Zubaan imprint.

Typeset by RECTO Graphics, 432 C, DDA Flats, Gazipur, Delhi 110 096
Printed at Raj Press, R-3 Inderpuri, New Delhi 110 012

Contents

Foreword

ANN WHITEHEAD

Competition and conflict over access and use of land are at a historical peak globally. Demographic growth and urbanisation, running at unprecedented levels, are one set of drivers, but the decades of liberalisation and commitment to market forces, as well as the more recent securitisation of economic objectives have shaped the contours of the scenario that presently prevails. Many regions have been, and are, witnessing new waves of land privatisation in which international actors, national elites and smaller local entrepreneurs are alienating the historical users of land from their own territory. These changes in the social relations of land ownership are accompanied by new uses and new values for the natural resources of the land, in which the newly dispossessed enter into new forms of work and production. Powerful global processes are being experienced locally as a complex combination of innovation, adaptation, resistance and struggle, with gains for some and losses for others.

This book is an important and exciting assessment of some of these issues. It explores the particular characteristics of globalisation at the beginning of the 21st century, especially the diverse changes wrought in the depths of rural areas in many parts of the majority world. Addressing the issues arising from the extensive transformation of rural society and economy across nations is of huge importance to a wide range of actors with deep concerns, who should make reading this book a top priority. Its contributions to a number of broad contemporary debates on the subject are indeed significant:

- the book explores the inter-connectedness of global processes and land tenure, land holding, and land use, a theme recently set aside as focus shifted to trade and economic growth—dominant themes in discussions of global processes.
- it makes an important contribution to the study of globalisation's effects on the social relations and social imaginaries of everyday lives.
- the gendered nature of its analyses points to not only the particular ways in which many other existing inequalities (for example those of class, race and caste) are reproduced and reconstituted, but the important connection of these inequalities with the creation of political subjects and agents who, yes, seek change, but do so within the constraints of powerful economic, political and social relations.

These broader themes are explored in this volume through its central focus on examining how globalisation and the associated changes in land use and tenure are affecting rural women. These processes are understood as mediated by gender relations which are themselves complexly constituted and the subject of re-workings both at the level of the everyday and in widespread political fora.

In its subject matter and approach this volume is a significant and stimulating heir to some of the central themes in contemporary feminist social science. In the 1970s, second wave feminism in Europe was a kaleidoscope of activities that included the formation of many informal study groups, which gradually moved more formally into the academy and became underpinned by the funding of specific programmes of research.

These study groups established a trajectory of ideas and developed skills of argument and analysis that were the foundation for the huge scope of contemporary feminist research. The Gender Unit at IDRC has played an important part recently in the institutional and intellectual foundation for that work in its successive funding of projects for gender research in the developing world and through the specific financial and organisational support being given to gender researchers. This excellent book is a product of some of these investments.

One of the key texts in the hugely formative, but quite short, period of 1970's feminist ferment was Frederick Engel's *The Origin of the Family, Private Property and the State*. The historical range of its theses and the grand vista of its linking of class, property and gender commanded our attention, but all too soon produced critical commentary. Its arguments were too universal, its theses too deterministic, its gender subjects too uni-dimensional, we cried. But what cannot be underestimated is the impetus its rediscovery gave to the study of gendered processes of historical change and of the relation between gender and property and the way it forced us to deepen and sharpen our arguments about what gender is. It also established the centrality of questions about gender to analysis of and theorising about core issues.

This book is influenced by the broad currents in these earlier debates, but it is a book very much of its time—of now. In the late 1960s we were about 25 years away from the ending of the global conflict termed the second world war by imperialist powers. Its legacies in neo-imperialist global conflicts were one of the backdrops to the radical ferments of those times.

The Bretton Woods institutions were only 27 years old and analyses of global relations focused, among other things, on the developing world as a source of extracted minerals and the destination of technology transfer. The language of development and underdevelopment and of cold war blocks and spheres of influence was dominant in discourses on these global relations. They had also begun to be about the countries of the majority world as the recipients of aid.

Thirty-five and more years of continuing financial, economic, political and institutional change on the global stage since then have produced complex, accelerated and arguably radically different processes of globalisation. These processes are well illustrated in the four comparative case studies that are at the heart of this volume. These closely observed and well designed empirical studies in Vietnam,

Cameroon, Ghana and the Amazon forests of Brazil, Bolivia and Peru deal with very different examples of contemporary global processes.

In Vietnam the context is the de-collectivisation of land occurring as part of the shift from a socialist to a market economy. In Cameroon, the study looks at the impacts on the communities along the Chad-Cameroon oil pipeline, which is financed, owned, and operated by a consortium of trans-national companies. In Ghana the studies compare communities newly exploiting small-scale gold resources and mangrove resources as a result of 20 years of national economic liberalisation. The Amazon forest communities are directly engaged with conflicts over resources with capitalist logging, cattle ranching and agri-business. Each example finds significant threats to livelihoods and significant changes in women's access to resources and the basis for their livelihoods.

Comparing the findings of these studies, the introduction to the book argues forcefully that the diversity that is found in the changes in women's relation to land shows how important understanding the particularities of contexts is. Context specific configurations of economic and political interests within nation states, the kinds of integration into markets and the attitudes and aspirations of local communities are all here shown to affect the outcome of particular kinds of changes in land use and ownership.

Nevertheless, the comparisons bring out important general themes both about the nature of contemporary globalisation and the centrality of gender issues to how these are experienced in people's everyday lives. The book shows clearly a theme in the wider literature—namely that market reforms rarely improve women's access to land, but it also shows different kinds of processes in play.

Commercialisation of land and natural resources is in some cases accompanied by a concentration of land in the hands of a much smaller group of men, and women are disproportionately the losers. The promise of changing tenure systems, that they will provide women with opportunities which they have hitherto lacked, is not borne out. In other cases, reforms and commercialisation interact with existing gender inequalities so that again, women cannot benefit.

The book is unusual in that in addition to a very substantial introduction, it contains three other chapters centred on thematic, theoretical, methodological and political reflection and analysis from experts who not only advised the project, but were participating researchers as well. This adds immeasurably to the value of the volume and helps to make the book greater than the sum of its parts.

One of the main initial messages I got from the book was how multifaceted land is. The debates, findings and discussions range over understandings of land variously as:

- Space
- Place
- Commodity
- Capital/assets
- Source of extracted resources
- Basis for livelihood
- Site of belonging
- Basis for citizenship
- Site of struggle
- Foundation for a delicately balanced ecosystem
- Part of the natural world

The authors of the main commentary chapters each have their own specific set of leading interpretations from within this diverse list and some of the value of the format of the volume lies in having these different approaches to land side by side.

A second main message for me, however, was just how contentious the issues are. As the authors make clear, they do not agree on some of the key terms and perspectives. They take, for example, different positions within the widely debated question of what globalisation is, and that too in the ways in which they conceptualise gender. While none of the writers treats gender as the unproblematic existing categories of national data collection and all see gender as fluid and negotiated, the insertion of this messy reality into social relations and social processes is conceptualised very differently within the chapters. Finally, although each author understands their work to reflect a profound political engagement, there are very different emphases on where the political takes place, who are its key actors and the potential for positive change within everyday resistance and in political movements around land.

These well articulated debates, together with the comparative discussions of the findings from the empirical case studies, make this an extremely important study of gender, land and globalisation. It is the book's simultaneous attention to political, economic and social forces that make it stand out. States, markets, communities and human subjects are all central to its analysis. From this point of view the volume has benefited from a lengthy process of writing.

The case studies were undertaken after a research competition in 2001, and completed 2-3 years later. So this volume would normally appear a rather tardy publication, but so much has been added by the scholarly and informed reflection on the set of the case studies, both by the initial researchers and by other academics, that this now appears as a strength.

The publication of the volume now is also very timely. Commercial interests in the extraction of ever more of the earth's resources are leading to increasingly exploitative expropriative activities in many regions. At the same time the effects of climate change are profoundly affecting the land surface and its productivity for agriculture. It is important to re-assert the centrality of gender as we respond to these difficult and challenging processes.

The book does not set out to explore in detail what might be done to prevent the deepening of gender inequities in relation to resources. It points rather to how important it is to examine both the macro and micro politics of response. The work that is begun here shows how significant are the constraints of the powerful economic, political and social relations around land. But it also shows—precisely because access to land and resources is so critical to many everyday lives—how challenges to that access are met with often very powerful and flexible responses of resistance, which often create new gender identities. This book has a part to play in building on these as the current priority for international cooperation and alliance building.

1

Introduction

DZODZI TSIKATA[1]

SETTING THE CONTEXT

The phenomenon of globalisation[2] has, over the years, generated a vast amount of literature wherein certain questions have been debated at length. One of these pertains to whether the phenomenon is essentially economic in nature, that is, involving the globalisation of production, trade and finance and deploying new technologies to great effect (Gills 2002), or whether it is multi-dimensional with economic, technological, cultural and political aspects, each of which can be privileged depending on the subject of discussion (Wanitzek and Woodman 2004). Related to this is the question of how to date globalisation; whether it has been with us since European adventurers sailed round the world in search of precious cargo, or whether it had its beginnings in the 1980s. While there is no simple alignment of positions on these issues—for example those who argue that globalisation is essentially an economic phenomenon are not in agreement as to its starting point—it is possible to discern that discussions which privilege the cultural and technological dimensions tend to focus less on the question of growing inequalities among nations and people, the rising power of trans-national corporations and the loss of sovereign decision-making in national spaces. Instead, they have sought to highlight the shrinking of space and time, the homogenisation of cultures and political systems, the importance of ideas and discourses in shaping the world, the creation of global knowledge systems powered by advances in communication technologies, and the impact of local processes on global developments.

There is also a general dichotomy in the analysis of globalisation's material and ideational elements. As Mackenzie notes in this book, these two elements are both important in the sense of being mutually constitutive. However, it is a challenge to sustain focus on both elements in the same piece of writing. This is also a function of the choice of analytical framework. Much of the literature on the discourses of globalisation is post-structuralist in approach while the analyses of material, particularly economic matters, are often within broadly structuralist frameworks. These questions about the literature are not idle. As Pape notes "how a researcher defines globalization shapes the focus of research and conclusions" (2000, p. 1).

The literature on globalisation also has gaps and silences. Commentators have argued that there has been greater focus on processes and discourses than on impacts (Jaggar 2001). Also, much more has been written on the globalisation of production, trade, investment and finance at national and multi-national levels (Khor 2000; Pearson 2000; Jaggar 2001; Gills 2002; Mcgrew 2000), than at the level of local communities and their members. Furthermore, only a few studies (e.g., Pape 2000; Pearson 2000; Jaggar 2001; and Bee 2002) have paid attention to the gender dimensions of globalisation. There are even fewer studies on the interconnections between globalisation, land tenure and gender (see Razavi 2003 for a seminal collection of articles), and so also on the implications of globalisation for legal systems and particular bodies of law such as land law (Wanitzek and Woodman 2004).

This book is a contribution to the literature on community and gendered experiences of globalisation. Anchored by four case studies located in the Amazon forests of Brazil, Bolivia, Peru (Porro), Cameroon (Endeley), Ghana (Awumbila and Tsikata) and Vietnam (Scott, Bélanger, Nguyen and Khuat), it tackles globalisation as an economic process with material consequences for land tenure systems, people's livelihoods and gender relations. Differences in orientation, approach and position on some of the key issues of globalisation notwithstanding, the case studies together provide theoretical and empirical insights into some of the debates among academics, policy makers and activists.

In the Amazon forests, the focus is on local mobilisation in defence of land and forest resources such as brazil nuts and babaçu palm; this in the face of state policies in support of the global market in logging, cattle ranching, agri-business, and competition from the global vegetable oil and nut industries. In Cameroon, the study focuses on the recently constructed Chad-Cameroon oil pipeline—financed, owned and operated by a consortium of trans-national corporations—exploring its implications for gendered land tenure regimes in the communities along the pipeline. The Ghana study explores the implications of over two decades of economic liberalisation for land-based livelihood activities in two rural communities—one involved in small-scale gold mining and the other in mangrove resource exploitation. In Vietnam, researchers explore agrarian transitions taking place in the context of a major shift from a socialist to market economy and the de-collectivisation of land. The study examines how the changes in the land tenure systems in communities in North and South Vietnam have interacted with kinship arrangements to affect women's land tenure interests.

Each of the four cases explores the relationship between land tenure and local people from a gender perspective, focusing on particular national dimensions of the workings of global capital, be they the processes of economic liberalisation or structural adjustment programmes, de-collectivisation, a trans-national capital project or direct competition for land in the interests of global capital. Unlike the studies critiqued by Jaggar (2001) for ignoring the agency of people, the studies in this book explore in detail peoples' responses along a continuum. This continuum embraces everyday livelihood activities in Ghana and Vietnam, temporary organisation for compensation in Cameroon and movements in Bolivia, Peru and Brazil. As Mackenzie and Porro argue in their contributions to this book, this range of responses—even the simple insistence on a particular way of struggling for survival and livelihoods which are sustainable—can be seen as resistance to the powerful global forces impinging on the lives of men and women in remote rural areas.

A unique feature of the book is the inclusion of two chapters—Mackenzie's survey of the literature on globalisation, gender and land from a post-structuralist perspective and Goebel's account of the methodological approaches of the case studies. These contribute significant theoretical and methodological insights and also affirm the book's value as a record of an ambitious collective research project, involving scholars from the global north and south, to push the boundaries of feminist knowledge about globalisation.

Goebel's contribution discusses the methodological strategies of the researchers in the light of debates in the literature about the politics and practice of feminist research. Critical material, which the case study chapters did not include because of space constraints have been brought to light in this chapter. What is most interesting is the author's discussion of the engagement of researchers with political questions of location, power and subjectivities. This introduction will explore some of Goebel's conclusions. Mackenzie's contribution tackles the three organising concepts, which all four case studies have in common as a result of their common history.[3] These are globalisation, gender and land. Her analysis showcases the invaluable contributions of post-structuralist analysis to knowledge. In particular, the elegant and powerful ways in which social phenomena are uncovered in all their fluidities and messy complications, the celebration of the human spirit and the agency of even the most powerless of persons and the reminder that change is constant and that things are not always what they seem, come to mind.

Mackenzie's detailed discussion of post-structuralist perspectives on globalisation, land and gender allows readers to situate some of the findings and pre-occupations of several of the case study chapters. However, it is pertinent to note that while all four case studies take up post-structuralist insights,[4] three of the four (Cameroon, Ghana and Vietnam) largely remain within a structuralist framework. This is probably due to the training of the researchers, but also because of the limitations of post-structuralist concepts for analysing questions of land tenure and livelihoods. This introduction will engage with some of the perspectives in the Mackenzie chapter, including the notion of globalisation as a struggle over meaning, the view of relations of gender as negotiated and performed, and land as constantly changing in meaning, through a discussion of some of the findings of the case studies and the insights of other literature within structuralist traditions.

On methodological questions, Porro's study raises the issue of the location of the researchers in relation to the research subjects, making clear some of the identities of the project team and arguing that their findings are their reading of field narratives, influenced by their locations and identities. This level of reflexivity distinguishes Porro's study from the other three studies, as Goebel notes. It is reflected in Porro's methods which have been largely qualitative, and also in her privileging of the voices of her research subjects throughout her chapter as well as in the extent to which the research made possible the meetings and collective action among the research subjects. While the other three studies have tended to remain silent on the politics of the research (the authors of the Vietnam study, however, do define their work as feminist and as promoting the participation of women from the research communities and training some of them in gender mapping and involving them as members of the research team), it is important not to assume that these questions did not exercise the researchers, as Goebel has argued. As a matter of fact, all three studies make extensive use of qualitative methods in order to privilege the voices of their subjects. Also, a key concern across the board has been to bring to the surface gender inequalities in land and resource tenures and explore how processes of globalisation have exacerbated some of these, with deleterious consequences for the livelihood prospects of poor women on three continents.

The silence on feminist methodologies and the power relations between researchers and research subjects is in part because of a consciousness of the wider politics of knowledge production involving donors, research institutions, researchers and research subjects. The power relations of the particular projects under discussion, therefore, were beyond those between researcher and research subjects. The IDRC, as the initiator and financier of the research projects, had laid down parameters which researchers had to follow to secure funding. For example, the call for proposals was intended to support feminist research couched within a framework which established a link between globalisation, land tenure and gender grounded in case studies. While different projects had particular interpretations of the brief, their research questions, selection of subjects and methods were influenced by the call, their institutional locations and how they intended to deploy the findings of the research. A project inception meeting with resource persons, while useful for creating space for developing ideas and networking among the selected projects, also did influence the design of the projects. This meant that there was a limit to the freedom to engage in the kind of action research and policy advocacy driven by the research subjects and not the researchers. Given these limitations, some research teams were cautious about overstating the feminist credentials of the studies. It would be fairer to argue that all the research teams at the very least brought feminist sensibilities to their work through the research questions they posed, their data collection methods and their analytical tools.

The multi-regional spread of the book's case studies is a strength, but has also posed challenges for comparative analysis; a strength because regional specificities have been highlighted, but a weakness because regions are not homogeneous and cannot be understood on the strength of one or two case studies. Indeed, the countries of the studies have their particularities in their relationship with globalisation processes: Ghana, with the dubious distinction of being seen as a sub-Saharan Africa success story in structural adjustment by many except its own citizens; Cameroon, oil rich and seeking to avoid the violence underpinning oil exploitation in neighbouring Nigeria, but clearly in the thrall of global capital; Vietnam, ex-communist and confidently striding forth under the banner of neo-liberalism; and the countries of the Latin American study—Brazil, Peru and Bolivia—with full direct engagements in global agri-business. That all four studies involve multiple cases, be it different regions within a country (Vietnam and Ghana) or different communities in the same region (Cameroon) or different communities in different countries (Brazil, Bolivia and Peru), further complicates their accounts.

The land tenure systems of all the case study areas also have specificities which make comparisons and conclusions tricky. In Cameroon, land is largely state owned while in Ghana, 80 per cent of land is held under customary land tenure systems. In Vietnam, collectivisation in North Vietnam changed the relationship between women and land in putting them formally on the same footing as male members of their collectives. The land came to be re-allocated to households in the period of de-collectivisation, with the state retaining its formal ownership. In Latin America, years of land concentration have created large swathes of landless rural dwellers with changing identities related to their labour relations with land owners and communal land resources.

In spite of these differences, there is a unity in the studies, forged by the common themes they tackle which help to uncover the commonalities and specificities in the lives of women and men in agriculture, gathering, and in other extractive activities across continents. This introduction highlights some of these common themes, which include the conceptions of globalisation as economic liberalisation, de-collectivisation, the increasing power of transnational capital and the growing significance of global trade rules and negotiations. Related to this, the nation state in the era of globalisation will be discussed, drawing especially on the Cameroon and Latin America cases. The bio-physical characteristics of natural resources, the economic, institutional and social arrangements for their exploitation and the implications for environmental and socio-economic impacts on local communities and their members are explored. Other thematic concerns discussed are the relationship between land and labour, the social relations of livelihoods and livelihood responses, resistance and organisation in defence of livelihoods threatened by processes of globalisation.

ECONOMIC GLOBALISATION AS CONTEXT, POLICIES AND PROCESSES

While the term globalization is the subject of intense discussion and debate, and globalization has an impact on virtually every aspect of life—cultural, political and social—I use the term here to refer principally to an economic phenomenon, the internationalization of production and financial services. For the third world, more specifically, globalization has signified the dominance of neo-liberal economic policies, the "Washington Consensus", promoting privatization and liberalization; these policies have been forcefully advanced by the three major international economic institutions, the World Trade Organisation (WTO), the World Bank (hereafter, "the Bank') and the International Monetary Fund (IMF) (Anghie 2005: 245).

The importance of situating discussions of women and land in the broader context of capitalist transformations in developing countries has been highlighted (Razavi 2007). The case studies do this in focusing broadly on rural livelihoods in the context of globalisation and the liberalisation of land tenure regimes. In keeping with the literature which focuses mainly on the economic aspects of globalisation (Khor 2000; Jaggar 2001; Gills 2002), the case studies have tended to privilege the material conditions of livelihoods in their considerations of globalisation.

Pearson (2000) argues that the economic focus of studies of globalisation reflects "the extraordinary concentration of international trade, investment, and financial flows in recent years" (Pearson 2000: 10).[5] She notes, however, that these unprecedented developments in production, trade, investment and finance would have been difficult without technological instruments such as electronic transfer and calculation of transactions, and developments in computer and telecommunications technologies such as the world-wide-web.[6] She also identifies other related aspects of globalisation such as the international and national movements of population resulting in the creation of world cities; the growing inequalities and a widening gap between the rich and poor, between and within regions, countries and cities; and global patterns of consumption and tastes (2000). Gills (2002) argues that while these changes have been made possible by technological developments, it is important not to see technologies as the "overwhelming determinants of economic restructuring, but only as its adjutants" (p. 109).

Jaggar (2001), for her part notes that globalisation is underpinned by neo-liberalism, which promotes the free flow of traded goods through the removal of tariffs and quotas, but seeks to control the flow of labour and seeks extensive privatisation of all resources, turning public services into private enterprises for profit and natural resources—such as water, minerals, forests and land—into global commodities. The focus on the economic and material has to do with the fact that the rendition of globalisation as being about form, ideas, images and imaginings, while correct, does not do justice to the material realities of globalisation as these are experienced through policies and contested processes. When trans-national corporations buy up large swathes of land in East Africa to be used for hunting lodges, thus depriving locals of farming land, these are hardly contests over ideas. While the hegemony of neo-liberal ideas is a factor which has enabled the imposition of structural adjustment, it is worth remembering the debt crisis and the coercion of aid conditionalities which have allowed the international financial institutions (IFIs) to impose their economic policy prescriptions.[7] The role of the IFIs, particularly the World Bank in promoting economic liberalisation goes way beyond the imposition of conditionalities. It has also been involved in guaranteeing projects of trans-national corporations against financial loss. In relation to large projects such as the Chad-Cameroon Oil Pipeline project, which has been described as the World Bank's most ambitious effort to date to establish good governance in resource extraction, the Bank's interventions are an important element of its support of globalisation (Pegg 2005).[8] The role of the Bank in a project outweighs the size of its investments. It also involves political risk management, credit mobilisation and resource curse risk management, which essentially involves protecting the investments and reputations of trans-national corporations. It is these activities that account for the questions about the Bank's poverty alleviation credentials.

Pegg's unproblematised account of state-IFI relations raises critical questions about state sovereignty and the responsibility of states to their citizens. He justifies an extensive conditionalities regime and state control as necessary for good governance in the management of natural resources (2005). This does not pay much attention to the freedom assumed by trans-national corporations and the threats to development represented by their acts of omission and commission. Current thinking is to let the corporations police themselves through corporate social responsibility programmes. However, as Fig (2005) has demonstrated in his study of South Africa, corporate social responsibility has not been effective in ensuring redress for communities affected by the activities of the corporations, thus making the case for regulatory mechanisms. The literature on the Niger Delta demonstrates this point very strongly. To succeed, corporate social responsibility requires vigilant states, a robust and independent media with strong traditions of investigative journalism, and well resourced civil society organisations and social movements (Fig 2005). The absence of such conditions in many developing countries is a factor in the current structure of investments by TNCs.

These discussions of economic globalisation or the globalisation of production, trade, investment and finance (Gils 2002), while compelling, often do not sufficiently address impacts on communities and peoples' livelihoods. There is, however, some literature focusing on the impacts of liberalisation, labour market flexibility, informalisation and gendered livelihoods on women's productive and reproductive labour. Such studies have noted that the emphasis on global competitiveness and export promotion has encouraged low wages and undermined labour rights. While women have found employment in export processing zones (EPZs) and the urban informal economy as home workers, home-based workers and employees; and in agri-business as wage workers and casual labourers, their conditions of work have been poor in order to guarantee the extraordinary profits demanded by foreign direct investment. Many such women have been drawn away from rural subsistence production in the countryside and are involved in several paid and unpaid activities to secure their livelihoods, their reproductive activities in effect subsidising capital (Gills 2002; see also Tripp 1997; Carr, Chen and Tate 2000; Darkwah 2002; UNRISD 2005; Hansen and Vaa 2004; Tsikata 2008 for similar analysis). With a few exceptions, however (Gills 2002; Whitehead 2004; 2008), most of these studies focus on livelihood activities in the urban informal economy. The case studies in this book take up similar issues of livelihoods but with emphasis on rural areas, and this shows in their definitions and characterisations of globalisation.

Endeley, for example, refers to the Chad-Cameroon Pipeline project[9] as a globalising project, arguing that it was large and involved complex technologies and expertise which brought rural communities in remote parts of Cameroon in direct contact with trans-national oil companies; their financiers and construction crew drawn from all over the globe. This resulted in processes whereby economic, financial, technical and cultural transactions between different countries and communities throughout the world became increasingly inter-connected.

Porro's chapter has identified several developments which illustrate the ways in which globalisation is affecting livelihoods in the Amazon. These include the paving of a trans-oceanic highway to integrate commodity markets in Bolivia, Brazil and Peru with those in Asia through the Pacific. Accompanying this process has been an intensification of land privatisation along the highway and its inter-connections. A second element is the competition between commodities and subsistence production on the same lands, represented by the conversion of brazil nut and babaçu palm forests into land for cattle rearing, logging and the production of soy for exports. In some cases, this has involved granting rights in the same piece of land to small scale farmers and then as concessions to nut gatherers and then again to people with land titles whose interests are considered stronger than concessions. A third element is the imposition of European regulations and standards of unestablished scientific bases on small producers, leaving them to shoulder the financial and labour burdens of meeting these standards. Last but not least, is the competition from Malaysian palm oil in the Brazilian market, facilitated by the elimination of import taxes on vegetable oils and aggressive marketing by Malaysian firms. Local and trans-national corporations operating in Brazil switched to palm oil and decreased their purchases of babaçu oils. This produced a fundamental change in the productive chain, resulting in the shutting down of processing companies and affecting local oil companies and the extractive activities of thousands of families. The local oil industry has not regained its market share even though the oil prices have been reduced in sensitivity to the competition. Some local companies have themselves begun producing palm oil, with land and labour taken from the locals.

Based on the above, Porro concludes that development policies in the Amazon have been driven by the imperatives of globalisation, favouring logging, cattle ranching and agri-business for commodity production, resulting in wealth and land concentration as well as environmental degradation.

These developments in the Amazon are occurring in contexts dominated by the impacts of structural reforms and neo-liberal policies undertaken by the national governments of the study, under pressure from the IFIs. The Awumbila and Tsikata chapter focuses on the ramifications of such policies in Ghana where the economic liberalisation of macro-economic policies, the extractive sectors (mining and timber), and the land tenure system have resulted in a massive expansion of gold mining, timber logging, large-scale farming and real estate development. The paper argues that these policies have had implications for the livelihoods of people in rural and urban Ghana in particular ways—the intensification of competition over land resulting in land scarcity and degradation; greater exploitation of hitherto marginal resources as a result of a more liberalised regime of access; the decline of other natural resources and an increase in poor livelihood outcomes. Similarly, Scott, Bélanger, Nguyen, and Khuat note that the changes analysed in their chapter on Vietnam are occurring within a context of economic globalisation and predominantly neo-liberal policy orientations among governments and international institutions.

Scott et al. also demonstrate that local contexts mediate the outcomes of national policies. Within the overall set of economic reforms, de-collectivisation of agriculture, which reversed decades-old agrarian reforms of a socialist policy orientation, was significant in Vietnam. Rural economic restructuring and quasi privatisation of land in Vietnam, considered as key to strengthening production, innovation and investment, while reflecting the global shift in rural governance towards private property rights, was fuelled by internal and external challenges facing Vietnam's agricultural sector.[10] Land tenure reforms were seen as central to this transition (known as *doi moi* or economic renovation), which began in 1986, and which signalled a move from egalitarianism and collectivism towards entre-preneurship and market competition.

The Vietnamese land tenure reforms, in keeping with similar reforms in sub-Saharan Africa, included the modernisation of the land administration system through the issuing of long-term land use rights certificates. The goals of the reforms were to improve security of tenure for land holders, increase domestic and foreign investment in land, reduce land disputes, ensure better infrastructure planning and coordination, and establish a fair, equitable and efficient taxation system, among other things (ADB 1997, quoted in Scott et al.). These discussions on globalisation in the case studies at once set out the context and processes of particular elements of globalisation. Several of these are discussed below.

THE NATION STATE AND MARKETS IN THE ERA OF GLOBALISATION

Peck (2002) tackles the scalar dimensions of the globalisation debate, drawing attention to the rescaling of analysis and reality which has been an integral component, particularly the rendering of the global as the most effective scale in economic terms for market forces and the local as the most effective for coping and adaptation. In this rescaling, the national welfare state is considered no longer important for policymaking and implementation (See also Khor, 2000 on the internationalisation of policymaking). Peck successfully draws attention to the continuing role of the nation state in making, and policing the implementation of the rules of globalisation, thus providing regulatory cover for the developments in global and local policy arenas. He argues that it is important to counter "the pervasive naturalization of the global as the economically optimal scale of market forces and the local as the politically optimal space of coping and adaptation" (p. 332). He therefore calls for a rescaling which involves a strengthening of the nation state in ways which are cognisant of the changing conditions under globalisation.

The nation state's importance in the regulation of the liberalisation agenda and in the land tenure reforms is highlighted in all four case studies. In Cameroon, it is in alliance with the oil transnational corporations (Endeley), in Ghana and Vietnam, it is presiding over economic liberalisation (Awumbila and Tsikata; and Scott et al.) while in the Brazil case it is doing both by rezoning land from extractives to land intensive agriculture and introducing policy reforms favourable to global capital.

In the Ghana study, the discussion focuses on the liberalisation of land tenure systems and the common goals of land tenure reforms across sub-Saharan Africa in the service of foreign direct investment. Peck's observation about the homogenisation which is attendant on the globalisation of economic policies creates a framework for understanding the ways in which land tenure reforms feed directly into the liberalisation agenda and how they are fuelling land concentration and significant changes in tenure arrangement which increase the land tenure insecurity of women, migrant farmers, and young people (Awumbila and Tsikata).

Endeley refers to the situation in the oil producing communities in neighbouring Nigeria, arguing that strong policies are needed to address the grievances of communities along the Chad-Cameroon pipeline in order to avoid the turmoil in the Niger Delta region. This is important because the literature on the Niger Delta and other oil producing communities shows very clearly that violence in petroleum producing communities is often fuelled by a combination of state and trans-national corporation responses to expressions of community grievances related to environmental pollution and threats to livelihoods (Watts 1997, 2001; Turner and Brownhill 2004; Ukeje 2005). Endeley's chapter focuses on questions of compensation, particularly the implications of the compensation regime for the developmental aspirations of the project. As she notes, the project's developmental potential can be assessed by examining how the revenue it generates contributes to economic growth, tackles poverty in Cameroon and more specifically, its contribution to the living conditions of affected people. This, she argues, can be situated within a broader discussion of state and corporate social responsibility in the petroleum industry. Compensation was selected as a focus because, as Endeley argues, all persons—whether as individuals or as community members—suffered one or more forms of dispossession of private and/or communal property because of the pipeline project, even if temporarily. Given the newness of the project, issues of oil spillage, environmental degradation, long-term livelihood disruptions, etc., were not yet serious. It seemed entirely appropriate to focus on compensation while situating it within wider questions of national development.

Already, compensation issues were proving to be a good indicator of the fraught relations between the state and affected communities. Endeley's study reveals four related issues around compensation: a) the law governing compensation; b) classes of beneficiaries—individual, community and regional, each with its own criteria for eligibility; c) the nature of compensation (whether in kind or in cash or both); and d) the quantum of compensation.

Endeley notes that while the decision to compensate actual land users for crop losses ensured that gender inequalities in land ownership were not transferred to the compensation regime, the long term loss of earnings of farmers, both male and female, was ignored. Even more importantly, women received less compensation than men because of the gendered nature of crops[11] and the location of farms.[12] Furthermore, while in-kind compensation may have insulated communities from abuse by their leaders, the downstream character of decision-making and the limits of community participation in decisions about compensation created suspicions of wrongdoing by chiefs, a situation which had the potential of undermining community solidarity. As in the Niger Delta, Endeley found that community-state relations were fraught, complicated by the poor treatment of communities by project staff. It was felt that the government was not doing enough to protect communities and instead often intervened on the side of the project whenever there were disturbances. The Cameroon case study is a powerful illustration of the relationship between the quality of participation, the degree of social inclusion and the achievement of social cohesion.

Considering the nation state raises questions about the role of markets, an important issue because policy documents referred to in the case studies were in support of private property rights and land titling as a strategy to encourage investment, improve land market efficiency and also strengthen women's land interests. In spite of this, all four case studies concluded that market reforms had not necessarily improved women's access to land. This is in agreement with the literature on gender and globalisation. Razavi (2007) for example argues that

> although the empirical base is far from comprehensive, a judicious reading of the existing evidence points to the severe limitations of land markets as a channel for women's inclusion. It is of course important not to homogenise women as a social group… but for the vast majority of women small holders, market mechanisms are not likely to provide a channel for their inclusion (p. 1486).

In the Ghana case, the already existing gender inequalities had affected women's ability to benefit from the commercialisation of small-scale mining land. In the mangrove areas, changing resource tenures resulting from the commercialisation of mangrove interests, while appearing to provide the opportunity for a levelling of land relations, had reinforced male-centred tenure arrangements in shrinking the ownership structure to a very small all male group. This meant that for the majority, market transactions and labour relations, which are gendered, would determine the levels of earnings from mangrove harvesting. Hence it was not surprising that women who leased mangrove stands earned less than men because of the higher labour costs they had to assume as a result of the sexual division of labour in mangrove harvesting. Women labourers in the mangroves also earned less than the men partly because men, who worked in teams, were paid by the day while women, who often worked on their own, had piece-rate arrangements.

The Vietnam case study is particularly interesting in its interrogation of markets because it examines what happens when women's access to land is no longer mediated by the state but rather by markets and kinship relations. Land markets allowed households with surplus land, at any point in time, to transfer some of it to those who did not have enough. However, this increased land speculation and concentration and landlessness.[13] Scott et al. argue that while landlessness often signals economic insecurity, it is not always the case. Their observation that landless peasants, mostly teenage girls and married women, were working as day labourers for other farmers, is nonetheless revealing. They also note differences in attitudes to land between the northern and southern communities, which they partly attribute to the variations in their land interests. In the north, many families fought to keep their interests in state-allocated land to which they had use rights by leasing it, as a measure to guarantee security in adversity. In the south on the other hand, households with ownership interests in land were more likely to sell and purchase land outright. Scott et al. conclude that although the emergence of land markets had deepened economic inequalities, peasants continued to have a socialist ethos which disapproved of land concentration and inequalities and favoured some periodic land redistribution. This had tempered the free operation of land markets and marketing principles in the management of land.

The four studies support the literature which suggests that states are actively involved in processes of economic liberalisation in their rule-making, policies and regulatory practices, and also in supporting trans-national corporations. At the same time, the global homogenisation of economic and social policy and legal reforms has fundamentally undermined the sovereignty of nation states with regard to decision-making. This has resulted in dilemmas as to how livelihoods can be protected and social inequalities reduced in this period. It also explains why communities bypass the state and appeal directly to global institutions and constituencies for redress. Besides, it supports the argument that markets are not likely to be able to address gender inequalities in land tenure arrangements.

LAND AND THE PARTICULARITIES OF NATURAL RESOURCES

One recurring question in the literature which rarely gets full attention is how the bio-physical, economic, strategic and social properties of certain natural resources determine the technologies, capital and labour relations of their exploitation, and therefore livelihood outcomes. This issue helps to clarify some of the specificities of the case studies and differences between the exploitation of forest resources such as nuts, palms and mangroves on the one hand and oil and gold on the other. Linking the bio-physical properties of oil with the social relations of its exploitation in the context of globalisation, Watts (2001) analyses the implications of oil, some of which are relevant to other natural resources. These include the commercial negotiability of oil globally and the colossal amounts of money circulating in the oil industry, which while generating great wealth for companies, their shareholders and other well-placed individuals, has resulted in immiseration and environmental degradation for communities. As well, the national and centralising character of oil has the effect of creating a mono economy, thus allowing states to accumulate resources for purchasing legitimacy and patronage and providing cover for the operations of the TNCs. The depression of non-oil sectors such as agriculture means that other sources of revenue such as taxation become irrelevant, and this displaces the accountability of government from citizens to oil companies (Watts 2001). The properties of particular natural resources and the mode of their exploitation, therefore, affect how local communities experience them. Like for other local communities affected by extractive activities in developing countries, fishing and farming were the main livelihood activities prior to the discovery of oil and these were largely disrupted by petroleum exploitation activities (Watts 2001; Ukeje 2005). The employment opportunities in the capital intensive oil industry have not been able to address the crisis in local livelihood activities in both oil and non-oil producing communities (Ukeje 2005). In addition, local populations have also suffered from extreme levels of environmental stress—24 hour long gas flares, oil spills from pipelines, blow-outs at well heads, contaminated water and soil and threats to their health.[14] The situation of Ogoniland has been attributed to the constantly depreciating share of oil revenues going to communities and the low levels of compensation for land acquired and oil spillage.[15]

Some of these issues may not be relevant for the Cameroon case partly because of the short life span of the pipeline and also because oil was not being directly extracted from the study areas. The case for taking resource specificity seriously is strengthened when one contrasts the oil case with that of forest extractives in the Amazon case study. In the Amazon forests of Brazil, Bolivia and Peru, the brazil nut, babaçu palm and rubber trees have provided a range of occupations involving large numbers of local men and women with various land interests and labour relations. The nature of these forest plant resources, some naturally generating and others planted on forest lands, had created a field of common property resources with livelihood possibilities for large numbers of people as harvesters and processors. Over time, though, land concentration has transformed common resource tenures into private property, creating exploitative and conflictual land and labour relations between a class of land owners and various categories of small holders and landless labourers. In spite of the changes in tenure relations, significant numbers of men and women still participated in the exploitation of these forest resources. In contrast, when land has been converted to cattle ranching and the production of agricultural commodities such as soy and oil palm, their capital intensive character has excluded the majority of people. Also, the loss of land as a common resource regulated by local people themselves has disturbed the livelihood activities of babaçu palm breakers and brazil nut gatherers.

In studying both gold mining and mangrove exploitation, the Ghana study found more evidence of the importance of resource particularities. Differences in nature between gold and the mangroves helped to shape their impact on livelihoods. Mangrove as a plant species which could be cultivated, the fact that its use and harvesting involved local knowledge and its capital requirements were not so high as to discourage poor people, made it easier for locals to participate widely in mangrove harvesting, although men and women did so on different terms. In the case of gold, the level of upfront capital investment needed, the fact that its technologies were not local and were distinct from those of agriculture, and its higher capital requirements excluded many people from participating in its exploitation. The gender division of labour established in the farming systems of northern Ghana also contributed to creating social differentiation in the mining industry between men and women and between locals and migrants. Women spent less time in the year and were involved in the least secure and most poorly paid activities compared to men, while locals worked in a range of labouring activities with a few progressing to the ranks of pit owners and sponsors, roles reserved for foreigners (Awumbila and Tsikata).

The question of resource specificities therefore provides an important dimension to our understanding of globalisation, land and resource tenures and their implications for gendered livelihoods. The studies in the book suggest that while minerals such as gold and oil presented particular challenges to agricultural livelihood activities, forest resources could also be exploited in ways which expropriated local communities, forcing them into unfavourable labour relations, leaving in its wake environmental degradation and impoverished and dispossessed local populations.

SOCIAL RELATIONS AND IDENTITIES IN LAND TENURE

All the studies underline the fact that different social relations and identities are implicated in the experiences of the impacts of global-isation on livelihoods. Some of the discussion notes that while these social relations predate the developments under discussion, it is clear that they have played a key role in the differentiation of impacts. This segment will focus on labour, kinship and gender relations as they intersect in various ways and structure land tenure relations.

Land-labour relations

Land and labour regimes have been analysed independently and each found to contribute to the gendered nature of livelihood activities and outcomes. However, these studies, while focusing on either land or labour, have also drawn attention to a land-labour nexus in livelihoods. Often, this latter aspect is not fully addressed in the literature, with the exception of studies of share contracts (e.g., Amanor 2000, 2002; Lavigne-Delville et al. 2001). This analytical gap has contributed to one of the more intractable controversies in the literature, i.e., whether there are gender inequalities in land relations or whether it is women who are unable to take full advantage of the land because of other constraints they have such as capital, credit, technologies and labour (see Razavi 2007 for a discussion of this issue). This debate can be made more productive with more serious attention to the connection between land interests and control over other resources, particularly labour as well as trends in the overall economy. A number of the case studies, particularly those that have focused on resource exploitation such as the Ghana and the Amazon studies, explore this issue.

In places where policies promote large-scale capitalist agriculture, as in the Vietnam and Amazon cases, land concentration results in women becoming landless labourers. The loss of farmlands also means that they do not have the cushion of growing their own food crops except in rare cases where they are able to enter into agreements with landowners for land on which to grow food crops. The labour-land nexus is illustrated by Porro's observation that in many places in the Amazon, people have established their connection to land through their labour, i.e., how much work they have done on this land and not necessarily on account of legal rights or the operation of land markets. The ability to claim land in this way had enabled certain women to establish control over land outside the power of male household heads (Porro). In this connection, Porro has also demonstrated that land is not just material in its implications. The social construction of land as territory, especially in the context of political contestations, has enabled poor peasant women to stand up to powerful land dealers and defy their efforts to deprive them of land. While these struggles by the poor are not always successful, these non-economic conceptions of land and rights to land afford their struggles some legitimacy. This is particularly important in a context where the land tenure system is highly layered and characterised by severe inequalities in the sizes of holdings and in the rights of small holders.

The Amazon study shows that while some companies have been interested in land, others have focused on processing, leaving extraction and production to small farmers and middlemen and thus avoiding land conflicts. This strategy has allowed these companies to assume green credentials while ignoring the destruction of forests and people's livelihoods—an integral element of the global market processes they thrive in. In Peru, there have been efforts to give land to small peasants through a land reform programme which started in 1969. Very few women benefited, largely because the beneficiaries were required to be household heads of over 18 years of age with dependents. This excluded certain categories of women from land rights and forest resources. For such persons—single women, teenagers and children—the only options for involvement were through processing activities. This suggests that it is important

to differentiate between categories of women in the analysis of the
impacts of land concentration. Some landless farmers, who work
as peelers in nut processing factories, are also involved in small-
scale farming on land rented from the Peruvian military on a share
contract basis, enabling them to grow food crops and small animals
for consumption.

GENDER, LABOUR AND LAND RELATIONS

The ways in which land tenure is discussed in the four case studies
highlights the salience of gender as a social category but also the
importance of analysing its embeddedness in other social relations
as well as its specificities in the different settings. Porro's chapter,
for example, critiques the homogenising role of gender discourses,
arguing that while they have played an important role in highlighting
gender inequalities and policies to mitigate them, specificities have
been lost, leading to sterile slogans which were heard among women's
groups in different parts of the Amazon, but which did not reflect
their complicated and multi-faceted realities and their everyday
lives. In her study therefore, she explored how gender discourses
propagated by development NGOs were deployed by women in the
negotiation of their relations with men and other dominant social
categories and how these interacted with their land rights in the
context of globalisation.

In problematising gender discourses, Porro has demonstrated
the salience of gender analysis but approached it in a way which
enables us to see its embeddedness in the emergence of social identities fashioned around work and relations to land which have enabled
women to struggle to maintain the viability of agrarian livelihoods
and ways of life in the face of powerful forces of change. Her chapter
also examines the significant gender relations in the lives of women
and comes to the conclusion that a number of women were in charge
of households with three to four generations of persons. For such
women, relations with husbands may be as important as those with
their sons and grandchildren. Therefore, the husband-wife dyad at the
heart of gender analysis of households is not complete in this context

and "gender relations along inter-generational vertical lines could be as significant as along matrimonial, horizontal lines" (Porro).

Awumbila and Tsikata demonstrate that gender relations are one of several social relations implicated in the organisation of livelihoods by examining how the intersections of gender with class, ethnicity, kinship and inter-generational relations, as well as the relations between migrants and locals, and between chiefs/land owners and land users, structure access to natural resources and livelihood options of men and women.

They also analyse how new social identities created by the labour and land relations of small-scale mining industry reproduce gender inequalities. Certain jobs, with names adopted and adapted from other mining areas—sponsors, ghetto owners, moya men, chisellers, loco boys, kaimen, shanking ladies and cooks—denoted roles and particular relations within the mining industry which were gendered. Power and influence within mining communities was heavily influenced by success in establishing and maintaining mining pits (known as ghettoes) and employing many people. Women who assumed roles played by men, such as sponsoring, could not fulfil some of the key labour requirements of successful sponsorship because of the sexual division of labour in the industry and therefore, could not secure the recognition and remuneration these positions afforded. Men's work-related identities in the mining industry were more permeable and easier to change while women's work identities were quite fixed. Similarly, in the babaçu palm and brazil nut industries in the Amazon, a division of labour has been in operation (Porro).

Scott et al. stress the fact that the particular identities which shape relations with land are not fixed or pre-determined. As they note, "at times, a woman's membership in her family, class or ethnic group, more than her gender can shape her identity and the decisions she makes." This point, while essentially correct, should not mean that we cannot privilege gender in our analysis as all four studies do, but that it be understood how gender intersects with other social relations in establishing land interests.

The Vietnamese case study has the most comprehensive discussion of kinship and its mediating role in land tenure. It focuses on those elements of kinship which constrain women's land interests—the patrilineal inheritance systems, patrilocal marital residence practices, and opposition to gender equity from within households and extended families. It also raises the issue of legal pluralism and its implications for women's land interests. These elements remind us of the continuities in conditions which influence how globalisation and economic liberalisation are experienced by local communities (see Whitehead and Tsikata 2003; Wanitzek and Woodman, 2004 for more detailed discussions of legal pluralism in the context of globalisation and economic liberalisation). As the authors argue, women and men's entitlements to land are mediated by three kinds of institutions—market, the formal legal system and beyond the market and legal systems, specifically kin networks, customary law, social conventions and norms (Scott et al.).[16]

The changing status of the household under de-collectivisation meant that state land was now accessed through the household while individuals could access land through the market. A result of these developments was that land inheritance, mediated by kinship now had a greater impact on the fortunes of individuals. In the northern Vietnam study communities, inheritance was largely through sons, justified on account of their social and ritual responsibilities for parents in old age and in death. There was more flexibility in the south with regard to women's inheritance, although sons received a larger share.[17] The inheritance picture was now being complicated by the fact that in recognition of the growing commercial value of land, women were beginning to assert their inheritance rights, moving away from the old practice of giving their share of land to their brothers.

Endeley has argued that the pipeline project was masculine in nature and therefore, its impacts were gendered, with women being the most negatively affected. This was because men were the more visible beneficiaries of the opportunities created by petroleum extraction projects in terms of employment opportunities, new technologies and human resource development, while women were the more affected by water pollution, oil spillage and soil degradation. This position is supported by studies of the Niger Delta communities affected by oil extraction (Turner and Brownhill 2004; Ukeje 2005).

Ukeje (2005) for example suggests that the differential impacts were on account of the fact that women were more sedentary, experienced more constraints in labour-related migration and their involvement in fishing and farming.

A formulation which stands out in several of the studies (Porro, Endeley) is the idea of gender as negotiated. Its roots lie in the post-modernist privileging of women's agency and the changing and contingent nature of gender identities. However, the idea of gender as negotiated downplays the structural and systemic manifestations of gender inequalities outside the negotiating power of individual women and men. While privileging agency is important for moving away from victimology in the study of gender relations, ignoring the structures and systems disables gender analysis from accounting for important commonalities in gender relations in women's lives the world over and in women's less than secure relationship with land and other resources.

In conclusion, the analysis of the social relations underpinning rural livelihoods has demonstrated clearly the role of globalisation processes in shaping national economic policies, and through that, labour and land relations. While women and men's experiences of global economic processes are influenced by pre-existing social relations of class, kinship and gender in their livelihoods struggles, new social identities related to land and labour relations are created. Women's agency is highlighted but discussed in ways which recognise the role of state policies, kinship systems and market transactions in shaping gender relations in unequal ways. While the case studies show many commonalities, their specificities demonstrate the importance of policies grounded in the local realities of Amazonia, Cameroon, Ghana and Vietnam.

RESPONSES TO GLOBALISATION: FROM EVERYDAY LIVELIHOOD STRUGGLES TO ANTI-GLOBALISATION MOVEMENTS

Responses to threats to livelihood activities are varied and can be differentiated by how they are organised and executed. Gills (2002) argues that the intensification of the exploitation of labour under globalisation has resulted in new forms of organisation and resistance. Escobar's (1995) characterisation of the exponential growth of particular local organisations as part of the new anti-development movements in the south, consequent to the failure of the modernisation project, has been taken up in studies by Watts (2001); Turner and Brownhill (2004); Pegg (2005); Ukeje (2005) in studies of Niger Delta movements. These studies privilege formal collectives. There is, however, literature which takes a broader view of resistance, for example, James Scott's work which identifies the weapons of resistance of relatively powerless groups such as "foot dragging, dissimulation, false compliance, pilfering, feigned ignorance, slander, arson, sabotage" (1985, p. 35).[18] In spite of some of the questions raised about Scott's concepts[19], they have been deployed in analyses of gender relations because of their salience for covert and indirect forms of resistance (Agarwal 1994).[20]

In keeping with this later tradition, Porro refers to all livelihood responses as resistance struggles whether or not they are formal or informal; organised or unorganised, visible or hidden, within the public or domestic spheres. She argues that while struggles of women within communities and families are invisible to researchers, they are nevertheless critical for their livelihood outcomes. Many such women do not belong to any recognised social movements. However, their situations are so serious as to legitimise their struggles. Awumbila and Tsikata discuss these as livelihood responses rather than struggles while Endeley, who focuses on the collective efforts to gain compensation, distinguishes different levels of protests. Looking at all these responses as resistance allows Porro to differentiate those in organised movements from those outside them, while insisting on the legitimacy of informal and hidden struggles. Separating struggles from responses has the limitation of preventing important linkages between levels of responses to be made. On the other hand, the language of struggle can raise expectations of what is actually taking place within communities, and with this comes the danger of romanticising the everyday responses of people to difficult living conditions and not taking into account whether or not such responses have transformatory potential.

There are insights from studies of new social movements which are supported by some of the findings of the case studies. These include the view that the globalised nature of the struggles has allowed local communities to take strength from struggles elsewhere, whether in terms of organisational strategies or demands. Another is the observation that local communities are dealing directly with trans-national corporations, thus raising questions about the role of the nation state, and last but not least, the finding that women struggle in different capacities, linked with the nature of the threat to their livelihoods and communities. Some of these insights are discussed in more detail below.

Endeley's study showed that the linear nature of the Chad-Cameroon pipeline had implications for the configuration of affected communities and their organisations. Whereas in the Niger Delta, whole communities with commonalities in their identities have been affected, in Cameroon, affected communities were found along the pipeline in four different regions and were therefore likely to have differences in their identities and language. As yet, they did not have the organisation which had made the Niger Delta protests so potent. Communities were represented by their chiefs and headmen in negotiations with the state and the pipeline project management over compensation.

The involvement of the TNCs in negotiations through the project management structures was changing the configuration of state community relations. Arguably, TNC experiences of communities elsewhere were being brought into play in this case. For example, Endeley has identified special arrangements made in the environmental management plan for the Bakola and Bagyeli pygmies which excluded other affected communities as a source of friction because it was considered discriminatory. This threat to inter-community cooperation and solidarity would not have featured in TNC concerns.

Peasant communities in the eastern Amazon have responded to threats to their livelihoods by mobilising locals to gain access to land which they then put to organic farming in order to benefit from international fair trade arrangements. Fair trade arrangements are a particular response to the imperatives of globalisation which take into account the livelihood needs of food growers. Local mobilisation has allowed communities to elect representatives to local and regional governments to enable them to struggle for changes guaranteeing their access to babaçu palms even on private property and also protecting organic farming.

Howsoever they may be positioned, all studies showcase women as independent agents making their livelihoods against the odds and establishing new identities in the process. Whether as *castaneras, seringueiras, extrativistas* or *zafreras* (labour categories) or *colonas, concessionarias, comunarias* or *assentadas* (relationship to land) in the Amazon, these work and land related identities confer on women the distinction of the ability to struggle for more gender equitable relations with men and more favourable livelihood outcomes, according to Porro. However, as she shows in her case study, there is no straightforward connection between these identities and more gender equitable relations. In Ghana, the magazia (who is the leader of the shanking ladies), the shanking ladies and women traders who act unofficially as sponsors in small-scale mining, have relations with mining concerns often mediated by male mining pit owners, and their livelihood outcomes often depend on the continued existence of unstable informal liaisons (Awumbila and Tsikata). Here, as in the Amazon, the labour relations women enter into are a function of their relationship to land, whether as local women or as strangers from other parts of Ghana.

CONCLUSION

This introduction has highlighted some of the book's contributions to the literature on gendered implications of globalisation for the social relations of land tenure and resource control. It has revealed striking commonalities which justify the continued analytical attention to gender relations. It has also thrown light on how the book's various contributors have tackled the role of states, markets and communities in the transformation of land and resource tenures in a globalised world.

The introduction has also discussed some of the themes tackled by the chapters which helped to uncover the commonalities and specificities in the lives of women and men in agriculture, gathering and other extractive activities across continents. These were the conceptions of globalisation as economic liberalisation, de-collectivisation, the increasing power of trans-national capital and the growing significance of global trade rules and negotiations. Related to this, the nation state and markets in the era of globalisation were discussed, drawing especially on the Cameroon and Latin America cases. The bio-physical characteristics of natural resources, the economic, institutional and social arrangements for their exploitation and the environmental and socio-economic impacts on local communities and their members, were also explored. Other thematic concerns explored were the connection between land and labour relations, the social relations of livelihoods and livelihood responses, resistance and organisation in defence of livelihoods threatened by processes of globalisation.

Considering the nation state raised questions about the role of markets, and all four case studies concluded that market reforms had not necessarily improved women's access to land. In some cases, it was found that the already existing gender inequalities had affected women's ability to benefit from the commercialisation of land and natural resources. In others, changing resource tenures resulting from the commercialisation and concentration of these resources, while appearing to provide the opportunity for a levelling of land relations, had reinforced male-centred tenure arrangements in shrinking the ownership structure to a very small all male group.

The issue of how the bio-physical, economic, strategic and social properties of certain natural resources determine the technologies, capital and labour relations of their exploitation, and therefore livelihood outcomes was discussed in some detail in the introduction. It was argued that while minerals such as gold and oil presented particular challenges to agricultural livelihood activities, forest resources could also be exploited in ways which expropriated local communities, forcing them into unfavourable labour relations, leading to environmental degradation and the impoverishment and dispossession of local populations.

Regarding social relations, the highlights presented were the discussions from the various chapters which conclude that while women and men's experiences of global economic processes were influenced by pre-existing social relations of class, kinship and gender, new social identities related to land and labour relations were created through their struggles to make a living. The introduction concluded that while the case studies showed many commonalities, their specificities also demonstrated the importance of policies grounded in the local realities of the Amazon, Cameroon, Ghana and Vietnam.

Responses to threats to livelihood activities in local communities, a common theme in the chapters, was highlighted. The four case studies showcased women as independent agents making their livelihoods against odds and taking on new identities in the process, thus establishing their ability to struggle for more gender equitable relations with men and more favourable livelihood outcomes. However, as the case studies showed, there was no straightforward connection between these identities and more gender equitable relations. The labour relations women were involved in were a function of their changing land interests in a context of land tenure liberalisation.

NOTES

1. I am grateful to Pamela Golah, Alison Goebel and Akosua Darkwah for useful comments on earlier drafts.
2. Mcgrew (2000) has classified the approaches to globalisation as neo-liberal, radical and transformational, based on whether they have defended the neo-liberal underpinnings of globalisation, critiqued it or have found some accommodation with different elements of the neo-liberal and radical approaches.
3. The four case studies came out of an IDRC research competition on globalisation, gender and land. Mackenzie provided intellectual support to the four research projects and was chief facilitator of several workshops held during the life of the projects.
4. Some of these insights of post-structuralism are the contingent and shifting character of gender identities, the struggle over meaning in the discourses of globalisation, the meaning of land and questions of resistance in everyday lives.
5. She cites some of the most striking indicators of this- the twenty fold expansion of foreign direct investment in production facilities, the fact that TNCs are responsible for 80 per cent of foreign direct investment and are responsible for a significant proportion of global employment and production as well as the unprecedented growth of financial flows across national borders for investment and speculation in goods and financial products and currencies.

6. These have enabled nonstop financial transactions, the ability to coordinate local production of fruit, flowers and vegetables on a global scale to serve markets across the world, and a range of new services and processes.

7. Anghie puts this well: 'the IFIs exercise enormous power over the workings of the international financial system, as reflected by the fact that half of the world's population and two-thirds of its governments are bound by the policies they prescribe' (Anghie 2005: 249).

8. Support for extractive sector investment is one of the main elements of the World Bank group's poverty reduction approach to sub-Saharan Africa.

9. The Chad-Cameroon Petroleum Development and Pipeline project was developed by an oil consortium and the governments of Chad and Cameroon with the assistance of the World Bank and other lenders between 1993 and 1999. It is operated by the oil consortium made up of Exxon Mobil (40 per cent), PETRONAS (35 per cent), and Chevron Texaco. At US$ 3.7billion, it is the largest single private sector investment in sub-Saharan Africa to date. It consists of the developing of oilfields in Southern Chad and the transportation of the oil through a 1,070 kilometre pipeline to a floating storage and offloading vessel near Kribi, Cameroon (Pegg 2005; Endeley, this volume).

10. These they enumerate as stagnation in productivity, breakdown in collective management structures and declining foreign aid from the Soviet Union.

11. Compensation was based on the local market prices of the commodities destroyed. More men than women were involved in growing world market crops such as cocoa and oil palm, while more women were engaged in food crop production for home consumption and the local market.

12. Men's farms were located in the outskirts of communities while women's farms were closer to home. The pipeline affected men's farms more because of a policy decision that the pipeline avoid settlements.

13. Scott et al. found that landlessness had doubled among rural households in five years according to Vietnamese national statistics.

14. The statistics offered by Watts (2001) is startling in its proportions: 76 per cent of natural gas in the oil producing areas in Nigeria is flared compared to 6 per cent in the USA. The gas burns 24 hours at temperatures between 13,000 and 14,000 degrees celsius, perpetually lighting up the night sky. (See also his statistics of oil spills and the discussion of impacts on streams). As Watts notes, the area's levels of misery and deprivation are unimaginable. The community where oil was first found has no all-season roads, few Ogoni households have electricity, doctor patient ratios are 1:100,000, child mortality rates are some of the highest in Nigeria, unemployment is 85 per cent, illiteracy 80 per cent, life expectancy is below the national average and there is large scale out-migration of the youth.

15. Shell was said to be making US$200 million profit from Nigeria annually but had provided only US$2 million to Ogoni communities in 40 years of operations. The company had also constructed one road and granted 96 school

scholarships in 30 years. Its employment record was no better. At one time, it had 88 Ogoni people out of 5,000 Nigerians in its workforce representing just 2 per cent (Watts 2001).

16. In other classifications, customary law is part of the formal legal system.

17. Inheritance inflexibility in the North had to do with the fact that only male children and relatives could take responsibility for death rituals for parents, while in the South, daughters could also be responsible.

18. In distinguishing between public/on-stage from private/off-stage scripts of both the powerful and their subordinates, he alerts one to the fact of responses that may not be public.

19. Among them is the critique that in characterising the decision of poor peasants to conform rather than resist openly as a rational response to the danger of sanctions or failure, Scott ignores the evidence of hegemony. Also, gender relations as well as intra-household relations are missing from his analysis (Kandiyoti, 1998).

20. As Kandiyoti argues, this is because, 'the fact that resistance did not necessarily have to take overt and organised forms but could be expressed through covert and indirect forms of bargaining was particularly well-suited to women's contestations of domestic power structures involving as they do face-to-face relations with intimates such as husbands, mothers-in-law, sons and daughters rather than encounters with the more impersonal workings of bureaucracies and state apparatuses' (1998, p. 141). Kandiyoti, however, cautions against the extension of frameworks developed to explain the relations between different social categories to account for gender relations.

REFERENCES

Agarwal, B., 1994, "Gender and Command over Property: A critical gap in Economic Analysis and Policy in South Asia", *World Development* 22(1): 1455–1478.

Akabzaa, T., 2000, *Boom and Dislocation: Environmental Impacts of Mining in Wassa West District of Ghana.* Accra: Third World Network.

Amanor, K.S. with M. Kude Diderutuah, 2000, "Land and Labour Contracts in the Oil Palm and Citrus Belt of Ghana", paper presented at IIED and GRET Workshop on June 2–6, Ouagadougou.

Amanor, K., 2002, "Shifting Tradition: Forest Resource Tenure in Ghana", in: Toulmin, C. *et al.* (eds), *The Dynamics of Resource Tenure in West Africa,* London: International Institute for Environment and Development, pp. 48–60.

Anghie, A., 2005, *Imperialism, Sovereignty and the making of International Law,* New York: Cambridge University Press.

Bee, A., 2000, "Globalization, Grapes and Gender: Women's work in Traditional and Agro-export Production in Northern Chile", *The Geographical Journal* 166(3): 255–265.

Carr, M., M.A. Chen, and J. Tate, 2000, "Globalisation and Home based workers", *Feminist Economics* 6(3): 123–42.

Darkwah, A. K., 2002, "Trading goes Global: Ghanaian Market Women in an Era of Globalization", *Asian Women* 15: 31–47.

Escobar, A., 1995, *Encountering Development: the Making and Unmaking of the Third World*. Princeton, NJ: Princeton University Press.

Fig, D., 2005, "Manufacturing Amnesia: Corporate Social Responsibility in South Africa", *International Affairs* 81(3): 599–617.

Gills, D. S., 2002, "Globalization of Production and women in Asia", *Annals of the American Academy of Political and Social Science* 581: 106–120.

Hansen, K. T. and M. Vaa, 2004, "Introduction" in Hansen, K.T. and M. Vaa (eds), *Reconsidering Informality: Perspectives From Urban Africa*, Uppsala: Nordiska Africainstitutet.

Jaggar, A. M., 2001, "Is Globalization Good for Women?" *Comparative Literature* 54(4): 298–314.

Kandiyoti, D., 1998, Gender, Power and Contestation: "Bargaining with Patriarchy" Revisited, in Jackson, C. and Pearson, R. (eds), *Feminist Visions of Development*, London and New York: Routledge.

Khor, M., 2000, Globalization and the South: Some Critical Issues, Third World Network, Penang.

Lavigne-Delville, P., C. Toulmin, J. Colin, J. Chauveau, 2001, *Negotiating Access to Land in West Africa: A Synthesis of Findings from Research on Derived Rights to Land*, London: IIED.

McGrew, A., 2000, "Sustainable Globalization? The Global Politics of Development and Exclusion in the new World Order", in Allen, A. and Thomas, A. *Poverty and Development in the 21st Century*. Oxford: Oxford University Press.

Pape, J., 2000, Gender and Globalisation in South Africa: Some Preliminary Reflections on Working Women and Poverty, Cape Town: International Labour Resource and Information Group (ILRIG).

Pearson, R., 2000, "Moving the Goalposts: Gender and Globalisation in the Twenty-First Century", *Gender and Development* 8(1): 10–19.

Peck, J., 2002, Political Economies of Scale: Fast Policy, Interscalar Relations, and Neoliberal Workfare, *Economic Geography* 78(3): 331–360.

Pegg, S., 2005, "Can Policy intervention beat the Resource Curse? Evidence from the Chad-Cameroon Pipeline Project", *African Affairs* 105(418): 1–25.

Razavi, S., 2007, "Liberalisation and the debates on women's Access to Land", *Third World Quarterly* 28(8): 1479–1500.

Scott, J.C., 1985, *Weapons of the Weak: Everyday Forms of Peasant Resistance*, New Haven: Yale University Press.

Tsikata, D., 2003, "Securing Women's Interests within Land Tenure Reforms: Recent Debates in Tanzania", *Journal of Agrarian Change* 3(1 and 2) January and April 2003: 149–183.

———, 2008, "Informalization, the Informal Economy and Urban Women's Livelihoods in Sub-Saharan Africa since the 1990s", in Razavi S. (ed), *The*

Gendered Impacts of Liberalization: Towards "Embedded Liberalism"? London: Routledge.

Turner, T.E., and L.S. Brownhill, 2004, "The Curse of Nakedness: Nigerian Women in the Oil War", in Ricciutelli, L., A. Miles, and M. McFadden, (eds), *Feminist Politics, Activism and Vision: Local and Global Challenges,* Toronto: Inanna Publications and Education Inc, London and New York: Zed.

Ukeje, C., 2002, Gender Identity and Alternative Interpretations of the Discourse of Social Protest among women in the Oil Delta of Nigeria, Paper for Presentation during the CODESRIA General Assemble December 2002, 8–12.

van den Berg, A., 1992, Women in Bamenda: Survival strategies and access to land. African Studies Centre 1992 Research Report No. 50 Welby, S., 2000. Gender, Globalization and Democracy, *Gender and Development* 8(1): 20–28.

Wanitzek, U. and G.K. Woodman, 2004, "Relating Local Legal Activity to Global Influence: A Theoretical Survey", in Woodman G. K., U. Wanitzek, and H. Sippel, (eds), *Local Land Law and Globalization: A Comparative Study of Peri-Urban Area in Benin, Ghana and Tanzania.* Transaction Publishers, USA and UK

Whitehead, A. and D, Tsikata, 2003, "Policy Discourses on Women's Land Rights in Sub-Saharan Africa." *Journal of Agrarian Change* 3(1 and 2): 67–112.

Whitehead, A., 2008, "The Gendered Impacts of Liberalisation Policies on African Agricultural Economies and Rural Livelihoods", in Razavi, S. (ed), *The Gendered Impacts of Liberalization: Towards "Embedded Liberalism*? London: Routledge.

World Bank, 2002, Land Use Rights and gender equality in Vietnam, Promising Approaches to engendering Development, No.1 (September).

| 2 | # Gender, Land Tenure and Globalisation
Exploring the Conceptual Ground

A. FIONA D. MACKENZIE |

INTRODUCTION

Through a series of case studies located in four places—the Amazon forests (of Brazil, Bolivia, Peru), Cameroon, Ghana and Vietnam—this book explores the diversity of ways through which gender is negotiated in situations of changes in land tenure and land use which are, in turn, interrelated with processes operating globally. Together, the case studies provide the empirical basis for tracing the specificities of the workings of global capital as these play themselves out with respect to the constitution of gender and land rights. This chapter considers the three main conceptual threads that inform the four studies—the "global", the "land", and "gender". There has been, as Gillian Hart (2004: 96) points out, a "stunning neglect of land/ nature and agrarian questions in huge swathes of the globalisation literature". But the intent here is not simply to add issues of gender and land to a literature whose objective has been to assess the "impact of globalisation". It is, instead, to explore how, through their inter-relations, the global, the land, and gender, are mutually constituted. The focus is on exploring *the processes* through which these concepts are negotiated. The case studies, conceptually diverse though they are, provide "windows" (see Hart 2004: 96) into these processes.

Working "the global"

> Just as none of us is outside or beyond geography, none of us is completely free from the struggle over geography. That struggle is complex and interesting because it is not only about soldiers and cannons but also about ideas, about forms, about images and imaginings (Said 1994; 7).

Edward Said's words, in the quotation from *Culture and Imperialism* cited above, are a cogent reminder that material struggles—for land, resources, capital—are at the same time struggles over the ideas or ways through which material interests are asserted. David Slater (2003: 48) makes this point clear in his discussion of the process of globalisation and North-South relations when he poses the question, "Global imaginations: Whose globe? Whose imagination?". In responding, his argument focuses on the particular "regime" or "domain" of truth that informs neo-liberalism[1] and whose source resides in Europe and the United States. Paralleling arguments of such critics of "development" as Arturo Escobar (1995) and James Ferguson (1994), Slater (*ibid.*: 50) proposes that, through "an invasive discourse of Western liberalism", "imperialism and the geopolitical penetration of other societies [was] constituted". This discourse, as discourses of development or modernisation, proceeds by constructing as "normal" that which reflected their own (European/North American) "truth", "whilst designating that which was different as other than truth and in need of tutelage" (*ibid.*: 49).[2] To draw on Foucault's analytics of power (for example, 1979), neo-liberalism acts as a political technology removing from the political arena deeply political, and material, questions of (global) social and economic (in)justice, casting them instead as something subject to technological fix—policies, or "dogma" (Patnaik 2003: 35), that frequently pose as "structural adjustment". As a discourse, neo-liberalism offers "the sole prescription for development and progress" (Slater 2003: 48), conveniently erasing from the visual field the extension of Western power that accompanies its practice. Slater (*ibid.*) refers to this process as "a crucial historical and geopolitical amnesia", a "forgetting" that "allows for the historical erasure of imperial politics, and additionally represses the record of contemporary forms of Western power over the non-West". This is "the colonial present", to borrow Derek Gregory's (2004) uncompromising phrase.

Neo-liberalism proceeds not only through the unwavering subscription to a "free" market economy and an ethos of privatisation, but also what Slater (2003: 53) defines as a "possessive individualism". It may be "produced" and "practised" in the North, but its "major deployment" is in the South through what are referred to as structural adjustment policies. In what is by now a familiar litany of measures, these policies, introduced most frequently by the International Monetary Fund (IMF) and World Bank as conditionalities for loans for indebted countries, centre on an externally oriented economy where what had been non-tradables are transferred to the tradable sector (for example, Mohan 1996; Elson 1994, 2002). They include currency devaluation, cutbacks in state expenditure in the economy (employment, wages, agricultural and other subsidies) and outwith it (social/welfare, specifically, health and education), the dismantling of protectionist barriers (trade liberalisation), and measures to support the export of specific commodities (see Bienefeld 1994; Hutchful 1989; Patnaik 2003). To these—since the early 1990s—have been added, as loan conditionalities, the implementation of "democratic" reform and "good governance" (Slater 2003: 53).

While there are obviously differences among states in the South with respect to macro economic performance, evidence demonstrates how such policies have led not only to a substantial redistribution of capital in favour of the North (Slater 2003: 54), but also to significant per capita economic and social costs which play themselves out most insidiously with respect to those increasing numbers of people who live in poverty, and which have specific effects on the issues with which this book is concerned—land rights and the negotiation of gender (see Patnaik 2003: 34). There is, as Utsa Patnaik (2003: 34) shows, a "global crisis of livelihoods" in Asia, in sub-Saharan Africa, and in Latin America. To cite but one indicator of this in sub-Saharan Africa, Patnaik (2003: 37) points to serious declines in per capita GDP (6 per cent in the period 1990–1999) and a rising number of people (from 300 to 380 million) in "absolute poverty (less than one US dollar a day)" over that same decade. She links the decline in levels of nutrition that accompanied this rise in poverty to the devastating effects of HIV/AIDS, arguing that this epidemic "might not perhaps have been as great" had nutrition been more adequate (*ibid.*). Adjustment, she concludes, can never have a "human face': "since the basic agenda is reduction in mass incomes along with a large rise in income inequality, neo-liberal reforms always imply a welfare worsening for the most vulnerable and push down hitherto viable producers into the mire of unemployment, indebtedness and asset loss" (*ibid.*: 38). In an argument reminiscent of Ferguson's (1994) regarding the "failure" of a World Bank financed integrated agricultural development scheme in Lesotho, Patnaik (*ibid.*, emphasis in original) suggests that the IMF and World Bank have not "failed" (as would be the case were rising rates of poverty and de-industrialisation to be taken as identifiers); rather they have "*succeeded*" in what they set out to do, "namely deflate mass incomes and open up third world economies in the interests of global finance capital".

Missing in so many accounts of globalisation, however, is an analysis not only of how gender and other axes of social differentiation such as class, race and age are reconstituted through global process (with respect to gender, for example, by intensifying "women's triple roles in production, reproduction and community management" [Nagar et al. 2002: 262]), but how the reconstitution of gender is central to its configuration. Globalisation, write Nagar et al. (*ibid.*: 273), "needs to be understood in terms of gendered and racialized culturally specific systems of oppression and struggles to negotiate and redefine those systems". Feminist scholarship has shown that "at the very heart (in the form of the constitutive outside) of neoliberalism is the nonmarket" (Roberts 2004: 137). In neo-liberalism, writes Susan Roberts (*ibid.*), what takes place in "informal economies, shadow economies, unpaid labor, subsistence work, barter, social reproduction, and care get[s] treated as nonmarketized", a "demarcation [which] is associated with gendered assumptions about what counts as the economy". Yet, Roberts (*ibid.*) continues, this "so-called nonmarket realm" is integral to the practice of neo-liberalism. Obvious examples include women's positioning as a social safety net for structural adjustment programmes or their work in sweatshops or homework (for example, Mies 1982; Beneria and Roldan 1987; Wright 1997). In both respects—as relations of (re)production—it is through gender that a neo-liberal agenda is subsidised (Nagar et al. 2002: 261; also, see Elson 1994; 2002).

By insistently calling into question the supposed binary of the local/global that works "epistemologically to relegate or contain gender" (Roberts 2004: 127), by recognising that such scales as "the local" and "the global" are themselves socially produced (Massey 1994) and that the "scales" of the body, the household, the community, are as necessary to an understanding of neo-liberalism as the "global" (see Nagar et al. 2002: 265), feminist research punctures the presumed boundaries between North and South, the local and the global. Roberts (2004: 129) refers to such boundary (or binary) making as the "colonialist spatialization" of neo-liberalism. This way of thinking disturbs, in Gibson-Graham's (2003: 49) words, "a global imaginary'—the hegemony, the given-ness, or the "normative insistence" (Massey 2000: 283), of the global. Thereby, it throws out "the neo-liberal mantra that there is no alternative" (*ibid.*). Doreen Massey (*ibid.*) writes, "The International Monetary Fund, World Trade Organization, World Bank and most governing elites, to say nothing of the world's multinational corporations, are deeply engaged in the double practice of describing as inevitable ... something which they are at the same time trying to produce". "It is that tendentially totalizing imagination of a necessary future", she continues, "which enables the imposition of strategies of structural adjustment ..." (*ibid.*). "It is of consummate importance", in her view, "that, as active producers of geographical imaginaries, we persistently question and try to hold open such discourses on the spatiality of power" (*ibid.*).

It is on such destabilisation of a deeply gendered colonialist imaginary and its spatial specifications that feminist and postcolonial scholars build an alternative configuration of the global/local. There is "a multiscalar focus on the connections, relations, and processes across cultures that constitute geographic unevenness" (Nagar et al.: 259) and, as a corollary, an awareness that the local and global are mutually constitutive. With this come "alternative readings of globalization" as "a contingent and constructed discourse" (*ibid.*: 262, 263)

666

and the theorisation of new, socially just, political possibilities, for
Gibson-Graham (2003: 53), a politics of the "otherwise". At times
and variously endorsed as "grassroots globalisation" (Appadurai
2000) or "grassroots post-modernism" (Esteva and Prakash 1998),
such politics privileges "place" as a theoretical construct. It does so,
not in order to romanticise a marginalised local, or to suggest that
there is such a thing as an autonomous "local" disconnected from
the circulation of global capital, but to challenge the ways through
which knowledge about the global has been produced and power
thereby exercised. It seeks to escape from the global/local binary of
the "capitalocentric imaginary" (Gibson-Graham 2003: 54), making
visible a counter-narrative whose principles and practices *"recognize
particularity and contingency, honor difference and otherness, and
cultivate local capacity"* (Gibson-Graham 2003: 54, 51, emphasis in
original).

For Gibson-Graham (2003), the notion of "resubjectivation",
drawn from Foucault's (1985: 28) distinction between principles and
practices of the self in his analysis of morality, is central to the cultivation of local capacity, and to the resignification of place. Graham
(2002: 19, cited in Roberts 2004: 130) defines the issue as follows:

> Globalization discourse has produced all of us as local subjects who are
> subordinated to, and contained within, a "global capitalist economy".
> Ultimately, then, the problem of locality is a problem of the subject, and
> the ethical challenge to a politics of place is one of re-subjectivation—
> how to produce ourselves and others as local agents who are economically
> creative and viable, who are subjects rather than objects of development
> (however we may want to define that term).

One way to take this line of argument forward, with the intent of
exploring further the workings of the local/global and, specifically, the
processes through which people reposition themselves with respect to
the capitalist economy (i.e. re-subjectivation), is to engage in research
which focuses on particular events—such as the construction of an
oil pipeline in Cameroon, the organisation of new trade networks
in the Amazon forests, the privatisation of land in Vietnam, or
the exploitation of resources (gold and mangroves) in Ghana. By
examining the *everyday* ways through which women and men,

differently placed in terms of class, age, race, for example, negotiate rights to land, resources, and trade relations, in historically and geographically precise places, such research has the potential to explore something of the complexity and contradictions of globalisation and how gender, among other axes of social differentiation, is constituted through such engagements.

A second area for investigation concerns considering the ways through which the workings of the local/global are bound up with discourses of "nature". This is not simply a matter of examining "environmental impact'—for example, of an oil pipeline, small-scale surface gold mining, or the privatisation of paddy fields—although it may be recognised that an intensification of exploitation of the environment in any of these sites is part and parcel of the exploitation of the land, tied in turn into the workings of global capital (see Peluso and Watts 2001; Peet and Watts 2004). It is rather a matter of exploring how "nature", as a social construct, enters the vocabularies of actors who seek to make claims to the land or to resources. If the arguments of such theorists of social nature as Bruce Braun and Noel Castree (1998; also see Castree and Braun 2001; Braun 2002) are accepted, this means conceptualizing nature not as something separate from humans (as conjured by the binary "natural"/"cultural"), as a given or a backdrop against which events occur, but as always in the process of becoming, caught up in the social, cultural, political and economic crossings of the past and the present. In Castree's words, nature is conceived as "*internal* to social processes" (2001: 15, emphasis his). And in this context, a key question for research whose aim is to examine the co-constitution of the local/global concerns how, through particular configurations of "nature", particular individual or collective claims to the land or to resources are created and legitimated.

Working "the land"

One of the first tasks of the culture of resistance was to reclaim, rename, and reinhabit the land. And with that came a whole set of further assertions, recoveries, and identifications, all of them quite literally grounded on this poetically projected base (Said 1994: 226).

Heralded by critic Samir Amin as a book that "rows against the current", *Reclaiming the Land. The Resurgence of Rural Movements in Africa, Asia and Latin America* (2005), edited by Sam Moyo and Paris Yeros, positions political mobilisation in rural areas in the South against the extension of neo-liberalism (structural adjustment), including land reform programmes and agro-food policies. It is rural movements, the editors argue, that, "despite ongoing problems of mobilization and political articulation, and under the most oppressive of circumstances, ... constitute the core nucleus of opposition to neoliberalism and the most important sources of democratic trans-formation in national and international politics" (2005a: 6). It is in "the countrysides of the periphery" that "the nucleus of anti-imperialist politics" is to be found (2005b: 9).

Centring their argument with reference to the debate in Marxism concerning the relationship between "the agrarian question" and "the national question", Moyo and Yeros propose that, through ongoing processes of "underdevelopment/neo-liberalism", a "semi-proletariat" has emerged—the result of "contradictory forces of proletarianization, urbanization, and re-peasantization'—and it is this that "constitutes the core social base of rural movements" (2005a: 5). Through case studies, the contributing authors trace the historical specificities of struggle and comment on the "strategies, tactics and ideologies" of each movement (*ibid.*). The movements range from those that are more "*organized*" (*ibid.*: 6, emphasis in original), such as the Movimento dos Trabalhadores Rurais Sem Terra (MST, or Landless Rural Workers' Movement) in Brazil (Fernandes; Mattei), the Zapatistas in Mexico (Bartra and Otero), the FARC-EP in Colombia (Revolutionary Armed Forces of Colombia—People's Army) (Ampuero and Brittain), and UNORKA in the Philippines (Feranil), to newer movements in sub-Saharan Africa. The last include the Landless People's Movement (LPM) in South Africa (Sihlongonyane) and the land occupation movement of Zimbabwe (Moyo and Yeros). Also evident in the book are "more embryonic, diffuse and spontaneous" land-based movements (Moyo and Yeros, 2005a: 6) in Ghana (Amanor), Malawi (Kanyongolo) and India (Pimple and Sethi). The movements, as the editors (*ibid.*: 6) point out, demonstrate considerable diversity both in terms of material response to a neo-liberal agenda and to the "ideologies" that inform them—"development", "human rights", "indigenous rights" and "national liberation", accompanied, *inter alia,* "by a growing emphasis on women's rights".

I introduce a discussion of the conceptualisation of land through this book because of its explicit objective of linking claims to the land to the extension or deepening of neo-liberalism in the South. It demonstrates both the centrality of land, and "the rural", to understanding the effects of neo-liberal structural adjustment programmes in the South and makes visible people's actions in the face of these—however inchoate they might be. Explicit interconnections are made between "the local" and "the global". But, for the purpose of this book and theorising the land, a troubling limitation is the book's unproblematised privileging of class over other axes of social differentiation. In stating this, I do not dispute that "class" is a critical category in understanding rural relations and people's mobilisation. And the editors (and contributors) acknowledge that class does not always act in isolation; in the cases of Mexico, Zimbabwe, and South Africa, for example, it is shown to be cross-cut by, and cross-cutting race in often complicated ways (2005b: 33). In India, Pimple and Sethi (2005: 235–256) show how caste intersects in important ways with class. But gender is far less visible, despite Moyo and Yaris's acknowledgement, first, of its analytical centrality to what they refer to as "functional dualism" as is race (2005b: 34) and, second, in the late 1990s, of rural movements' adoption of equity policies (2005b: 49–50). But there is virtually no exploration of how gender works with class/caste/race to reconfigure rural relations, and specifically, contemporary claims to land, through social movements. In his work on Malawi, Fidelis Edge Kanyongolo (2005: 124, 129–130) briefly identifies the intertwining of class and gender with respect to the reforms of 1967 and, more particularly, the recent land occupations. He cites the lack of documentation of the gendered dynamics of land occupations, but notes that there is "sufficient evidence" to show not only that both women and men have taken part, but that the same gendered inequalities evident in the national political economy may be seen in women's "limited involvement ... in the decision-making echelons of the land occupiers" (*ibid.*: 129).

Brief mention of the significance of gender is also made by Mfaniseni Fana Sihlonganyane (2005: 149–150) with respect to the land occupations in South Africa and by Moyo and Paris (2005c: 196–197) in the context of Zimbabwe. In India, Minar Pimple and Manpreet Sethi's (2005: 249) sole mention of women concerns their gaining of rights of land ownership in the Bodhgaya struggle in Bihar. More useful, analytically, is Igor Ampuero and James Brittain's (2005: 369) discussion of women and men's participation in FARC-EP, Colombia, on "increasingly equal terms'—women now comprising about 40 per cent of the membership. They surmise that "while the dynamics of poverty and violence affect women and men differently, [both] have joined together in the FARC-EP in a spirit of solidarity towards the defense of agrarian reform and socio-political transformation, against the hegemony of the national and international elite and business classes" (*ibid.*). With these very limited exceptions, the semi-proletariat—however otherwise sophisticatedly theorized that concept might be claimed to be—remains resolutely male.

This state of affairs is rendered all the more problematic by the considerable number of studies which demonstrate how gendered rural spaces and mobilisation around claims to land are. Brief examples of research attest to this point. To turn first to the MST in Brazil, Carmen Diana Deere (2003: 272) draws on a substantial body of research—including that conducted by herself and Magdalena León—to argue that, since its beginning in the 1980s, women have been "very visible" in the MST-led *assentamentos*, the land occupations, comprising between one-third and one-half of the participants and frequently positioning themselves at the forefront of confrontations with the police. Deere also shows that women's participation in the MST, and particularly in the leadership, has been a site of struggle linked to their growing politicisation in rural unions and their own autonomous rural movement. She indicates how, before the late 1990s, although women's formal rights to land were guaranteed under the constitutional reform of 1988, none of these organisations prioritised women's land rights. Women's organisations themselves focused, instead, on membership in the unions and on gaining social security benefits (for example, paid maternity leave and retirement benefits) for rural women workers (2005: 263). Women were fighting against their representation as "housewives" or "unpaid family workers", to claim a position as "rural workers" (Deere, 2003: 275). And it was also the case that until the end of the 1990s—despite growing visibility within the MST of gender issues, evident for example in a chapter on "The Articulation of Women" in the first edition of the *General Norms of the MST* (1989) (Deere, 2003: 273)—gender issues were seen as divisive and thus gender was eclipsed by class by the leadership. As Deere (2003: 274) explains, particularly at times when the struggle for agrarian reform became more difficult, as under the Collor Government (1990–1992), the unity of the movement was paramount. At the same time, it is important to note that the MST's lack of consideration of women's rights to land, for example through titling of land in couples' names, had to do with the MST's definition of land rights as collective rather than individual; use rights were to be individual, but the title was to be collective, assigned to all the *assentados* (Deere, 2003: 274).

That the situation changed at the end of the 1990s, Deere (2003: 278, 279) attributes, in part, to the growing realisation within the MST leadership that "the exclusion of most women from land rights has meant their exclusion from participation in the associations and cooperatives that make the crucial decisions governing production plans and infrastructure and social investments, etc., on the *assentamentos*". This had an effect on the "well-being" of the *assentamento* and, more broadly, the movement itself. Women's lack of participation played itself out in terms of both "general apathy" for collective activities within the *assentamento* and at the level of practicality where, for example, a woman was unable to obtain credit in the absence of her husband. In the face of some continuing ambiguity on the part of the MST, Deere (2003: 280) sees as significant women's growing visibility in the national leadership (9 of the 21 members of the National Directorate are now women) and in the "gender discourse at the base", frequently linked to the number of leadership positions at the level of the *assentamento*, sub-region or state now occupied by women. In part, the change was due to action outwith the MST. Here, the march of 15,000 to 20,000 women on Brasilia on 10 August 2000, known as the *Marcha das Margaridas* (after Margarida Alves, a union leader from the Northeast who was assassinated), organised by other rural organisations, including autonomous women's groups, is seen as a catalyst. Among other demands of the march, women's claim to rights to the land were made explicit (Deere, 2003: 281). As Deere (2003:282) notes, "gender-progressive measures" on the part of INCRA, the national institute of agrarian reform, have since followed, although the particular problems faced by women-headed households have not yet been addressed.

As a second example, reference may be made to research in India where Bina Agarwal's (1994) discussion of the Bodhgaya Struggle in Bihar (1978 to early 1980s) makes visible the limitations of Pimple and Sethi's (2005) work cited above, and Patnaik's (2003: 60–62) analysis of Operation Barga in West Bengal. To make a brief reference to the latter first, Patnaik (2003: 60) shows how Operation Barga (the term means "share'), begun in 1978, together with a revival of the *Panchayat* (the system of decentralised local government) in the 1980s under a Left Front state government which has been in power since 1977, contributed to a reversal of rural insecurity. In turn, this has led to sustained agricultural growth and, second only to Kerala, the highest rates of decline in rural poverty in India. Patnaik (2003: 60) attributes Operation Barga's importance to its giving "owner-like security to the mass of poor peasants by recording them and making eviction difficult, and fix[ing] fair limits to the share of the crop payable as rent". She notes that although the issue of gendered rights to land was not addressed in the early days of reform, this has now changed, largely owing to the lobbying of women's organisations (2003: 62). Land is now registered in the names of both spouses or, where a household is female-headed, in the woman's name alone (*ibid.*). Thus, she writes, "Bengal now leads in implementing land rights of women" (*ibid.*). This research, together with that cited on Brazil, makes clear that the negotiation of gender is part and parcel of a re-thinking of relations of (re)production and that it is not simply inadequate to conceptualise the rural semi-proletariat through a male-centric optic, but misleading too.

Agarwal's (1994) discussion, *inter alia*, of the Bodhgaya Struggle is instructive in leading forward the discussion thus far of the conceptualisation of land—as imbricated in the negotiation of what may be several axes of social differentiation (gender, class, race and caste) as these interrelate with the local, the state/nation and the global. Agarwal's position, echoed in substantial work which falls under the rubric of post-structural political ecology (as examples, Carney and Watts 1990; Escobar 1995; Mackenzie 1998; Paulson and Gezon 2005; Peet and Watts 1996, 2004; Schroeder 1999; Watts 1998, 2001, 2004) is that, material as are the struggles for land as the means of production, they are also struggles over the meanings of the land, the discourses through which rights are constituted. She demonstrates this with respect to the Bodhgaya "peasant movement", "probably the first land struggle in South Asia in which *women's* land interests were explicitly taken into account and carried forward with some success" (Agarwal,1994: 108, emphasis in original). Basing her account on Manimala's (1983) research, Agarwal (1994) points to how women drew on discourses (to be accurate, she writes of "ideologies') of gender equity, including women's right to economic resources, to a life free from domestic violence, to education, in their claim to land. These discourses, she notes, were simultaneously becoming more visible on the national and international stage (*ibid.*: 109) and thus women in Bodhgaya could draw on notions of gender-based solidarity outwith their particular area for their specific claims. She shows that the movement itself, located in one of India's "most caste-factionalised states", Bihar, was a struggle by a heterogenous group of people—landless labourers and sharecroppers—to secure rights to land they had long cultivated but which were "controlled" by a "monastery-cum-temple complex", a Hindu Math (*ibid.*). In turn, it drew on "a Gandhian-socialist" youth organisation, founded in 1975, whose focus was the alleviation of poverty and in which women played an integral role (*ibid.*). Agarwal cites evidence of women's active and visible participation in the struggle, supporting it both as a class struggle but also, importantly, making evident their gender-informed demands, including women's independent rights to land and participation in decision-making within the organisation from which they had largely been excluded (*ibid.*: 104, 106). In this, following a significant period of debate and opposition they had to counter from within the family, from some male activists within the movement, and from government officials charged with registering title, they were successful. Women gained rights to land as individual title holders, joint holders of title with their husbands, as widows, people who were impoverished or disabled and, in a few cases (and where land was more abundant) as unmarried adult daughters (*ibid.*: 105).

But if we are to understand land struggles, as Cecile Jackson (2003: 461) notes, we need to pay attention not only to such visible mobilisation as that cited above, but also to the struggles of the everyday, the myriad ways through which rights to land are defined by people who are differently positioned with respect to the land. Recognising that the everyday is constructed through social relations scaled from the body, the household, and the local to the global, I turn now to research where the negotiation of rights to the land is part of the everyday constitution of identities. My objective is to "unpack" how, conceptually, the land is worked. Congruent with the line of argument already developed, my concern is to demonstrate through reference to specific research how land, as property in Nicholas Blomley's (2003: 122) discussion, "depends on a continual, active 'doing'".

As a point of departure for this discussion, I focus on "the customary" as it pertains to land rights in selected studies in sub-Saharan Africa in order to demonstrate the analytical importance of recognising that rights to land—of access, control, and more recently "ownership"—as a material resource, are constituted through claims to the meanings of that land. This point is brought out forcefully in the post-structural literature cited above. Judith Carney and Michael Watts's (1990) research in the irrigated rice fields of the Jahaly-Pacharr swamps in The Gambia provides one example. In an extended case study where intra-household relations are positioned with reference to colonial and post-independence state policies, the workings of a multilateral donor agency (International Fund for Agriculture and Development [IFAD]), and kinship relations, Carney and Watts show how the gendered struggle for the redistribution of land following the introduction of irrigation in the mid-1980s centred on the re-negotiation of the meanings of individual (*kamenyango*) and household or collective (*maruo*) rights to land and labour. As they explain, the success of the scheme depended on an intensification of women's labour (double-cropping) in the cultivation of rice under contract farming. Following women's successful mobilisation, plots which had initially been allocated, for the most part, to men were re-registered in women's names by IFAD, but only because men had already achieved *de facto* control of the land through an agreement with the project management (Carney and Watts 1990: 224). As Carney and Watts (*ibid.*, emphasis in original) demonstrate, "[p]roject management had intervened to overcome male resistance to donor wishes by concurring with men that the household, and not the individual woman, irrespective of prior claims had *final* control over crop disposition on the irrigated plots". Thus male household heads, by classifying the irrigated land as *maruo*, and regardless of who had registered rights in the land, were able to exercise rights to women's labour. Such new demands on women's labour were at the expense of their "customary" *kamenyango* rights (*ibid.*).

Among women's responses to their loss of individual rights, particularly where they were not recompensed for their labour through the allocation of non-irrigated land or by being given a proportion of the harvest, was the withdrawal of their labour from rice irrigation (with clear effects on crop productivity). "Proletarianised" by the scheme, such women drew on the customary idiom of *kafos*, a reciprocal labour group, to effect greater control over their individual earnings as wage labourers on the rice schemes (Carney and Watts 1990: 229). Carney and Watts (*ibid.*) show how in *kafos*, "organizational framework in which women pool their labour for hire in transplanting, weeding, harvesting or threshing, but in contrast to the pre-project period, payment is no longer retained for the mutual need but is divided up among the members as a *de facto* wage".

Similar arguments are made by Fiona Mackenzie (1995) regarding *ngwatio* in Murang'a District, Central Province, Kenya. In this case, Mackenzie shows how "custom" provides the discursive means through which women both re-work collective work arrangements for their individual gain and try to gain security in rights to land generally registered in their husband's name. "In Murang'a, for instance, paralleling arguments made in the study in The Gambia, women's re-working of *ngwatio*, reciprocal work groups, is linked to their lack of control over the proceeds of their labour, specifically from the production of coffee. Payment for coffee is routed through cooperative societies where membership is assigned to the landholder, generally a man. The research shows how women's withdrawal of their labour from coffee production, and the resultant decline in the quality of coffee exported from the district, led to a drive for joint accounts in the cooperative's Savings and Loans societies. With respect to land, the Kenyan research demonstrates how women and men contest rights to land through customary idioms (for women, the notion of female husband is noticeable here) and that such rights are central to the ongoing configuration of land tenure even where land tenure reform (the registration and titling of land) has occurred. Customary law is here but one legal discourse, through which rights are contested and, as the research shows, to which women and men differentially positioned with respect to class, age, marital status, race, *inter alia*, have access (Mackenzie 1990, 1995, 1998). Customary law is shown to be not some "dead hand of tradition" (Chanock 1985: 237), but as malleable and manipulable as any legal discourse in the contemporary struggle for land. In other words, customary law, as state law, is not an essentialised legal order but, together with other legal orders, provides the political spaces through which rights to land are contested.

   This line of argument may be extended, in part, by reference to recent research published in Muthoni Wanyeki's (2003) edited volume, *Women and Land in Africa: Culture, Religion and Realizing Women's Rights.* With the intent of exploring the relationships among culture, religion and human rights in so far as they concern women's rights to land, and with considerable conceptual plurality, contributors expand the discourses through which rights are legitimated. As an example, Hussaina Abdullah and Ibrahim Hamza's (2003) discussion of land rights in Northern Nigeria is instructive. The primary aim of the research is to analyse "the ways in which women use tradition, religion and natural justice to assert and/or defend their land rights" (Abdullah and Hamza 2003: 134). But, the authors note, as such notions as custom or tradition and interpretations of Islam and Christianity are constantly under dispute, they also aim to examine how such disputes work to women's advantage or disadvantage (*ibid.*). With a focus on "actual practice on the ground", they choose three study sites to provide a window into the many ways through which land rights are negotiated (*ibid.*). Their first site, Muslim areas of Kano and Sokoto states, provides the basis for a nuanced study of "radical" and "conservative" variants of Islam and how these are played out with respect to women's land rights. The second site, Christian areas of Southern Zaria emirate, provides insights into land relations where Christianity is dominant. The third site, Maguzawa areas of Kano state, was selected on account of the large numbers of people who adhere to an indigenous religion which, the authors contend, provided significant economic autonomy for women, for example in terms of controlling the product of their labour on the land (Abdullah and Hamza 2003: 143–144). Interestingly, the study found that, with the deepening of economic crisis, conversions to both Islam and Christianity became more common among the Maguzawa, with implications for how gendered land rights were negotiated (*ibid.*).

One of the interesting outcomes of the research discussed in the book edited by Wanyeki is the detailed list of recommendations provided by each author as to how to move towards securing women's rights to land. As one might expect, and reflecting Ann Whitehead and Dzodzi Tsikata's (2003) discussion of the views of other African feminists, there is considerable diversity. There is no attempt at proposing one-size-fits-all prescriptions (on this issue, also see Jackson, 2003). Thus, for example, Patrice Bigombe Logo and Elise-Henriette Bikie (2003), writing about Cameroon, cite the need for changes in state as well as in customary law, with considerable emphasis placed on the means of increasing women's awareness of their (human) rights (particularly through women's organisations), an emphasis that is endorsed by Ngoné Diop Tine and Mohamadou Sy's (2003) work in Senegal. These recommendations run parallel to those of Abdullah and Hamza (2003) in Nigeria, but in the context of Nigeria, the authors explicitly emphasise women's independent rights to land, including the enforcement of rights recognised in the Sharia law. With respect to Ethiopia, Zenebeworke Tadesse (2003) addresses the broader social context (polygamy, labour rights and the gendered division of labour) of women's rights, while at the same time recognising the need for the implementation of existing legislation, for example, the 1997 Rural Land Redistribution Proclamation in Amhara National State that contains provisions for gender equality. Similarly positioning rights to land within the broader social and economic context, Winnie Bikaako and John Ssenkumba (2003: 310) call for more "effective conflict resolution mechanisms" than those found in "customary courts, local council courts and courts of law" in Uganda.

In moving forward the conceptualisation of the land as constantly "becoming", as constantly re-worked through the daily negotiations of its meanings, Whitehead and Tsikata's (2003) focus on the implications for gender justice of a "re-turn to the customary" in policy discourses is valuable, not least because it both problematises the customary and makes explicit connections between individuals' everyday experiences *vis à vis* the land, the state, and a global (World Bank), modernist, "language of custom". To reiterate a point made above, I am using the notion of "customary" here for heuristic purposes to demonstrate how, as a discourse, it mediates the material and the metaphorical. I draw briefly on the authors' arguments which call into question the emerging consensus among policy institutions, including the World Bank and non-governmental organisations (NGOs), that the route forward is through the "customary".[3] They note that, while "non-gender specialists" now propose to encourage "the evolution of customary practices", "gender specialists" are less sanguine, the majority advocating that "women's land and property rights ... be enshrined in statutory law" in order to achieve gender justice (2003: 69).

To turn to key aspects of their argument, Whitehead and Tsikata (2003: 76–77) stress the embeddedness of local legal practices in social relations, still bound up in complex, multiple and interlocking ways—with respect to use and disposal—to people. To borrow Martin Chanock's (1995) pithy phrase, claims to land in African tenure systems have, or at least had, to do with claims to people, not to things (property). Claims to land are constantly negotiated as social relations are re-worked. And whereas such research as that of H.W.O. Okoth-Ogendo (1978, 1989) questions the idea that such claims or rights used to be hierarchical—for example, that (frequently women's) rights of use were secondary to those of (frequently men's) rights of disposal[4]—Whitehead and Tsikata (2003: 78) observe that the significant issue is what has happened to gender-differentiated "historically-constituted" interests in land with profound socio-economic change. Importantly, they note, *contra* "a legal centrist model" of the relationship between customary and statutory law—implying separate legal domains—that contemporary negotiation of interests in land suggest "a more messy reality" (*ibid.*: 95). Drawing on such work as that of Takyiwa Manuh (1994) in Ghana and Anne Griffiths (1998, 2001) in Botswana, they question both the dichotomising and hierachisation of these legal orders. For example, with reference to the latter's findings, they write that "the concepts and objectives from one system seem to slip quite easily to the other and that actors ... do not treat the legal idea in the two systems as hermetically sealed off" (Whitehead and Tsikata, 2003: 95). They go so far as to propose that a "more appropriate model of legal pluralism [than the legal centrist one] would see them as mutually constitutive" (*ibid.*). They refer to situations of "forum shopping" where individuals draw on different legal orders and institutions in their search for justice, using whichever they can access or which they can work to their advantage (*ibid.*). And, of course, individuals have differential access to these legal orders according to gender, class, age ..., success being linked to the negotiation of power relations.

For Whitehead and Tsikata (2003: 97–98), it is precisely because land claims are socially embedded, because decision-making processes cannot be unravelled from local power relations, and because the latter, on balance, favour men over women, that customary law is limited with respect to working towards gender justice. It is "the inequalities in power relations in rural societies, played out in a modern context", they continue, "that are the mechanism by which women lose claims to land as individual proprietorship evolves" (*ibid.*: 98). The implication is that "the rural customary cannot be left to muddle along without widening the gap between men's and women's land access" (*ibid.*). Hence, they find deeply problematic the World Bank's recent espousal of the customary, following its decades-long adherence to the mantra of registered, individual, freehold title. For them, the Bank's endorsement of "local-level systems of tenure and rental" is "closely linked to its objectives of deeper and better land markets, and a belief that customary law will deliver, more cheaply, and with less conflict, precisely the individual forms of possession that foreign capital requires" (*ibid.* 100). "In this scenario", they continue, "the language of the customary masks modernization and marketization" (*ibid.*: 101).

But such re-invention of custom may also serve the interests of the governing elites of African states. For many, the construction of the binary "African/traditional/good versus Western/new/bad" has been of considerable rhetorical moment (Whitehead and Tsikata 2003:101). Here, the language of custom hides the play of "a contemporary form of political power", particularly where such power is allied, for example, to the institution and practices of chieftaincy (*ibid.*). There are, Whitehead and Tsikata (2003: 103–104) write, "too many hostages to fortune in the language of the customary at a national level for it to spearhead democratic reforms and resistance to centralized and elite-serving state power". But there are also a number of problems with advocating that gender justice be pursued primarily through the state. One example concerns the gender bias of state legal orders and practices, displayed in such instances where the state deploys a discourse of custom in order to subvert women's claims which are articulated through a rights discourse, itself located within "modern legal frameworks" (*ibid.*: 99, drawing on Stewart 1996). Whitehead and Tsikata (2003: 103) are of the view that the answer lies in "democratic reform and state accountability ... not [in] a flight into the customary". "At a more detailed level", they continue, "women's land claims need to be based on a nuanced and highly sensitive set of policy discourses and policy instruments—ones which reflect the social embeddedness of land claims, the frequent gender inequality in such relations and the rights to livelihood of African women" (*ibid.*).[5] Recognising the complexity of this issue in Zimbabwe, the Women and Law in Southern Africa Research Trust poses the question "whether justice is, ought to be or in reality can be, the prerogative of the state and its authorized agencies or is something that can be found and delivered in a multiplicity of ways and at many sites, including those not recognized by the state" (Stewart *et al.* 2000: 20, cited in Goebel 2005a: 160). "The implication for women and land rights", Allison Goebel (2005a: 160–161) continues, "is that, while state intervention is crucial to support improved access and control of land for women, at the end of the day women will be faced with negotiating those rights through the complex social field of formal and informal institutions (especially families), customary and general law practices and values" (also see Goebel 2005b).

In order to conceptualise "the land", I have argued in this part of the chapter that there is a need to unpack the meanings of the term. I have illustrated what this means both by exposing inadequacies of recent theorising of social, land-based, movements in the South and exploring the need to go beyond Marxian theorising of relations to the land by searching for the meanings through which struggles for the land are constituted. In order to develop this line of thinking, I have explored the ways through which "customary" rights may be entangled in attempts to exercise power or to resist its extension. This argumentation is extended in the final section of the paper by focusing on the need for a fine-grained analysis of the complex social relations, including gender, through which claims to the land are made.

Working "gender"

> There is first of all the possibility of discovering a world *not* constructed out of warring essences. Second, there is the possibility of a universalism that is not limited or coercive, which believing that all people have only one single identity is. ... Third, ... it does mean thinking of local identity as not exhaustive (Said 1994: 229).

In this quotation, Said is referring to the possibilities that arise when essentialisms (here, specifically, to do with identity—'nativism') are eschewed in the process of decolonisation. He writes, that to "leave the historical world for the metaphysics of essences like *négritude*, Irishness, Islam, or Catholicism is to abandon history for essentializations that turn human beings against each other" (1994: 228–229). His work, as well as that of other post-structural and post-colonial theorists of identity, centres on questioning the notion of identity as fixed and singular or "exhaustive", drawing attention to the negative political consequences that follow from such conceptualisation. Whether it concerns race, class, or gender—

among other axes of social differentiation—such theorists focus their concern on exposing the assumptions that underlie the construction of identity as essentialist, universal, or in some sense pre-given.

In feminist scholarship, this (post-colonial) conceptualisation of identity does not simply have to do with disputing claims of homogeneity among women on the basis of biology or "nature" but, as Chandra Mohanty (1991: 56) states in her widely cited article, "Under Western Eyes. Feminist Scholarship and Colonial Discourses", it concerns the production of women "on the basis of secondary sociological and anthropological universals", specifically "the 'sameness' of their oppression". There is "an elision", she argues (*ibid.*), between "'women' as a discursively constructed group and 'women' as material subjects of their own history". The result is the assumption that women comprise "an always already constituted group", characterised by such adjectives as "powerless" or "exploited", and thus that "the material and ideological specificities of women's experiences are left unexplored" (*ibid.*, 56–57).

While there are obviously important political consequences of challenging such essentialising and universalising assumptions (in addition to Mohanty [1991] see, for example, Haraway [1990], Flax [1992]), what is significant here are the conceptual issues that follow from such a line of questioning. Anne McClintock's (1995) penetrating analysis of imperialism is instructive. Gender, race and class are, for her, "articulated categories"; they are not "distinct realms of experience" that exist "in splendid isolation from each other; nor can they be simply yoked together retrospectively like armatures of Lego" (1995: 4–5) "Rather", she continues, "they come into existence *in and through* relation to each other—if in contradictory and conflictual ways" (*ibid.*: 5, emphasis hers). So the story that needs to be told "is not simply 'about the things that have happened to women and men and how they have related to them; instead it is about how the subjective and collective meanings of women and men as categories of identity have been constructed'" (Scott 1988: 6, cited in McClintock 1995: 16) in particular historical contexts. This is exactly what Judith Butler (1992) means when she writes about the "contingency" of identity. An identity, for example that of "woman", for her does not pre-exist its construction; it is performed through everyday social/political encounter (Butler, 1993).

What this line of argument signifies is that "gender" (or race, or class) is not a descriptive category, but "a site of permanent openness and resignifiability" (Butler 1992: 16)—for men as well as women. This does not mean that the categories "woman" and "man" are not of enormous political moment; it does mean that the terms "woman" and "man" are opened up to multiple meanings which shift as people continuously reposition themselves through the everyday exercise of household, kinship, community, national or global relations. In terms of research into gender and land, one implication of such theorisation is that there is a focus on *how* such a subject position as that of "woman" or "man" is brought into being through the negotiation of rights to the land rather than on women and men as fixed and undifferentiated analytical categories. These rights are undoubtedly time and place specific, related both to changes in life cycle and history. Jackson (2003: 465–469) gives some idea of the instability of the term "woman" and the complexity of relations through which this identity is constructed when she refers to the different subject positions that women may occupy simultaneously—as wives, mothers, mothers-in law, sisters, daughters, kin—and to their differing subjectivities.[6] With reference to women's subject positions, and in response to Agarwal's (2003) work in India, she writes that, "As a daughter, a woman appears to have the obvious interests in claiming a share or parental property that Agarwal outlines, but as a wife she may also be against the land claims of her husband's sister, and as a mother she will not necessarily support a daughter against the claims of a son" (Jackson, 2003: 467). "These intersecting interests", she continues, "which reflect the multiple subject positions occupied by any one woman, mean that we should expect a diversity of opinions on the desirability of land rights for women". Such diversity will necessarily reflect how women make sense of their individual worlds—their subjectivities— as, for example, they make choices about how to negotiate marriage or kinship relations.

Nowhere is a narrative of the reworking of the subject positions of "women" and "men" clearer than in Richard Schroeder's (1999) nuanced narrative of the conflicts that accompanied two "development" projects in Kerewan, on The Gambia's North Bank. The first, in the 1980s, concerned a Non-Governmental Organisation (NGO)-led initiative to support market gardening for women; the second, an initiative to promote agro-forestry in the 1990s. Both are located temporally with reference to a national economic crisis and structural adjustment programmes negotiated with international financial institutions, matters of food security and persistent drought, and the availability of substantial development capital bound up with global discourses, first, of WID (Women in Development) and, second, the environment. With respect to the earlier project, Schroeder shows how market gardening provided women (differentiated primarily by age and marital status) with the material and discursive means to rescript household relations, specifically the conjugal contract. In the struggle to gain the moral high ground in a local economy where women were becoming the financial mainstay as men's earnings from groundnuts declined, both genders deployed such metaphors as that of "second husband" to reposition themselves as "wives" or "husbands". Threatened by the loss of income from groundnuts, men accused women of neglecting their marital responsibilities—they now had a new husband, the gardens. Women's response was to state that to all intents and purposes the gardens had indeed replaced husbands in terms of providing for the household. Schroeder (1999: 42) relates how women insisted that they "might just as well be married to their gardens". He then goes on to cite how one woman "underscored the point dramatically by asserting that not just her garden, but the *well bucket* she used to irrigate her vegetables was her husband because everything she owned came from it" (*ibid.*, emphasis in original). Initially encountering opposition, women later managed to earn their husband's cooperation, albeit their "new carefully crafted autonomy" came with a certain amount of ambiguity as husbands found ways to extract money from them (*ibid.*: 60).

The story continues in the 1990s with a change in donor (NGO) priority, "women's gardens [becoming] men's orchards, all in the name of environmental stabilization" (Schroeder, 1999: 77). Here, Schroeder shows how an "elite group of senior men" were able to rework land rights to their benefit, diverting funds and materials from women's groups and planting trees (mangos) under the legitimating guise of environmental security (*ibid*: 136). These men conscripted women's labour to plant and then water the seedlings which, as they grew, shaded the vegetables and eventually led to their decline. As women in turn tried to reposition themselves in what in this case was a conflict defined in terms of a reworking of class as well as gendered relations, they engaged in high profile mass demonstrations, "arson, sabotage and benign neglect" (*ibid.*: 132). "The net result", Schroeder (*ibid.*: 115) argues, "was a highly varied social and political ecological landscape embracing gendered patterns of land use and control that tilted in favor of gardeners on one site and back toward landholders in the next".

The critical point in terms of the argument here is that Schroeder makes evident the *processes*—at once material and discursive— through which women and men negotiated what it meant to be a "wife" or a "husband", a landowner or a tenant on the land. These were not fixed positions—what it meant to be a woman or a man in a situation of rapid economic change was not pre-given, but the subject of contestation within as well as outwith the household. The articulation or "becoming" of gender/class was here linked to the "becoming" of the land whose meanings changed as the land was worked for market gardening and then agro-forestry.

That gender is no more fixed than the meanings of the land, itself bound up in contested rights of control and access—one might say that gender/class/kinship (among other axes of social differentiation) is co-constituted with the land—is further evident in such research as that of Melissa Leach and James Fairhead (1995) in the Kissidougou Prefecture in a forest-savanna transition zone in Guinea. They show, for example, how ecological change brought about through the practice of "soil-ripening"—a process of soil enrichment and improvement—is linked to a reworking of social relationships. For Kuranko farmers, they write, "soil ripening is not just an irreversible change in the soil, but also a categorical change in people's relationship to that place" (Leach and Fairhead 1995: 26). The gendered dynamics of this change are, however, far from linear. Some women farmers, they state, "regard the greater socioeconomic autonomy linked with extended soil-ripening as positive in some respects, although ambivalently in others" (*ibid.*: 32).

Conceptualising gender, like the land, as constantly "a-doing" has obvious implications for theorising the "household", "kinship" or "community", all much debated concepts in contemporary social science scholarship. With respect to the household, there is a clear need to escape from a definition of the household in terms of "joint utility function" where a singular corporate interest is assumed (see Elson 1994), "a monolithic decision-making unit" in Sara Berry's (1984: 84) terms; there is, similarly, a need to move beyond the conceptual confines of "conflictual and bargaining models" which may, as Razavi (2003: 28) observes, insufficiently "capture the *common* interests that all household members have in the overall success of their households". Addressing this issue, Jackson (2003: 472) refers to women's and men's "shared and separate interests" in households. It is because of the working through of shared and separate interests, she writes, that gender struggles are complicated and "why women may not act as might be expected from an analysis based on the idea of women as a separate category with interests entirely separate from men's" (*ibid.*: 473). To substantiate her argument that women may indeed subscribe to inequitable gender relations in the household as they negotiate these interests, Jackson cites a number of studies, including Cherryl Walker's (2003) analysis of South Africa's land reform programme.

Drawing on primary research carried out in KwaZulu Natal, Walker (2003: 143) views as problematic gender activists' claim for independent land rights for women as "a major goal". Instead, she argues that "the focus on individual rights for women needs to be tempered by a deeper appreciation of the importance of household membership in poor women's lives" (*ibid.*). Few women, she continues, considered that their problems would be resolved through separating their interests from those of their husbands or families. Rather, their priority was to secure or extend shared rights within their households, "including through such mechanisms as joint title and individual copies of title deeds" (*ibid.*). Household relations were "complex and multi-dimensional—and increasingly vulnerable to dissolution in ways that do not necessarily enhance women's life chances", a situation which can only be made worse by the growing HIV/AIDS crisis (*ibid.*). Thus, while women may experience oppressive gendered relations within the household, it nevertheless remains a site where they mobilise support. Referring to one of her case study areas, Mahlabathini, Walker (*ibid*: 144) notes how important are the household and community networks for "the survival and (relative) well-being of very poor people". Thus, she considers as important as the promotion of individual rights for women where this is "an option (whether out of choice or circumstance)", "a more gender-equitable reconfiguration" of household and community "ties", not "a politics of withdrawal from patriarchal institutions" (*ibid.*).

Despite the lack of visibility of gender in her analysis, Berry's (1997) discussion of social institutions in Kumawu, Asante, Ghana, is useful in moving forward the conceptualisation of the household, family and community. These are not, she proposes,

> clearly bounded, consensual social entities, but rather ... constellations
> of social interactions, in which people move, acquire and exchange
> ideas and resources, and negotiate or contest the terms of production,
> authority and obligation. People interact, within and across various social
> boundaries, in multiple ways and relations among them are constituted
> less through the uniform application of written or unwritten rules, as
> through multiple processes of negotiation and contest which may occur
> simultaneously, or in close succession, but need not be synchronized or
> even mutually consistent (Berry 1997: 1228).

Membership in such institutions as the family, household or community, Berry continues, provides "opportunities" for people to "engage in negotiation and/or struggle, rather than guaranteeing outcomes (subsistence, identity, etc.) or reproducing stable, consistent social relationships" (*ibid.*). Thus, what is required "is attention to the processes of negotiation and debate through which institutions themselves are constituted and people conduct their affairs within and among them" (*ibid.*: 1229). Such an analytics—which focuses on the operationalisation or exercise of power—as Berry (*ibid.*) notes, has to do with Foucaultian discourse. It concerns specifically how people, differently positioned with respect to gender, age, marital status, class ... negotiate, contest, and redefine household, kinship, or community. None of these "institutions" is given; they are constantly claimed in the exercise of shared and separate interests.

This line of thinking parallels that of Lila Abu-Lughod (1993:13) with respect to kinship. She insists on the need to "write against culture'—in other words, to tell stories that "unsettl[e] the culture concept and subvert [...] the process of "othering" that [generalization] entails" (*ibid.*) Thus, she suggests with respect to the practice of polygyny, as an example, that we ask how a particular group of people "live the 'institution' that we call polygyny", rather than "typifying" or making generalisations about it (*ibid.*) Similarly, one could suggest that people be asked how they "live" the practice of "patriliny" or "matriliny", rather than assuming that certain prescribed gender relations follow from either institution. By taking this approach, she continues, one undermines those enduring and problematic features of "culture'": "homogeneity, coherence, and timelessness" (*ibid.*: 14).

CONCLUSION

If nothing else, this discussion of the conceptualisation of the global, the land and gender, demonstrates the need for careful and detailed research documenting the everyday practices of women and men who negotiate rights to land and resources, to their labour, and to the products of their labour. People's lives and daily practices create "windows" (Hart 2004: 96) into the processes through which the global, the land and gender are mutually constituted. It is this evidence, to follow Nagar et al.'s (2002: 274) reasoning, that allows the analytical mediation "between larger structural processes and finer-scaled contextual realities in ways that underscore the complex workings of political, economic and socio-cultural processes at scales ranging from the body and the household to the local, national, and transnational". Richly empirical data allow the analysis of "the messy" and "entangled" ways through which power operates, rejecting as simplistic generalisations that project globalisation as "either totally victimizing or completely liberatory, [rather] illuminat[ing] the subtle ways in which power relations, interdependencies, negotiated constructions of femininity and masculinity, and multilayered politics of difference constitute the everyday politics and realities of globalisation" (*ibid*: 275; also, see Mohanty 1991). The case studies which make up this book demonstrate "an openness" to analysing "how gender works" through the construction of the global (Roberts 2004: 132) and suggest ways through which different political positionings and practices may be created.

NOTES

1. Susan Roberts (2004: 135) provides a useful definition: neo-liberalism is "a shorthand term used to identify the bundle of discourses and social practices that in large part animate the dynamics of the contemporary global economy". Its focus is, first, on the "opening of markets through the dismantling of legal barriers to trade" and, second, "the extension of markets (marketization) through the privatization of previously socially or communally held assets ... and the commodification of previously un- or less-commodified things and practices" (*ibid*.).

2. Slater (2003) develops his discussion with reference to "the North" and "the South". It must, of course, be recognised that these conceptual monoliths need to be unpacked, both in terms of recognising that particular interests (class, gender, race ...) are privileged in the North and the South through neo-liberalism, and that discourses countering neo-liberalism have emerged in both the North and the South.

3. For a recent discussion of the World Bank's approach to land tenure in Africa, see Yngstrom, 2002 (also, Platteau, 1996).

4. Okoth-Ogendo (1978: 60–61, 508) demonstrated how the subjection of the right to allocate land to the economic functions of the right of access (a distinction not recognised by English property law) meant that, where customary law prevailed, women's "proprietary position" in economies that depended so heavily on their labour was both legally visible and defensible. In such contexts, women's rights - of use - were central, not secondary, in the exercise of tenurial relations.

5. On the basis of parallel arguments, Ingrid Yngstrom (2002: 34) suggests that women's tenurial rights "would be far better tackled as issues of family law" than through land tenure reform itself.

6. Jackson (2003: 465) defines "subject position" as: "the particular locations within social structures and discourses occupied by women". "Subjectivities" refers "to that mental interior that is both psychological and social" (*ibid*.). It is, of course, also the case that the subject positions of men are constantly re-negotiated in complex ways.

REFERENCES

Abdullah, H.J. and I. Hamza, 2003, "Women and Land in Northern Nigeria: The Need for Independent Ownership Rights", in L.M. Wanyeki (ed), *Women and Land in Africa: Culture, Religion and Realizing Women's Rights*, London: Zed, pp. 133–175.

Abu-Lughod, L., 1993, *Writing Women's Worlds. Bedouin Stories*, Berkeley: University of California Press.

Agarwal, B., 1994, "Gender, Resistance, and Land: Interlinked Struggles Over Resources and Meanings in South Asia", *Journal of Peasant Studies* 22(1): 81–125.

————, 2003, "Gender and Land Rights Revisited: Exploring New Prospects via the State, Family and Market", *Journal of Agrarian Change* 3(1, 2): 184–224.

Amanor, K. S., 2005, "Night Harvesters, Forest Hoods and Saboteurs: Struggles over Land Expropriation in Ghana", in S. Moyo and P. Yeros (eds), *Reclaiming the Land. The Resurgence of Rural Movements in Africa, Asia and Latin America*, London and New York: Zed, pp. 102–117.

Ampuero, I. and J. J. Brittain, 2005, "The Agrarian Question and Armed Struggle in Colombia", in ʿ Moyo and P. Yeros (eds), *Reclaiming the Land. The Resurgence of Rural Movemenus in Africa, Asia and Latin America*, London and New York: Zed, pp. 359–382.

Appadurai, A., 2000, "Grassroots Globalization and the Research Imagination", *Public Culture* 12(1): 1–19.

Bartra, A. and G. Otero, 2005, "Indian Peasant Movements in Mexico: The Struggle for Land, Autonomy and Democracy", in S. Moyo and P. Yeros (eds), *Reclaiming the Land. The Resurgence of Rural Movements in Africa, Asia and Latin America*, London and New York: Zed, pp. 383–410.

Benería, L. and M. Roldàn, 1987, *The Crossroads of Class and Gender. Industrial Homework, Subcontracting and Household Dynamics in Mexico City*, Chicago; University of Chicago Press.

Berry, S., 1984, "The Food Crisis and Agrarian Change in Africa: A Review Essay", *African Studies Review* 27(2): 59–111.

————, 1997, "Tomatoes, Land and Hearsay: Property and History in Asante in the Time of Structural Adjustment", *World Development* 25(8): 1225–1241.

Bienefeld, M, 1994, "The New World Order: echoes of a new imperialism", *Third World Quarterly* 15(1): 31–48.

Bikaako, W. amd J. Ssenkumba. 2003, "Gender, land and Rights: Contemporary Contestations in Law, Policy and Practice in Uganda", in L.M. Wanyeki (ed), *Women and Land in Africa: Culture, Religion and Realizing Women's Rights*, London: Zed, pp. 232–277.

Blomley, N., 2003, "Law, Property, and the Geography of Violence: The Frontier, the Survey, and the Grid", *Annals of the Association of American Geographers* 93(1): 121–141.

Braun, B. and N. Castree, 1998, *Remaking Reality. Nature at the Millenium*, London: Routledge.

Butler, J., 1992, "Contingent Foundations", in J. Butler and J. Scott (eds), *Feminists Theorize the Political* (New York and London: Routledge, pp. 3–21.

———, 1993, *Bodies that Matter*, New York and London: Routledge.

Carney, J. and M. Watts, 1990, "Manufacturing Dissent: Work, Gender and the Politics of Meaning in a Peasant Society", *Africa* 60(2): 207–240.

Castree, N., 2001, "Socializing nature: theory, practice and politics" in N. Castree and B. Braun, (eds), *Social nature. Theory, practice and politics*, Oxford: Blackwell, pp. 1–21.

Castree, N. and B. Braun, (eds) 2001, *Social nature: Theory, practice and politics*, Oxford: Blackwell.

Chanock, M., 1985, *Law, Custom and Social Order: The Colonial Experience in Malawi and Zambia*, Cambridge: Cambridge University Press.

Cleaver, F., 2000, "Moral Ecological Rationality, Institutions, and the Management of Common Property Resources", *Development and Change* 31(2): 361–83.

Deere, C.D., 2003, "Women's Land Rights and Rural Social Movements in the Brazilian Agrarian Reform", *Journal of Agrarian Change* 3(1, 2): 257–288.

Elson, D., 1994, "Micro, Meso, Macro: Gender and Economic Analysis in the Context of Policy Reform", in I. Bakker (ed), *Strategies of Silence. Gender and Economic Policy*, London: Zed.

———, 2002, "Gender Justice, Human Rights, and Neo-liberal Economic Policies", in M. Molneux and S. Razavi (eds), *Gender Justice, Development and Rights*, Oxford: Oxford University Press, pp. 78–114.

Escobar, A., 1995, "Towards a Post-structural Political Ecology" in R. Peet and M. Watts (eds), *Liberation Ecologies*, London: Routledge.

Esteva, G. and M. S. Prakash, 1998, *Grassroots Post-Modernism*, London: Zed.

Feranil, S. H., 2005, "Stretching the "Limits" of Redistributive Reform: Lessons and Evidence from the Philippines under Neoliberalism", in S. Moyo and P. Yeros (eds), *Reclaiming the Land. The Resurgence of Rural Movements in Africa, Asia and Latin America*, London and New York: Zed, pp. 257–284.

Ferguson, J., 1994, *The Anti-Politics Machine*, Minneapolis: University of Minnesota Press.

Flax, J., 1992, "The End of Innocence", in J. Butler and J. Scott (eds), *Feminists Theorize the Political*, London: Routledge, pp. 445–463.

Foucault, M., 1979, *Discipline and Punish. The Birth of the Prison*, New York: Vantage.

Gibson-Graham, J.K., 2002, "Beyond Global vs Local: Economic Politics Outside the Binary Frame", in A. Herod and M.W. Wright (eds), *Geographies of Power*, Oxford: Blackwell, pp. 25–60.

———, 2003, "An Ethics of the Local", *Rethinking Marxism* 15(1): 49–74.

Goebel, A., 2005a, "Zimbabwe's "Fast Track" Land Reform: What about women?", *Gender, Place, and Culture* 12(2): 145–172.

Goebel, A., 2005b, *Gender and Land Reform. The Zimbabwe Experience*, Montreal: McGill-Queen's Press.

Gregory, D., 2004, *The Colonial Present*, Oxford: Blackwell.

Griffiths, A., 1998, "Reconfiguring Law: An Ethnographic Perspective from Botswana", *Law and Social Inquiry* 23(3): 587–620.

———, 2001, "Gendering Culture: Towards a Plural Perspective of Kwena Women's Rights", in J. Cowan, M. Dembour and R. Wilson (eds), *Culture and Rights*, Cambridge: Cambridge University Press.

Haraway, D., 1990, "A Manifesto for Cyborgs: Science, technology, and Socialist feminism in the 1980s", in L. Nicholson (ed), *Feminism/Postmodernism*, New York: Routledge, pp. 190–233.

Hart, G., 2004, "Geography and development: critical ethnographies", *Progress in Human Geography* 28(1): 91–100.

Hutchful, E., 1989, "From "revolution" to monetarism: the economics and politics of the Structural Adjustment Programme in Ghana", in B. Campbell and J. Loxley (eds), *Structural Adjustment in Africa*, New York: St Martin's Press.

Jackson, C., 2003, "Gender Analysis of Land: Beyond Land Rights for Women", *Journal of Agrarian Change* 3(4): 453–480.

Kanyongolo, F. E., 2005, "Land Occupations in Malawi: Challenging the Neoliberal Order", in S. Moyo and P. Yeros (eds), *Reclaiming the Land. The Resurgence of Rural Movements in Africa, Asia and Latin America*, London and New York: Zed, pp. 118–141.

Leach, M. and J. Fairhead, 1995, "Ruined Settlements and New Gardens: Gender and Soil-Ripening among Kuranko Farmers in the Forest-Savanna Transition Zone", *IDS Bulletin* 26(1): 24–32.

Logo, P.B. and E. H. Bikie, 2003, "Women and Land in Cameroon: Questioning Women's Land Status and Claims for Change", in L.M. Wanyeki (ed), *Women and Land in Africa: Culture, Religion and Realizing Women's Rights*, London: Zed, pp. 31–66.

Mackenzie, A. Fiona D., 1990, "Gender and Land Rights in Murang'a District, Kenya", *Journal of Peasant Studies* 17(4): 609–642.

———, 1995, ""A farm is like a child who cannot be left unguarded": gender land and labour in Central Province, Kenya", *IDS Bulletin* 26(1): 24–32.

———, 1998, *Land, Ecology and Resistance in Kenya, 1880–1952*, Edinburgh: University of Edinburgh Press.

Manuh, T., 1994, *Women's Rights and Traditional law: A Conflict*, International Third World Legal Studies Association and Valparaiso University School of Law.

Massey, D., 1994, *Space, Place and Gender*, Minneapolis: University of Minnesota Press.

———, 2000, "Entanglements of power: reflections" in J.P. Sharp, P. Routledge, C. Philo and R. Paddison (eds), *Entanglements of power*, London: Routledge, pp. 279–286.

Mattei, L., 2005, "Agrarian Reform in Brazil under Neoliberalism: Evaluation and Perspectives" in S. Moyo and P. Yeros (eds), *Reclaiming the Land. The Resurgence of Rural Movements in Africa, Asia and Latin America*, London and New York: Zed, pp. 341–358.

McClintock, A., 1995, *Imperial Leather*, New York and London: Routledge.

Mies, M., 1982, *The Lace Makers of Narsapur. Indian Housewives Produce for the World Market*, London: Zed.

Mohan, G., 1996, "Globalization and Governance: The Paradoxes of Adjustment in Sub-Saharan Africa" in E. Kofman and G. Youngs (eds), *Globalization: Theory and Practice*, London: Pinter.

Mohanty, C. T., 1991, "Under Western Eyes. Feminist Scholarship and Colonial Discourses", in C. T. Mohanty, A. Russo and L. Torres (eds), *Third World Women and the Politics of Feminism*, Bloomington and Indianapolis: Indiana University Press, pp. 51–80.

Moyo, S., and P. Yeros, 2005a, "Introduction", in S. Moyo and P. Yeros (eds), *Reclaiming the Land. The Resurgence of Rural Movements in Africa, Asia and Latin America*, London and New York: Zed, pp. 1–7.

———, 2005b, "The Resurgence of Rural Movements under Neoliberalism", in S. Moyo and P. Yeros (eds), *Reclaiming the Land. The Resurgence of Rural Movements in Africa, Asia and Latin America*, London and New York: Zed, pp. 8–66.

———, 2005c, "Land Reform and Land Occupations in Zimbabwe: Towards the National Democratic Revolution", in S. Moyo and P. Yeros (eds), *Reclaiming the Land. The Resurgence of Rural Movements in Africa, Asia and Latin America*, London and New York: Zed, pp. 165–208.

Nagar, R., V. Lawson, L. McDowell, and S. Hanson, 2002, "Locating Globalization: Feminist (Re)readings of the Subjects and Spaces of Globalization", *Economic Geography* 78: 257–285.

Okoth-Ogendo, H. W. O., 1978, "The Political Economy of Land Law: An Essay in the Legal Organization of Underdevelopment in Kenya, 1895–1974", PhD Dissertation, Law School, Yale University.

———, 1989, "Some Issues of theory in the Study of Tenure Relations in African Agriculture", *Africa*, 59 (1): 6–17.

Patnaik, U., 2003, "Global capitalism, Deflation and Agrarian Crisis in Developing Countries", *Journal of Agrarian Change* 3(1, 2): 33–66.

Paulson, S. and L. L. Gezon (eds), 2005, *Political Ecology across Spaces, Scales and Social Groups*, New Brunswick: Rutgers University Press.

Peet, R. and M. Watts (eds), 1996, *Liberation Ecologies*, London: Routledge.

———, 2004, *Liberation Ecologies*, Second Edition, London: Routledge.

Peluso, N. and M. Watts, 2001, *Violent Environments*, Ithaca: Cornell University Press.

Pimple, M. and M. Sethi, 2005, "Occupation of Land in India: Experiences and Challenges", in S. Moyo and P. Yeros (eds), *Reclaiming the Land. The Resurgence of Rural Movements in Africa, Asia and Latin America*, London and New York: Zed, pp. 235–256.

Platteau, J.P., 1996, "The evolutionary theory of land rights as applied to sub-Saharan Africa: a critical assessment", *Development and Change* 27: 29–86.

Razavi, S., 2003, "Introduction: Agrarian Change, Gender and Land Rights", *Journal of Agrarian Change* 3(1, 2): 2–32.

Roberts, S., 2004, "Gendered Globalization", in L. A. Staeheli, E. Kofman and L. Peake (eds), *Mapping Women, Making Politics. Feminist Perspectives on Political Geography*, New York and Abingdon: Routledge.

Said, E., 1994, *Culture and Imperialism*, New York: Alfred A. Knopf.

Schroeder, R., 1996, ""Gone to Their Second Husbands": Marital Metaphors and Conjugal Contracts in The Gambia's Female Garden Sector", *Canadian Journal of African Studies* 30(1): 69–87.

———, 1999, *Shady Practices: Agroforestry and Gender Politics in the Gambia*, Berkeley: University of California Press.

Scott, J., 1988, *Gender and the Politics of History*, New York: Columbia University Press.

Sihlongonyane, M. F., 2005, "Land Occupations in South Africa", in S. Moyo and P. Yeros (eds), *Reclaiming the Land. The Resurgence of Rural Movements in Africa, Asia and Latin America*, London and New York: Zed, pp. 142–164.

Slater, D., 2003, "Rethinking the Geopolitics of the Global. The case of North-South relations", in *Globalization: Theory and Practice*, eds. E. Kofman and G. Youngs, London: Pinter, pp. 48–63.

Stewart, J., Sithole, E., Ncube, W., Noyo, T., Gwaunza, E., Nzira, T., Degu-Zuobgo, K., Mashingaidze, D., Donzwa, B., and Kazembe, J., 2000, *In the Shadow of the Law. Women and Justice Delivery in Zimbabwe*, Harare: Women and Law in Southern Africa Trust.

Tadesse, Z., 2003, "Women and land Rights in the Third World: The Case of Ethiopia", in L.M. Wanyeki (ed), *Women and Land in Africa: Culture, Religion and Realizing Women's Rights*, London: Zed, pp. 67–95.

Tine, N. D., and M. Sy, 2003, 2003, "Women and Land in Africa: A Case Study from Senegal", in L.M. Wanyeki (ed), *Women and Land in Africa: Culture, Religion and Realizing Women's Rights*, London: Zed, pp. 207–232.

Tsikata, D., 2003, "Securing Women's Interests within Land Tenure Reforms: Recent Debates in Tanzania", *Journal of Agrarian Change* 3(1,2): 149–183.

Verma, R., 2001, *Gender, Land and Livelihoods in East Africa: Through Farmers' Eyes*, Ottawa: IDRC.

Walker, C., 2003, "Piety in the Sky? Gender Policy and Land Reform in South Africa", *Journal of Agrarian Change* 3(1, 2): 113–148.

Wanyeki, L.M., 2003, *Women and Land in Africa: Culture, Religion and Realizing Women's Rights*, London: Zed.

Watts, M., 1998, "Nature as artifice and artifact", in B. Braun and N. Castree (eds), *Remaking Reality. Nature at the Millenium*, London: Routledge, pp. 243–268.

Watts, M., 2001, "Petro-Violence: Community, Extraction, and Political Ecology of a Mythic Community", in N. Peluso and M. Watts (eds), *Violent Environments*, Ithaca: Cornell University Press, pp. 189–212.

———, 2004, "Violent Environments: petroleum conflict and the political ecology of rule in the Niger Delta, Nigeria", in R. Peet and M. Watts (eds), *Liberation Ecologies*, London: Routledge, pp. 273–298.

Whitehead, A. and D. Tsikata, 2003, "Policy Discourses on Women's Land Rights in Sub-Saharan Africa: The Implications of the Re-Turn to the Customary" *Journal of Agrarian Change* 3(1, 2): 67–112.

Williams, G., 1994, "Why Structural Adjustment is Necessary and Why It Doesn't Work", *Review of African Political Economy* 60: 214–225.

Wright, M. W., 1997, "Crossing the Factory Frontier: Gender, Place and Power in the Mexican *Maquiladora*", *Antipode* 29(3): 278–302.

Yngstrom, I., 2002, "Women, Wives and Land Rights in Africa: Situating Gender Beyond the Household in the Debate Over Land Policy and Changing Tenure Systems" *Oxford Development Studies* 30(1): 21–40.

3 | Gender, Globalisation and Land Tenure
Methodological Challenges and Insights

ALLISON GOEBEL[1]

INTRODUCTION

The major methodological challenge of the research represented in this book is its engagement with issues of gender, land tenure and globalisation in the early 21st century. This engagement incorporates the specificities of context, research topic, team perspectives, background, available resources and institutional and other factors of each project. The intent of this chapter is to map this process, and to relate it to the broader methodological literature. In particular, some of the preoccupations of feminist and post-colonial methodological writing are addressed. While not all team members identified as feminist researchers (an issue discussed later in this chapter), the concerns of feminist scholarship resonated in some ways with all the teams. Their work also contributes to a growing body of research and epistemological reflection by southern women that is critical to the transformation of feminist research globally (see Narayan 1989; Meena et al. 1992).

This chapter is based on an analysis of the teams' accounts of their methodologies in project reports, discussions at a workshop held in Ottawa in September 2005, and subsequent correspondence with team members. First, a general discussion on researching gender, land tenure and globalisation is presented. This is followed by a consideration of the projects in relation to research about and for social change, a focus that proved useful in researching the effects of globalisation. Next, the chapter addresses the research methodologies used in the projects and how these were linked to analysis. Finally, the implications for the methodological literature are explored.

RESEARCHING GENDER, LAND TENURE AND GLOBALISATION

While the researchers differed in some aspects of their theoretical and practical approaches, a commonality among southern researchers was, "challenging the way knowledge is produced and whose view of the world it represents" (Kirby and McKenna 1989: 15). All the projects participated in "the search for new ways of being—at the individual, collective and global levels—and the knowledge to support the political, economic and cultural changes required" (Pereira 2002: 1). Interested in disrupting a sense of the inevitability, and certainly the rightness of globalising forces, the methodologies chosen allowed the highlighting of the crises in land-based livelihoods among diverse peoples. As such, a central challenge was the question of scale. All four teams addressed the inter-relatedness of larger structural processes, associated with globalisation, with the lived realities of local people in specific contexts as land tenure and gender relations changed:

> ...it is critical for feminist studies of globalisation to identify and interrogate the local, regional, and transnational scales, the multiple sites and their intersection, through which the global dimensions of restructuring and resistance strategies are refracted and reproduced (Zeleza 2002: 12).

A key methodological move was the case study approaches adopted by the teams. These allowed the specificities of locations and lived realities to be detailed, while at the same time enabling the identification of the similarities in the footprint of globalising processes in diverse corners of the world. To achieve this, all four teams engaged in extensive empirical fieldwork in their local contexts, drawing on the tools of social science and anthropology to generate new knowledge about the complex and changing social and environmental realities, particularly of people's livelihoods as related to land and gender. The teams also employed comparative approaches to deepen their case studies. The Ghana group compared two different resource-based activities (gold mining and mangrove use) in different regions in Ghana. The Vietnam team did research in both northern and southern areas, which were differentiated by history and land tenure regimes. The Amazon team utilised inter-regional comparisons across Brazil, Peru and Bolivia, also researching multiple sites within each of these countries. Finally, the Cameroon team selected communities along an oil pipeline project, including sites in two out of the four affected provinces in the country, and hence including different ecological and social/cultural contexts. Teams also researched documents and literatures illuminating the roles and activities of their governments and relevant international bodies and processes implicated in globalisation, and in some cases conducted interviews with the concerned officials. As such, the multi-methodologies chosen resisted a binary view of the local and the global, and instead sought to reveal their interconnections. As Peggy Antrobus puts it: "The word 'glocality' has been coined to highlight the ways in which global trends affect local experience" (Antrobus 2004: 20). For Paul Zeleza,

> The challenge for feminist research on globalisation is not simply to insert the local into the global… but to consider local forms of globalisation as constitutive ingredients in the changing shape of globalisation, whether of trade, commodities, capital, culture, politics, ideologies; in short, to integrate macro and micro levels of analysis, to engender theories of globalisation by examining relationships between and across the analytical levels—spatially of the local, the national, regional, and global—and socially of the household, community, race, class—all of which are imbricated with gender (Zeleza 2002: 12).

As discussed in Mackenzie's chapter, both "land" and "gender" are understood not only as material (that is physical places and bodies), but as negotiated meanings, relationships and struggles. The methodological implication of this with regard to land issues was the investigation of the discourses or contested ideological realms that have accompanied changes in land tenure or entitlements to land, its productive resources, associated institutions and other social relations (such as families, traditional authorities and the state) that play key roles in these discourses and negotiations. As such, the teams made use of some methodological practices developed in natural resource and land tenure research, much of which is associated with post-structural and/or feminist political ecology (see Rocheleau et al. 1996; Fortmann 1996; Goebel 1998). Most importantly, this meant understanding the complexity of people's relation to land, with numerous types of control, access and entitlements, often depending on the particular resource and activity involved. For example, women may have access to arable land to grow particular food crops for the household, but not be able to grow cash crops for sale, nor formally hold title to land. All people in a community may have access to fruit from wild trees in common property areas, but only a traditional leader would be allowed to gather wild fruits for sale. These types of social relationships involved in land and resource tenures tend to be culturally specific, and are subject to change, such as in the cases discussed in the projects. Feminist political ecology also draws particular attention to marriage and households as central mediating factors in women's relationship to land and other natural resources. In many agriculture based communities in the south, women often have access to land only through marriage. Hence a divorce or widow-hood could spell the end of their entitlements. Researching the particularities of these gendered relations in each context is therefore critical, as it is to identify women and their interests, as well as to study their relationships (particularly marriages, households and families) and social networks, and how their (and men's) entitlements change through negotiation, struggles, alliances and the manufacturing of new meanings of gender (Goebel 2002). The teams researched deepening inequalities and hardships for women, and how these were produced through ideological, social, political, environmental, as well as economic processes of change. As such, many standard methodological features of feminist social science research—such as focusing on household/domestic dynamics and power relations, shifting ideological constructions of gender roles and relations, women's relationships to community and political institutions, and their access to productive resources—emerged as useful. Examples of these aspects of the projects are developed in the sections below.

RESEARCH FOR AND ABOUT SOCIAL CHANGE

An important aspect of the desire to produce "knowledge to sup-port the political, economic and cultural changes required" (Pereira 2002: 1) in this era of globalisation, was the engagement of the teams in research for and about social change. All teams were focused on understanding the processes of change, mostly emphasising this aspect in their work over any deliberate alignment with action research or engagement with change processes themselves. In what follows, I first discuss how the teams researched processes of social change and with what outcomes; this is followed by an analysis of how the projects can be considered "action research" in some ways.

The Cameroon project was strongly focused on change, especially in relation to land and gender as affected by the pipeline project. Areas of interest in this included the social and economic effects, on communities, of the presence of the travelling pipeline work crews and their followers, including prostitutes and other service providers; temporary employment opportunities for some community mem-bers; gendered aspects of compensation packages for crop loss; and impacts on land tenure regimes. The focus on gendered change revealed that customary land tenure practices afforded women good access to land for food production, and this access was not much affected by the pipeline process because of the abundance of land in most communities (see the Cameroon case study chapter for a discussion of how project compensation mechanisms helped to ensure that women enjoyed some compensation for their crop and labour losses). The Cameroon team's detailed attention to the micro dynamics of gender and livelihoods provided important cautions against generalising about impacts of globalising projects. Perhaps the most important impact in terms of social change will come in the future, as communities reflect on what has happened, develop contact with other affected communities, and begin envisioning new roles for themselves and the state as a result.

For the Ghana team, researching social change was a strong focus in both the study of the emergence of small-scale mining in an area in Northeast Ghana and a case study of the intensified importance of mangrove use in South-eastern Ghana. In the gold mining case, the team studied the impact of migration, mainly on resource use; the emergence of new social identities, particularly with regard to new labour relations linked to new resource-based livelihood activities; changes in land and resource tenure; and more broadly, changes in gender relations. The mangrove study also documented changes in resource tenure, livelihoods and gender relations more generally. Centring social change in the analysis helped capture the dynamism in processes such as customary land tenure, and the impacts of tenure changes such as the introduction of land titling, negotiation of gender relations and livelihoods in highly fragile eco-systems, and the importance of seeing labour as a set of relations rather than as positions occupied by different categories of people. For example, the highly complex, gendered and hierarchical labour categories and relations emerging around small-scale mining were studied in detail by the team, revealing the operation of power relations of gender and class.

Unlike the Cameroon study, the Ghana team's work on social change revealed extensive transformations occurring in gender, livelihoods and land/resource tenure as a result of the globalising forces of neo-liberal policy, particularly related to the need for rural people to exploit formerly marginal natural resources. The focus on social change in the Ghana study, as with the Cameroon study, led to concerns with environmental degradation and sustainability issues. In the Cameroon case the main concern was the pollution and deforestation left behind by the pipeline construction; in Ghana, environments were being destroyed by mining activities, workers were exposed to dangerous chemicals such as mercury, and natural resources such as mangroves were under threat of overexploitation, likely to lead eventually to the collapse of this livelihood resource. In both cases, the approach helped to highlight the links between environmental health and social well-being.

The Amazon project sought to study how gender was negotiated under conditions of change in land tenure linked to processes of globalisation. The latter included both development policies in the Amazon that favoured cattle ranching and agri-business (and compromised resource-based livelihoods of indigenous forest people), and the emergence of new international markets for these same forest resources. Focusing on women gatherers and peelers of brazil nuts and women breakers of babaçu fruits, this project documented how women identified themselves in these social change processes. Emerging from this research were stories of how women's social identities were produced in ongoing interactions between public processes such as women's social movements and domestic arenas in households with husbands and other family members. The Amazon project also emphasised the production of identities in historical and ongoing struggles in relation to land and resources, struggles characterised by the desire to enact and maintain relations to land as territory, a particular cultural/historical belonging to a place that was severely under threat in contemporary conditions.

The dramatic changes sparked by the de-collectivisation of agri-culture, and the shift from a centrally planned to a market economy starting in the mid-1980s was the focus for the Vietnam project. Interested particularly in the implications for women's entitlement to land, the team investigated the changes in women's vulnerability to land loss and land scarcity as young women, new wives, divorcees, widows or second wives, and changes in gendered inheritance patterns. Land entitlements in this case could not be understood without drawing attention to the micro context of gender ideologies and relations. In all cases, then, researching social change allowed the inter-relationships of the micro and the macro, the local and the global, to come into focus.

A deliberate linking of research with positive change outcomes or action has often been associated with feminist and other critical approaches in western scholarship such as community action research (see Israel 2005 for a non-feminist example). Critical social research seeks to challenge, rather than support the "relations of ruling" (Smith, D. 1996) in some way. This can be done through the demysti-fication of power relations and inequality, evaluation of programmes or policies, prevalence or needs assessment research, research that is in and by itself action, such as in building networks among groups, or research that shifts hierarchies of knowledge production such as participatory research (Reinharz 1992). Actions can occur along a continuum of involvement of research participants themselves: from the expert generation of new knowledge necessary for change, which generally involves participants primarily as informants, to research that empowers through participatory processes that encourage participant roles in problem definition, learning, analysis and action (Burt and Code 1995; Devault 1999; Gottfried 1996; Harding 1987; Kirby and McKenna 1989; Reinharz 1992).

In the projects there is a range of ways in which research is linked to social change. As expected, this depends on the concepts used, and each team's methodological approach in general. For example, the Amazon research was from the beginning committed to an action-based participatory project with social movements, and hence had direct and purposeful approaches to research *as* social change:

> This research-action is about producing and exchanging knowledge with and among women and men who have lived on forest resources throughout the history of transformations of the natural and social environments in the Amazon… Our research design also integrated research and collective action. Crossing national borders, groups of babaçu-breaker and Brazil-nut-peeler women exchanged simple, but concrete experiences dealing with alternative products and markets, trying to establish partnerships and disseminate information, and lobbying for policy change (Amazon Final Report: 3; 12).

The Cameroon project began with the recognition that gender research was rare in general in Cameroon, so one of the team's initial goals was to raise the profile of gender research in the university and policy settings, and enhance its institutionalisation in those locations. Institutional change, then, was a strong focus of the research, while the work was envisioned as having quite indirect links to change for the participating communities. The marginalisation of gender research is not unique to Cameroon. Writing about feminist and gender research in African intellectual institutions, Amina Mama has traced an enduring gender blindness and sexism in what she calls "malestream research", which has gone hand in hand with adherence to traditional western methodological approaches in social science. In 1994 she and co-author Imam noted that in the social sciences, positivism and quantitative methods dominated:

> The dominance of logical positivism in the social sciences has led to a hierarchization of knowledge which privileges quantitative over

qualitative, and assumes a narrow range of research tools to be the only "scientific" way of producing knowledge (Imam and Mama 1994: 83).

Like Linda Tuhiwai Smith, writing from an indigenous scholar's perspective about (still) colonial New Zealand, African scholars have inherited

> the way research became institutionalized in the colonies, not just through academic disciplines, but through learned and scientific societies and scholarly networks. The transplanting of research institutions, including universities, from imperial centres of Europe enabled local scientific interests to be organized and embedded in the colonial system (Smith, L. 1999: 8).

This together with disciplinary hierarchies (e.g. the primacy of economics and its focus on economic growth), censorship, discrimination against women, and material constraints (for example in research funding and conference travel) that have differentially impacted women scholars and alternative research methodologies and theories, these institutional conditions have worked to marginalise feminist scholarship: "Most African social science scholarship demonstrates an almost complete neglect of gender and a bias against women" (Imam and Mama 1994: 84). Sadly, more than 10 years later, despite a groundswell of feminist intellectual and activist work in Africa, much of which has gone on in institutions outside the university, "mainstream academic institutions... insist that feminism, and therefore GWS (gender and women's studies), has no local currency" (Mama 2005: 105). The marginalisation of feminist or gender analysis has persisted even in independent, radical intellectual institutions such as CODESRIA, where feminist, gender-focused research "runs *parallel* to the malestream of scholarship in which gender blindness is accepted as the norm, a situation which raises the broader question of how successfully feminist thought has permeated non-feminist 'progressive' scholarship on Africa" (Pereira 2002: 5).

Seen in this context, the concern of the Cameroon team to intensify the institutionalisation of gender research is critical. They also had to work hard to promote the acceptance of qualitative research in the academy. The team felt, however, that the research had good potential to spur actions amongst affected communities toward social change or to draw the attention of other actors such as the World Bank, the government of Cameroon, international organisations (e.g. the human rights agencies) and the pipeline consortium. These powerful players seemed to operate with nearly no gender analysis whatsoever. For example, the team was shocked to discover scant mention of women or gender issues in the pipeline project blueprint document, and the neglect of women's rights as guaranteed by CEDAW,[2] particularly in terms of access to employment, in communities along the pipeline:

> The information gathered would enable the government, researchers and other interested bodies (such as civil society, human rights and development agencies) to verify if there were major flaws in the transnational investment agreements signed between the government of Cameroon and the pipeline consortium, especially with respect to fulfilling their human rights obligations under international law for those affected by the pipeline project (Cameroon Final Report: 4).

In furtherance of the project's potential for action, the Cameroon team held a post-research workshop to disseminate and gather feedback regarding the research results. This workshop provided a unique opportunity for representatives from the 27 study communities to meet and share experiences, in the process discovering commonalities in their communities' concerns. Assisted by legal, development and other experts, community representatives were inspired to organise and take action such as lobby policymakers and others in positions of power. For example the communities resolved, at the end of the workshop, to put forward a memorandum to the Prime Minister of Cameroon regarding the negative impacts of the pipeline project on their communities. The workshop also enhanced awareness among community representatives of the role of the University of Buea as a partner in helping the communities in their efforts to seek redress, a relationship they wanted to continue.

For both the Ghana and Vietnam teams, the research was designed deliberately to have an impact on policy at critical moments of land policy reform in those countries. The communities worked with were therefore more a representation of processes and dynamics that the researchers wished to bring to the attention of policymakers, rather than immediate subjects for action and change:

> The team provided preliminary feedback to policymakers at the regional and district levels in Bolgatanga and Sogakope and this drew their attention to the research findings. It is expected that after publication of research reports, more policymakers will be conscious of the gender and social dimensions of land tenure and reform. The researchers have also contributed their knowledge to activities involving various NGOs and policymakers and it is our hope that more will be realised when the research is completed (Ghana Final Report: 20).

The Vietnam team plan to report back to the provincial government and other officials on their findings, which they suggested was critical for the impact of the research on later state interventions in land policy. The Ghana, Cameroon and Vietnam projects, then, had a different approach to "research as action" from the Amazon project, which was committed to the particular social movements and their actors as they struggled with the processes of globalisation:

> The Amazon proposal indicated potential for contributions to policy-making processes, but as the research design implies, the women themselves were the actors to present the results to the policymakers. On December 8–10, 2004, during their V Inter-state Meeting, 240 "babaçu breaker women" and 8 invited Bolivian and Peruvian female leaders discussed the results of the Amazon project in a specific workshop. The resulting document was sent to the Brazilian Agency of Cooperation and to policymakers in other governmental agencies. (Amazon Technical Report 2004 and V Inte-state Meeting of the Babaçu-Breaker Women 2005).

It may be tempting to locate these differences in approach in major paradigmatic differences between the Amazonian and the other three projects. Certainly, principal investigator Noemi Miyasaka Porro has utilised a radical critique of development following Escobar (1995) as well as a post-modern critique of knowledge production following Foucault (1972) in order to develop her ethnography. As such, her research resists and critiques development interventions as processes of continued imperialism and post-colonial exploitation. Development is to be resisted, not "fixed" by, say, a good gender analysis. Therefore, it is southern women's actions of resistance and survival that Porro wishes to reveal and assist in her research. On the other hand, the remaining three projects are located more in the field of attempting to influence the development interventions that are occurring, mostly by interacting with the state and its policy development arms. However, as is evident from the Cameroon project process, unanticipated critical community-based actions may be sparked by research primarily designed to influence the state and other powerful actors. Strict divisions between "radical" and what may be viewed as "reformist" approaches to social change, are not always easily drawn. The struggles of those whose livelihoods, social relations and institutions are negatively impacted by globalisation, are nevertheless bound to engage with its processes, including the need to engage with the state in the hopes of improving the outcomes for those who have little influence on the larger structures and processes that so profoundly affect their lives. A radical critique does not provide exemption from the need to engage with the realities of development and globalisation. As Porro reflected in an editorial comment:

> Knowing and contesting does not necessarily mean to be powerful to live it differently, but many times means "reforming" something to the acceptable point. In sum, our discourses and practices are constantly challenged by the contradictions in which we live.

Hence, while it is possible to identify different paradigmatic approaches to the relationship between research and social change among the projects, as well as attendant methodological choices, it is possibly more relevant that teams made strategic choices in their institutional contexts to maximise the potential for their research to make change.

Another element to consider, as evident in the Ghana, Vietnam and Cameroon projects, was that the question of whether social change is directly or indirectly linked to the research process, also depends upon the research questions pursued and the identity and location of the key players or targets of the research. For example, in all of these projects, base-line data on the issues under study were lacking, and hence there was a heavy knowledge generation component to the projects. This was seen as critical before any direct actions at either the policy or the local levels could be meaningfully engaged in. Also, different actors had different mandates: the Latin American project worked with social movements, which have social change and action as their main reason for existing. In all other projects, while informing research participants as well as the public in general was important, the key actors were more likely to be policymakers, with the role of researchers therefore more generally cast as generating information to inform their policy making and decisions. The next section discusses the particular research strategies used by the teams and how these strategies led into analysis.

RESEARCH STRATEGIES USED

There was a wide array of research methods used in the projects, including ethnography, in-depth interviewing, life histories, participatory rural appraisal (PRA) tools (transect walks, resource mapping, etc), survey questionnaires, observation, photography, documentary research, etc. Teams' selection of methods was strongly driven by the research questions, and the different scales at which these questions were directed.

All projects used multiple methods, with quantitative methods typically chosen to produce base-line descriptive data needed at the level of communities or regions, and qualitative approaches used in complimentary fashion to investigate meanings, micro-level relations, power and perceptions. Quantitative data, particularly on the prevalence of particular livelihood strategies, were important for the Ghana team which administered 240 questionnaires at two research sites. The Vietnam project completed 500 questionnaires at their two study sites, as well as 45 in-depth interviews of women and men with varying positions, and 10 focus groups. Quantitative data were very important for the Vietnam team in establishing scientific legitimacy for the project in their institutional context and for gaining the attention of government policymakers. Having the base of quantitative research also helped smooth the way for the appreciation of the rich qualitative data produced by the team—the narratives of family, kinship and gender change emerging as highly significant in the Vietnam project. Choice of methods also reflected the desire of team members to experiment, to learn new methods themselves, to train research assistants and involve research participants in ways that were empowering. For example, the Cameroon and Ghana teams were keen to enhance gender research training through the involvement of research assistants from their universities in their fieldwork. The Vietnam team was very gratified to learn the use of PRA methods, which they found were also enjoyed by village parti-cipants, who gained important knowledge about themselves and their communities in the process. This became part of what they felt they left behind in the communities as a positive contribution.

The use of qualitative methods was particularly important in researching social change. For the Ghana team, recognition of the need to hear people's voices, their own narratives, clearly suggested life histories and in-depth interviewing as critical approaches. These techniques allowed the team to map the emerging new social identities, and the operations of power in new social relations. The transect walks and resource mapping were essential in understanding the environmental context and social-spatial relationships. For the Amazon research, qualitative, ethnographic approaches were central for similar reasons. The desire to reflect how women identified themselves as subjects in a globalising process was a central goal. The Amazon team utilised interviews, but also extensive participant observations, focusing particularly on the systematic observation of diverse social situations. Following Gluckman (1958), the Amazon team sought through this strategy to read the contours of the broader context—to identify larger social, political, economic and environ-mental patterns and processes as implicated in the individual and collective lives of the women in the research. A qualitative approach was also privileged in the Cameroon project. A stratified and pur-poseful sampling method was used to select 27 of the possible 53 accessible communities along the pipeline. Reconnaissance visits also provided an opportunity for community members to influence the design of the research questions and strategies. For the main fieldwork, in each community five different research instruments were used for different groups of people with the types of experiences and positionalities of interest in the study, and included key informant, group and individual interviews. This purposeful sampling is characteristic of qualitative research, which selects participants with the relevant experiences. This contrasts with a quantitative approach, which randomly selects a sample from a population with the purpose of displaying variability and generalisability across that population (Kirby and McKenna 1989; Layder 1993). The team selected group interviews as the best means to unearth shared understandings, an approach used heavily in PRA and RRA (Rapid Rural Appraisal) following Robert Chambers' influential work (Chambers 1992), and important in feminist approaches as well (Montell 1999; Wilkinson 2004). Groups were organised along apparent pre-existing social categories (women, men, and youth), allowing the team to compare and contrast the views of the major social groups.

There has been a tendency in feminist research to prefer qualitative methods, such as life histories, in-depth interviewing, journaling, focus groups, workshops and participant observation, that allow participants' self-expression and definition, and a conversation between researcher and participants to deepen understanding (Reinharz 1992; Anderson et al. 1990; Oakley 1981). Quantitative methods such as random sample survey research, clinically-based experimental methods often used in psychology or medicine, or naturalist observation were thought to impose categories and analyses through predetermined sets of research questions and misunderstandings of women's lives (Armstrong and Armstrong 1987; Caplan and Caplan 1999). Later feminist work lost this distrust of quantitative methods (see Smith, M. 1994 and Greaves et al. 1995 for examples), especially in cases where base-line data are not available. However, feminist research still favours multi-methods to generate both quantitative and qualitative data. The teams also did not carry negative views of quantitative methods, taking a more pragmatic stance. As Porro pointed out in an editorial comment:

> I have seen both: qualitative methods that misinterpret women's lives and quantitative methods that do not result in production of scientific knowledge. The adequacy of either qualitative or quantitative method

depends on the research question we want to answer. I am convinced that life histories, in-depth interviewing, etc., are scientific methods, as much as surveys, GIS, etc.

Whether the methods were quantitative or qualitative in nature, there were differences in the ways in which subjects or participants in the research were treated or conceptualised as "subjects". The most notable contrast exists between the Cameroon and Amazonian projects. In the Cameroon project, social categories that the researchers observed people had "naturally" organised themselves into (women, men, leaders, youth, etc.), became the basis for disaggregated data collection and analysis. This approach yielded very important information about gender relations and women's entitlements, and was complimented by individual interviews. On the other hand, the Amazon project followed an approach where research subjects "identified themselves", and wherein the research engaged in the existing lives and patterns of the research participants as they defined them, particularly in terms of their collective identity as women in their social movements. Indeed, it is how they lived their lives, engaged in struggle and formed identities, which constituted how the project viewed them as "subjects". These differences in approaches to the "subject" of social research can be associated with traditions and debates in social theory and methodology. For example, the Amazon project fits with the surge of post-modern feminist interest in subjectivity in the late 1980s and 1990s in feminist scholarship (some of it originating with southern women theorists), which seeks to de-stabilise homogenous and uninterrogated categories such as "third world woman" (see Mohanty 1991; S. Smith 1993; Ong 1988). This is achieved through the study of how subjectivities and identities are formed, contested and transformed in different contexts. Elements of this interest in subjectivity were also found in the Ghana project. The Cameroon project, on the other hand, adhered to a more traditional approach to "the subject" in social science research, that focuses less on subjectivity than on how people are affected by macro and micro processes, and how they respond to these. The "subject" itself is more stable in this approach. Both approaches, however, ultimately produced critical insights into a common research question: changing social relations and identities in the context of globalisation.

ANALYSIS

Commitment to multi-method research automatically means complicated analysis, not least because of the sheer volume of data collected, and the various skills needed to work with different kinds of data. Just to start with language issues, the Cameroon team, for example, needed to draw on linguistic expertise in their university and local interpreters (fluent in French) to help interpret local languages they encountered in different communities. The Ghana team had local language interpretation challenges and the Vietnam team faced challenges with transcription of tapes because of differences in local dialects. All teams had to deal with the process of statistical analysis of quantitative data, as well as the transcription and analysis of interviews and other qualitative data. Some of the teams used software packages such as SPSS for analysing quantitative data and N-Vivo for interview-based data.

Common threads to emerge in the post-fieldwork workshop included the uses of the different kinds of data collected. The Amazon team, for example, utilised descriptive quantitative data on material conditions such as area of land, number of cattle, volume of brazil nuts, etc., in order to help identify patterns and contexts for the experiences and discourses emerging in women's lives. The qualitative material was used to investigate how people interpreted these material conditions. The critical use of quantitative approaches allowed the Amazon study to discover that it was not the quantity of nuts being sold in the international market that mattered most for the women involved, but their perceptions of the process and its effects on their lives that explained the intensity of the impact of globalisation. However, qualitative approaches were also used critically and in interpretive fashion. For the Amazon team this meant understanding that people's narratives were socially constructed accounts, not "historical truths", both because of the strategic shaping of the accounts by the research subjects, as well as the interpretation of those accounts by the researchers:

The life trajectories we discuss in this work do not intend to be historical truths about the subjects, but are accounts of what and how we heard and selected parts, and presented them in ways that made sense to us and the reader we are aiming at (Amazon Final Report: 14).

This approach finds parallels in feminist and certain strands of social science approaches to life history or personal narrative research (PNG 1989). In these approaches, memory itself is "part of an active social process", and the researcher must "understand and disentangle the elements of that process" (Thompson 1978: 109). People create themselves through speaking about their lives, using stories "to make sense of the temporal flow of their lives" (Stivers 1993: 412). Hence, personal narratives are "true" in that they have personal meaning, sense, and order for the speaker, but are not necessarily "factually" correct.

Teams also found that insights gained through one method helped build the next stage or method of the research. In the Vietnam study, for example, knowledge gained in resource mapping and transect walks made subsequent in-depth interviews much more productive than they would have been otherwise. The comparison of the case studies of the northern and southern locations, with their differing land tenure regimes and kinship systems, also allowed the Vietnam team to identify the role of land scarcity versus land abundance, the effects of private tenure, and the implications of patrilineal versus bi-lineal inheritance patterns for gendered land entitlements. The Ghana team also gained insights through designing their research as comparative (mining and mangrove based resource activities). In particular, the importance of legal pluralism, and the relationships between labour and gender were thrown into strong relief as they emerged in both case studies.

In all projects, issues arising from the data led to the investigation of new literatures, or re-engagement with literatures used in the early development of the research in new ways. The Vietnam team, for example, found that the profound regional differences revealed in their study led to a need to deepen the historical elements of their literature search. They also found that the policy literature, and literature on the state were woefully inadequate for analysing the emergent issues. Hence there was an urgent need to re-theorise the state, particularly in relation to gaps between policy and implementation, and the mediation of policies through institutional levels and kinship systems.

The Amazon project revealed grassroots challenges to the concept of "empowerment" and the whole package of "development" as passed down from bodies such as the World Bank. In their work they found that women felt disempowered by official development projects and discourses, that it was the World Bank that took away their power. As such, researchers engaged critically with these concepts in the literature through the voices of grassroots women.

The Cameroon study also raised issues that contradict the literature or conventional wisdom, such as the idea that "women don't control or own land" because patriarchy does not permit it. The realities are less rigid, and hence theories of women and land tenure require revision. Further, the fieldwork raised critical questions about the relationships between different social actors such as communities, NGOs and the state. Communities felt marginalised and isolated from the state, elites and the pipeline consortium. This pointed to the absence of civil society groups and NGOs in efforts to mitigate this profound disjuncture between the state and affected communities. More detailed aspects of the analyses and findings of the projects are discussed in Chapter 1 and in the subsequent case study chapters.

INSIGHTS FOR METHODOLOGICAL LITERATURE

The discussion thus far has revealed a number of points relevant to the methodological literature, including feminist and other critical research traditions. For example, the linking of research to positive change for people marginalised or disadvantaged by globalising forces was common to all the projects. Interest in multi-methods research was another point where the projects echoed feminist research preferences. The projects showed interest in the micro context of women's lives, their families, relationships and identities, which are common features of feminist research. In this final section, teams' work is considered more deliberately in relation to feminist methodologies, both as these have been articulated by feminist researchers, and as teams have taken them up as southern researchers.

Were the methods "feminist"?

In the 2005 workshop, teams reflected on whether or not they would identify their methods as feminist. Overall, teams felt that it was not the methods themselves that made the research feminist, but the attention to women and gender. The Vietnam team stated that they were committed to look at gender relations and women in the research from the beginning, and this is what made it feminist research. First, the project specifically involved local women as project leaders at the community level, and second, the project attempted to focus on single women and young widowed women (groups who are usually excluded from policy making). While these were quite simple steps, their impact for the project was profound. The Cameroon team reflected on the need to find the best entry points to study gender and women, and how critical systematic observation of communities and social groups was to this process. In a later editorial comment, the Cameroon team suggested:

> Our study was guided by a feminist research perspective with consideration to the female prism and consciousness raising. We deliberately focused on gender bias and included women in the focus of our inquiry as we researched the reality of the oil pipeline project in the affected communities. This was contrary to other research and general impressions, which have viewed the oil pipeline operations through a "male prism". By using gender graduates as field research assistants we hoped that they possessed a "double vision" and were therefore better equipped to identify, understand and interpret women's and men's experiences. As Cook and Fonow (1990) in Sarantakos (1998:69) have argued, this orientation is important in consciousness raising in feminist research. We were also informed by Shulamit Reinharz (1992), especially the chapters on feminist interview research including group interviews such as focus groups.

For Porro of the Amazon team, however, it was neither techniques/methods, nor even that the research aimed to work against power imbalances between men and women that made research feminist.

While many in the Amazon teams adopted methodologies that were associated with feminist research, the team members themselves, and certainly the research subjects or participants, mostly did not identify as feminists.

Since the 1980s and 1990s, a consensus has developed in western feminist social science and humanities scholarship regarding critical elements of feminist methodologies. Early pioneers forged the way with the very simple points that women could be knowers, and that gender relations and women's lives were interesting and important topics of study (Anderson et al. 1990; Harding 1987). All research teams deliberately sought out women as research participants, and generated new knowledges about their lives as they were changed by globalisation and transformations in land and resource tenure. This aspect of feminist methodology, expressed here by an Indian scholar based in North America, seems to wear quite well across cultures and locations:

> A fundamental thesis of feminist epistemology is that our location in the world as women makes it possible for us to perceive and understand different aspects of both the world and human activities in ways that challenge the male bias of existing perspectives... The inclusion of women's perspective will not merely amount to women participating in greater numbers in the existing practice of science and knowledge, but it will change the very nature of these activities and their self-understanding (Narayan 1989: 256).

Hill Collins (1991) has insisted that race had to be added deliberately to this point, identifying the invisibility and/or misrepresentation of Black women in social science scholarship, and hence the need for research that centred the experiences of Black women. An important collection from Southern Africa, for another example, embraces the feminist study of women and gender, but calls for the importance of generating scholarship from the perspectives of African feminist researchers (Meena et al. 1992). Narayan also inserts colonial domination as critical to understanding Indian women's identities and culture, and the tensions this causes in the application of what she calls "the predominantly Anglo-American project of feminist epistemology" (p. 258) (see also Bannerji 1994):

The imperative we experience as feminists to be critical of how our culture and traditions oppress women conflicts with our desire as members of once colonized cultures to affirm the value of the same culture and traditions (Narayan 1989: 259).

These concerns of southern and Black feminist theorists are echoed in the project approaches. While for all the teams, the feminist practice of focusing on women's experiences and gender relations was important, the research projects did not produce a "universal southern woman" but women shaped by their cultures and social relations, their livelihoods, their relationships with their environments and the operations of globalisation.

One major concern in western feminist scholarship that does not seem to travel south very well, is the focus on issues of positionality, reflexivity and power in the research process (Gibson-Graham 1994; Kirby and McKenna 1989; Laurie et al. 1999; Reinharz 1992; Rose 1997; Wolf 1995). These issues were of significant interest to only the Amazon research team. In western feminist research, the class and race privilege of researchers in relation to their participants has been interrogated, in efforts to make space for marginalised women's voices and experiences and to acknowledge the politics and power in research and representation. Central concerns within this have been the ethical issues related to the operation of power at various moments of a research process, including conceptualisation of research questions, fieldwork, analysis and publication (see PNG 1989; Wolf 1995). Some feminist scholars of colour in North America have indeed suggested that it is not possible to do ethical work as a white western scholar across the divides of race, class and nation (Patai 1991). Such thinking has caused near paralysis in some white feminist scholars working cross-culturally (Wolf 1995). Within the teams, Porro considered extensively the research implications of her location as a professional researcher working among grassroots women in the extractive industries of the Amazon, and engaged with literature concerning knowledge and power in her reflections on these questions:

In our research design, we took into consideration that the authors' (who are also social agents) engagement with the issues approached in the research affects the definition and implementation of the research. This consideration brings a specific perspective, which should be taken into account in the analysis of the results. Warned by the critique about the problems regarding the authoritarian representation of the "Other" (Marcus and Fischer 1986) and the risks and contradictions of imperial translations of "Other's" narratives (Fine 1994), we applied to ourselves as researchers and practitioners, the constant exercise of asking ourselves the questions proposed by Foucault (1972: 50–55): Who is writing? What kinds of qualification do we, as authors, have? From which kind of social relations does our enunciation emerge? (Amazon Final Report: 12).

These sentiments, however, were not representative of the other teams. While all teams worked across divisions of class and often ethnicity in their work, the implications of these relative locations did not emerge as issues warranting a great deal of attention.

All teams did incorporate consideration of the broader social relationships that are produced through research processes and interactions. Consistant with a focus in feminist research (see Wolf 1995), teams grappled with issues such as community expectations, and the frustrations of some communities that have seen researchers come and go, while their own situations stay the same or even deteriorate. In the Vietnam case, the existence of many NGO projects that produce some kind of immediate result or benefit, meant that it was very hard to promote an informed understanding of the nature of research, which may only have long term impacts. In many communities in Ghana, "research fatigue" has emerged as a result of many NGO and research projects carried out but resulting in no subsequent benefits. This raises complex ethical dilemmas about research. Should we only engage in research that is guaranteed to bring benefits to participants? How can we control the post-research usage of knowledge produced?

A positive element in this was that it was often possible to do small things in the field that were appreciated by local participants and/or their communities, and this helped to create goodwill and some reciprocity in the research relationships. The Ghana team made a contribution to the community through the local school, and the Vietnam team made contributions to poorer families in the communities.

Most of the teams showed little interest in western feminist preoccupations associated with the post-modern turn in western feminist theory that gathered steam in the 1990s. Most obvious among these was the destablisation of "women" as a category that posed fundamental challenges to feminist epistemology and research:

> If we accept that there is no unity, centre or actuality to discover for women, what is feminist research about? How can we speak of our experiences as women? Can we still use women's experiences as resources for social analysis? Is it still possible to do research *for* women? (Gibson-Graham 1994: 206).

Except for the Amazon team, the teams did not address such questions in their work. The fact that issues of positionality, reflexivity, and deconstructed categories were marginal in the studies could signal at least two important insights for feminist research. Firstly, perhaps these preoccupations are one more way that feminism is "white" and "western". Western feminist methodologies have been informed mostly by the experiences and thinking of relatively privileged women working across power divides of race, class and often nation (Narayan's "predominantly Anglo-American project of feminist epistemology"), and hence bear the marks of that work. So while western feminist methodologies have provided useful points of departure for many of the team members, these reflections recounted here pose a challenge to the universal applicability of some of western feminist's research concerns. Secondly, the epistemological perspectives and concerns of southern researchers need to be further sought out and invited to transform feminist research. Publications by southern women on epistemology and methodologies remain few and far between. We need more writing "that privileges the indigenous or southern presence, that uses "the words" (such as colonialism, decolonisation, self-determination), and... which situates research in a much larger historical, political and cultural context and then examines its critical nature within those dynamics" (Smith, L. 1999: 6).

CONCLUSIONS

This chapter has sketched the processes of four research teams as they grappled with questions of gender, land and globalisation in diverse locations in the global south. The research methodologies were multi-method, critical, action-oriented, and in some respects, feminist. In some cases and aspects, we can trace colonial legacies that cling to many southern institutions in ways that shape both methodological choices and gender research. Mostly, though, teams chose the strategies that best answered their research questions within the constraints they faced. The creativity, insight and excitement of this collection of scholarship, speak of how well this has been done.

NOTES

1. I acted as a facilitator in two workshops held in Ottawa with the project teams, the first in September 2002 on methodology, and the second in September of 2005 on writing and publication. I have been invited by the editors of the book to write this chapter from my own perspective, so while I at all times attempt to represent the teams' views and experiences as accurately as possible, I take full responsibility for the analysis and interpretation, and any errors therein.
2. Convention on the Elimination of All Forms of Discrimination Against Women (1979), of which Cameroon is signatory.

REFERENCES

Anderson, K. et al., 1990, "Beginning where we are. Feminist Methodology in Oral History", in J. McCarl Nielsen (ed), *Feminist Research Methods. Exemplary Readings in the Social Sciences*. Boulder: Westview Press, pp. 94–112.

Antrobus, Peggy 2004, *The Global Women's Movement. Origins, Issues and Strategies*. London: Zed Books.

Armstrong, Pat and Hugh Armstrong 1987, "Beyond Numbers: Problems with Quantitative Data", in Greta Hofmann Nemiroff (ed), *Women and Men: Interdisciplinary Readings on Gender*. Toronto: Fitzhenry and Whiteside, pp. 54–79.

Bannerji, H., 1995, "But who speaks for us? Experience and Agency in Conventional Feminist Paradigms", in *Thinking Through. Essays on Feminism, Marxism and Anti-Racism*. Toronto: Women's Press, pp. 55–89.

Burt, S. and L. Code (eds), 1995, *Changing Methods: Feminists Transforming Practice*. Peterborough, ON: Broadview Press.

Caplan, P.J. and J.B. Caplan, 1999 (Second Edition), *Thinking Critically about Research on Sex and Gender*. New York: Harper Collins/College Publishers (Addison Wesley).

Chambers, Robert 1992, *Rural Appraisal: Rapid, Relaxed and Participatory*. Institute of Development Studies, University of Sussex.

Devault, M. L., 1999, *Liberating Method. Feminism and Social Research*. Philadelphia: Temple University Press.

Escobar, A., 1995, *Encountering Development: the Making and Unmaking of the Third World*. Princeton, NJ: Princeton University Press.

Fortmann, Louise 1996, "Gendered Knowledge: Rights and Space in Two Zimbabwe Villages", in D. Rocheleau et al., *Feminist Political Ecology. Global Issues and Local Experiences*. London: Routledge, pp. 211–23.

Foucault, M., 1972, *The Archeology of Knowledge*. New York: Pantheon Books.

Gallin, R., Ferguson, A. and Harper, J.1995. *The Women and International Development Annual*, volume 4. Boulder, CO: Westview Press.

Gibson-Graham, J. K., 1994, "'Stuffed' if I know!' Reflections on post-modern feminist social research", *Gender, Place and Culture* 1(2): 205–224.

Gluckman, M. 1958. *Analysis of a Social Situation in Modern Zululand*. Manchester: published on behalf of the Rhodes-Livingstone Institute by the Manchester University Press.

Goebel, Allison 1998, "Process, Perception and Power. Notes from 'Participatory Research' in a Zimbabwean Resettlement Area", *Development and Change* 29(2): 276–305.

———, 2002, "Gender, Environment and Development in Southern Africa", *Canadian Journal of Development Studies* XXIII(2): 293–316.

Gottfried, H., 1996 (ed), *Feminism and Social Change. Bridging Theory and Practice*. Urbana and Chicago: University of Illinois Press.

Greaves, L. et al., 1995, "Women and Violence: Feminist Practice and Quantitative Method", in Sandra Burt and Lorraine Code (eds), *Changing Methods: Feminists Transforming Practice*. Peterborough, ON: Broadview Press, pp. 301–325.

Harding, Sandra 1987, "Introduction: Is there a Feminist Method?" in *Feminism and Methodology*. Bloomington: Indiana University Press, pp. 1–14.

Hill Collins, Patricia 1991, "Learning from the Outsider Within. The Sociological Significance of Black Feminist Thought", in M. M. Fonow and J. A. Cook (eds), *Beyond Methodology. Feminist Scholarship as Lived Research*. Indiana University Press, pp. 35–59.

Imam, A.M. and A. Mama, 1994, "The Role of Academics in Limiting and Expanding Academic Freedom", in Mamadou Diouf and Mahmood Mamdami (eds), *Academic Freedom in Africa*. CODESRIA Book Series. Dakar, Senegal, pp. 73–107.

Israel, Barbara A. et al., 2005, *Methods in community-based participatory research for health*. San Francisco, CA : Jossey-Bass.

Kirby, S. and McKenna, K., 1989, *Experience, Research, Social Change*. Toronto: Garamond Press.

Layder, Derek 1993, *New Strategies in Social Research. An Introduction and Guide.* Cambridge: Polity Press.

Mama, Amina 2005, "Gender Studies for Africa's Transformation" in Thandika Mkandawire (ed), *African Intellectuals. Rethinking Politics, Language, Gender and Development.* Dakar, Senegal: CODESRIA Book Series, pp. 94–116.

Marcus, G. and M.M.J. Fischer, 1986, *Anthropology as Cultural Critique: an Experimental Moment in the Human Sciences.* Chicago: University of Chicago Press.

Meena, Ruth (ed), 1992, *Gender in Southern Africa: Conceptual and Theoretical Issues.* Harare: Southern Africa Political Economy Series (SAPES) Publishers

Montell, Frances 1999, "Focus Group Interviews: A New Feminist Method", *NWSA Journal* 11(1) Spring: 44–71.

Mohanty, Chandra Talpade, (1991), "Under Western Eyes. Feminist Scholarship and Colonial Discourses", in C.T. Mohanty, A. Russo, L. Torres (eds), *Third World Women and the Politics of Feminism.* Bloomington: Indiana University Press.

Narayan, Uma 1989, "The Project of Feminist Epistemology: Perspectives from a Nonwestern Feminist", in A. Jagger and S. Bordo (eds), *Gender/Body/Knowledge: Feminist Reconstructions of Being and Knowing.* New Brunswick, NJ: Rutgers, pp. 256–269.

Oakley, Ann 1981, "Interviewing Women: A Contradiction in Terms" in Helen Roberts (ed), *Doing Feminist Research. .* London: Routledge and Kegan Paul.

Ong, Aihwa 1988, "Colonialism and Modernity: Feminist Re-presentations of Women in Non-Western Societies", *Inscriptions* 3(4): 79–93.

Patai, Daphne 1991, "U.S. Academics and Third World Women: Is Ethical Research Possible?", in Sherna Berger Gluck (ed), *Women's Words: The Feminist Practice of Oral History.* New York: Routledge, pp. 137–53.

Pereira, Charmaine 2002, "Between Knowing and Imagining: What Space for Feminism in Scholarship on Africa?", *Feminist Africa* Issue 1. (http://www.feministafrica.org/index.php/between-knowing-and-imagining) Accessed December 11, 2009.

PNG (Personal Narratives Group) (ed), 1989, *Interpreting Women's Lives. Feminist Theory and Personal Narratives.* Bloomington and Indianapolis: Indiana University Press.

Reinharz, S., 1992, *Feminist Methods in Social Research.* Oxford University Press.

Rocheleau, Diane, B. Thomas-Slayter, and Ester Wangari (eds), 1996, *Feminist Political Ecology. Global Issues and Local Experiences.* London and New York: Routledge.

Rose, Gillian 1997, "Situating knowledges: positionality, reflexivities and other tactics", *Progress in Human Geography* 21(3): 305–320.

Sarantakos, Sotitrios 1998, Social Research. London: Macmillan Press Ltd: 62–71.

Smith, Dorothy E., 1996, "Contradictions for feminist social scientists" in H. Gottfried (ed), *Feminism and Social Change. Bridging Theory and Practice.* Urbana and Chicago: University of Illinois Press, pp. 46–59.

Smith, Linda Tuhiwai 1999, *Decolonizing Methdologies. Research and Indigenous Peoples*. London and New York: Zed Books; Dunedin: University of Otago Press.

Smith, Michael D., 1994, "Enhancing the quality of survey data on violence against women: A Feminist Approach", *Gender and Society* 8(1): 109–127.

Smith, Sidonie 1993, "Who's Talking/Who's Talking Back? The Subject of Personal Narratives", *Signs* 18(2): 392–407.

Stivers, Camilla 1993, "Reflections on the Role of Personal Narrative in Social Science", *Signs* 18(2): 408–425.

Thompson, Paul 1978, *The Voice of the Past: Oral History*. Oxford: Oxford University Press.

Wilkinson 2004. "Focus Groups: A Feminist Method" in Sharlene Nagy Hesse-Biber and Michelle L.Yaiser (eds), *Feminist Perspectives on Social Research* New York and Oxford: Oxford University Press, pp. 271–295.

Wolf, Diane (ed), 1995, *Feminist Dilemmas in Fieldwork*. Boulder, CO: Westview.

Zeleza, Paul Tiyambe 2002, "African Universities and Globalization", *Feminist Africa* Issue 1. (http://www.feministafrica.org/index.php/african-universities-and-globalisation) Accessed December 11, 2009.

4

Economic Liberalisation, Changing Resource Tenures and Gendered Livelihoods
A Study of Small-Scale Gold Mining and Mangrove Exploitation in Rural Ghana

MARIAMA AWUMBILA AND DZODZI TSIKATA

INTRODUCTION

This chapter discusses the implications of economic liberalisation, environmental change and the increased competition over natural resources for land and resource tenures in rural Ghana. Through an exploration of two cases—small-scale gold mining and mangrove harvesting—the chapter explores the implications of changing resource tenures for the livelihoods of men and women, paying particular attention to changes in gender relations in this context. The importance of the case studies lies in their contribution to debates about the linkages between globalisation, gender relations and land tenure. They also draw attention to the significance of labour relations in the constitution of land relations and the importance of land for structuring labour relations.

The mangrove study focuses on how long-term environmental degradation and socio-economic decline arising from the damming of the Volta River in the 1960s to produce hydro-electric power for national development has been compounded by economic liberalisation, resulting in the intensification of exploitation of mangroves in the South Tongu District of the Lower Volta. This, in combination with the gendered character of mangrove exploitation, has led to increasing insecurities, tensions and differential benefits from mangrove resources and other livelihood activities for men and women. The gold mining study, for its part, follows the introduction of small-scale mining into the Talensi-Nabdam District in the Upper East Region, in the early 1990s, as a result of the liberalisation of gold mining in Ghana and the decriminalisation of small-scale gold mining. The study examines the participation of locals and migrants in mining and the emerging hierarchies of labour relations based on a combination of ethnicity, gender, migrant status and access to capital in an area which is in one of the three poorest regions in Ghana.

Land and natural resources remain critical to the economies and livelihoods in sub-Saharan Africa in the foreseeable future. Economic globalisation of the 1980s, which Africa experienced as economic liberalisation or structural adjustment policies under the direction of the World Bank and International Monetary Fund (IMF), restructured economies in general and had two significant effects on land. Firstly, these policies reinforced the agrarian character of most economies, reversing efforts at economic diversification and encouraging the commercialisation of land and expansion in land markets. Secondly, these developments were accompanied by contra-dictory processes of concentration (in the hands of certain economic interests) and fragmentation (of the already small holdings of rural families), resulting in significant inequalities in access to land and its resources.

An aspect of economic liberalisation was the rehabilitation and promotion of export agriculture and extractive economic activities such as gold mining and timber logging. These activities put pressure on land, a situation exacerbated by massive labour retrenchments in the urban economy. The policy response was to extend liberalisation policies to the land sector through titling and registration, and insti-tutional reforms to increase tenure security and the effectiveness of land markets. There are suggestions that both the crisis and the pro-posed solutions will deepen inequalities in land tenure and weaken the land interests of social groups such as women, young persons and migrants (Wily and Hammond 2001).

Studies of land tenure have tended to focus on land used for farm-ing and housing. This study extends these insights by exploring the changes in tenure arrangements in relation to the exploitation of natural resources as livelihood activities. The chapter also contributes to debates in the literature, specifically on issues such as the gendered implications of legal pluralism for tenure security and the nature of new social identities created or modified in the struggle over natural resources. Also of interest are the issues of the intersection of several social relations in the organisation of resource tenure and livelihoods and the linkages between labour and land relations in the creation of resource tenures.

The chapter is structured thus: The introduction is followed by a section on conceptual issues. The background to the study areas is then set out, followed by two sections which focus on the case studies. Section 6 then draws out the implications of the findings of these for the literature on gender and land tenure. A summary and conclusions are then drawn.

ECONOMIC GLOBALISATION, LAND AND RESOURCE TENURES AND GENDER RELATIONS: SOME CONCEPTUAL ISSUES

This section explores briefly the organising concepts of the study—globalisation, land tenure, gender and other social relations—and their inter-connections. There are different emphases in the definitions of globalisation. While some highlight cultural dimensions, others focus on technological changes or economic processes. Certain definitions highlight the integrative properties of globalisation while others draw attention to the widening inequalities between regions, countries and social groups arising from the logics of its processes. The World Bank's definition of globalisation as "the growing integration of societies and economies around the world as a result of reduced costs of transport, lower trade barriers, faster communication of ideas, rising capital flows and intensifying pressure for migration" emphasises integration between countries even while conceding that there are winners and losers[1] (World Bank 2002). The UNDP's globalisation emphasises the role of technologies in increased trade and the creation of new markets, and suggests that processes of globalisation are inevitable. What is needed, therefore, is to fashion rules and institutions to create an ethical globalisation (UNDP 1999). Khor's discussions have focused on economic globalisation, the most important elements of which are "the breaking down of national economic barriers; the international spread of trade, financial and production activities; and the growing power of trans-national corporations and international financial institutions in these processes" (Khor 2000:1). In emphasising the economic aspects of globalisation, Khor (2000) thus situates the economic liberalisation policies of the 1980s within the globalisation processes. Besides, he departs from the World Bank and UNDP approaches of putting technological and other aspects of globalisation on the same footing as the economic. Khor argues that economic processes drive other aspects of globalisation, and has structured them in particular ways. Thus a focus on economic processes demystifies globalisation, drawing attention to the fact that it is the outcome of deliberate rather than natural or inevitable processes, and driven by powerful constituencies and ideas (Khor 2000).

Among most definitions of globalisation though, there is a general agreement that while the processes discussed under the rubric of globalisation may have started earlier, the unprecedented economic liberalisation underpinned by neo-liberal economics, which is the hallmark of globalisation, can be dated from the 1980s. This approach to globalisation links the global with the national by its focus on the economic liberalisation policies of the last two and a half decades. The reforms, also known as structural adjustment programmes, which were instituted across Africa from the early 1980s, combined an IMF stabilisation loan with conditionalities, with a longer term Structural Adjustment Programme overseen by both the World Bank and the IMF (Olukoshi 1998; Tsikata and Kerr 2000).

A result of liberalisation programmes was that agriculture experi-enced a short-term boom made possible by investments in export crops. Since the 1990s, however, agriculture has been in stagnation as a result of the removal of subsidies and vital support to farmers (Mkandawire and Soludo 1999). This has been detrimental to many rural livelihoods and has been a contributing factor to the poverty of farmers, especially food crop growers and those involved in unpaid labour in agriculture most of whom are women (Whitehead and Kabeer 2001). Missing from this literature is the consideration of the liberalisation of land and resource tenures as a factor in the agrarian crisis and the poor outcomes of rural livelihoods. This issue is taken up in other literature on economic liberalisation and land tenure.

Within Sub-Saharan Africa the need for land tenure reforms is long felt and predates the economic reforms instituted in the 1980s. Since the colonial period, processes of agrarian change have exerted pressure on land tenure systems and vice versa. In the last few decades, the twin processes of land concentration for big business (tourism, large-scale agriculture, dams and industrial production) and land fragmentation for small peasants has been observed in several countries (Mbilinyi 1999; Wily and Hammond 2001; Whitehead and Tsikata 2003). Also, growing land shortages and the rapidly rising prices of land in both urban and rural areas have been accompanied by a transformation of customary norms of land tenure in ways which have weakened collective interests at the expense of individual interests in land. Incomplete processes of titling and registration since the 1960s have also exacerbated tenure insecurities. Strenuous efforts to promote foreign direct investment (FDI) since the 1980s have resulted in a massive expansion of gold mining, timber extraction, large-scale farming and real estate. At the local level, these developments have squeezed the stock of land available for traditional livelihood resources, leading to increased exploitation of hitherto marginal natural resources and exacerbating competition and conflicts in the use of these resources. All these factors have resulted in tenure insecurity and landlessness which affects a larger proportion of land users than is recognised.

For women, the situation has several particular elements. As a result of the erosion of customary tenures, they have experienced the loss of land in conditions of scarcity but also gained access to land in some instances of male migration. Buying and leasing land are not easy options because of transaction costs, women's poorer access to resources, the insecurities and inequities of customary tenancies and gender discrimination in the treatment of potential land purchasers. While there is increasing recognition of gender inequalities in land tenure systems, this issue has not been central in either the past or current land tenure reforms which have been instituted under the guidance of the World Bank, with the support of bilateral aid agencies. This is in spite of the large body of literature on women's land interests which has documented unfavourable changes since the colonial period.

Land tenure and the intersection of social relations

In much of the gender and land literature, it has been argued that unequal land rights are an important factor in the reproduction of gender inequalities as well as women's poverty, particularly in agricultural economies (Wanyeki 2003; Butegwa 1991). There are, however, suggestions that in certain situations, labour, women's increased workloads, their lack of access to capital, extension services and technologies are much stronger constraints than land, even if land is an issue (Himonga and Munachonga 1991). Some have gone so far as to discount completely gender inequalities in land as an issue in agriculture (Benneh et al. 1995; See Whitehead and Tsikata 2003 for a discussion of this debate). More generally, there is widespread recognition in the literature of the link between access to land and access to other resources such as labour (Butegwa 1994). The ways in which the land and labour relationships are manifested has been explored in the two case studies of the chapter. In both the mangrove and gold mining areas, labour relations are gendered and structure the ability to access land and natural resources.

In the literature on livelihoods, centrality is given to social relations, especially in situations of livelihood crises which result in the intensification of competition for natural resources. This is because under such conditions, what determines which households are poor and which are not are the social relations which structure their access to resources (Tsikata 2006). Gender relations are one of several social relations implicated in the organisation of livelihoods. They intersect with class, ethnicity, kinship and other inter-generational relations as well as the relations between migrants and locals, and between chiefs/ land owners and land users to structure the livelihoods of men and women. In situations of increased competition over particular resources, certain social groups might find that their access to and control of resources becomes more uncertain as the rules of access become more formalised and subject to market principles.

The conceptual framework of the studies focused on livelihood processes and outcomes in order to include the physical, financial, social, political, human and natural resources in the analysis of resources. This framework has allowed an analysis of the social relations which govern livelihood activities and affect their outcomes. It also takes account of the institutions and the broader political economy within which livelihoods are organised (See for example Bebbington 1997; Murray 1999; Ellis 1998, 2001; Whitehead and Kabeer 2001).

THE STUDY AND RESEARCH METHODS

The chapter is based on research conducted between November 2003 and May 2005 in two sites—the Datoko-Sheaga area in the Talensi-Nabdam District[2] of the Upper East Region, located in north eastern Ghana and the Gamenu area which is part of the South Tongu District in south eastern Ghana (Figure 1). The Talensi-Nabdam district is in the Guinea Savannah zone which has a long history of environmental degradation, seasonal out-migration and a more recent history of surface gold mining as a result of legalisation and regulation of small-scale mining as part of economic re-structuring policies. The Gamenu area is located in the Lower Volta Basin area, in the south eastern coastal zone of Ghana. As a result of the construction of the Akosombo and Kpong Dams over the Volta River, this area has suffered environmental stress including changes in rainfall patterns, soil quality and the character and flow of the Volta, resulting in the loss of traditional sources of livelihoods. These two sites, located in two different ecological zones and operating different land tenure systems, provided micro level data on the inter-linkages between economic and resource pressures, land and gender relations in different environments.

A three-stage approach using a combination of qualitative and quantitative data collection methods was employed in the research. A pilot study was first undertaken in November 2003, in the two areas using mainly PRA techniques—transect walks, resource mapping, focus group discussions and in-depth interviews. This enabled familiarisation with the study site, collection of background information, choice of study communities and the testing of research instruments. It also enabled the identification of key informants and the development and modification of research issues and key concepts and approaches. A glossary of mining terms was also compiled during the pilot survey to facilitate the researchers' understanding of the industry.

This was followed by the main survey in the Datoko-Sheaga area in June –July 2004, and in the Gamenu area in March—April, 2005, which involved the administration of a sample of 120 structured questionnaires in each of the two study areas. The questionnaires were administered to an equal number of male and female respondents, in each of the two study areas. In both study

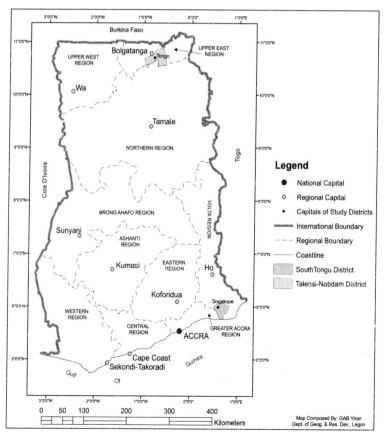

Figure 1   Regional map of Ghana showing the study districts

areas, the sample of 120 was selected purposively with 50 per cent from the mining or mangrove communities and the other 50 per cent from the nearby farming communities of Datoko and Sheaga, for the Talensi Nabdam area, and Amedormekope for the South Tongu area (see Figures 2 and 3). In the Gamenu area, survey respondents were residents of 4 of the 13 settlements in the Gamenu area—Hawui, Agorkpokope and Norsakope for the mangrove communities and Amedormekope for the non-mangrove communities. Out of the respondents, 61 (50.8 per cent) were male while 49 (49.2 per cent) were female. This was to provide basic base-line information on the nature and extent of the research issues, as well as to enable an examination of mangroves/mining in women and men's livelihood activities. To enable better insights into the inter-linkages among liberalisation policies, livelihood activities and social relations, 15 key informant interviews in the Regional and District capitals of Bolgatanga and Sogakope and in the research communities, as well as 40 life histories of men and women involved in mining, mangrove and farming activities were undertaken. Key informants included chiefs and community elders, other custodians of customary law, e.g., *tendama* (see Rattray, 1932) or earth priests, community-based organisations, women's groups, policymakers and implementers at the district level including District Chief Executives and District Assembly Sub-Committee Heads, the Ministry of Lands, Mines, and the Minerals and Forestry Commission.

Setting the context: economic liberalisation and environmental change in the Talensi-Nabdam and South Tongu Districts

The Talensi- Nabdam District

The Datoko-Sheaga area (Figures 1 and 2) is in one of the poorest and most rural parts of Ghana. It has a dry savannah climate and vegetation, poor soils, and irregular rainfall patterns leading to poor crop yields and inadequate levels of food production. Agricultural production is mainly rain-fed and largely non-mechanised, and is a mixture of cash-cropping and subsistence food crops. The area experiences high net out-migration, especially of males, but increasingly of females to the south of Ghana as a result of historical factors.[3]

More recently, structural adjustment policies of the mid-1980s and 1990s, such as the removal of subsidies on fertiliser, health care and other social services, have seriously affected development in many parts of Ghana. These have contributed to northern Ghana's low welfare indicators and high concentration of the poor in Ghana. In the Upper East Region, 70 per cent of the population live below the poverty line, compared to the national average of 29 per cent (Ghana Statistical Service, 2007).

Under Ghana's structural adjustment programme (SAP), the mining sector was one of the key areas of liberalisation. In 1986, a mining sector reform programme was initiated with the aim of increasing production by streamlining policies and rehabilitating the infrastructural base to attract new investors. In line with this, the Minerals and Mining Law was promulgated in 1986, and the Minerals Commission (MC) was constituted to provide a more flexible and open mining regime for potential and existing investors, formulate policies for the sector and provide a one-stop service for investors. Almost all state–owned mines were divested or privatised (Akabzaa 2000)

Small-scale mining of gold and diamonds which had traditionally played an important role in the economy of Ghana until 1905 when the colonial authorities made it illegal, also received attention under this new liberalised mining environment. Under the minerals sector restructuring reforms, the government legalised small-scale mining activities through the enactment of the Small Scale Gold Mining Law (PNDC Law 218), in 1989. The liberalisation of the mining legislation and the resultant liberal mining investment climate opened up the mining sector to an estimated 50,000 small-scale miners extracting gold and diamonds from alluvial and primary deposits (Hinson 2001). However, despite the legalisation of their operations, many small-scale miners still operate illegally (a practice known as *galamsey*), partly because of the frustrations they face in the process of registering and licensing their operations. In the Upper East Region, the discovery of gold deposits in the mid-1990s led to an influx of unregistered small-scale miners into the region, thereby increasing the importance of gold mining to the local economy.

The South Tongu District

The Gamenu area is part of the Agave traditional area in the southern-most part of the South Tongu District, located in the south eastern part of Ghana in the Volta Region (See figures 1 and 3). The district is generally low lying by virtue of its location within the coastal plain, but rises gradually to a height of 75 metres above sea level (South Tongu District Assembly, 2003). This location is unique in its access to both the Volta River and the Atlantic Ocean (see Figure 3). There are also numerous streams, which run across the district, with a number of lagoons in the southern section, thus accounting for its marshy nature. The creeks in this area were fed by both the Volta River and salt water from the sea at different intervals in the year. Since the construction of the Akosombo Dam, many of the creeks have dried up, but the area remains marshy and saline and is still influenced by this river/sea interface. The district is located within the coastal savannah vegetation zone, with the southern section—where the study area is located –covered by swamps and mangroves, while the northern section is predominantly savannah woodland. The area has a dry equatorial climatic zone and unlike north eastern Ghana, experiences two rainfall seasons, although rainfall is at times low and erratic.

The Gamenu area is made up of dispersed hamlets with very small populations and has a poor road network. The high rate of salinity of underground water in the mangrove area makes access to drinking water one of the major challenges facing the area. Only 21 per cent of the population have access to potable water. Poverty levels for the Volta Region are relatively high, at 31 per cent, which is slightly higher than the national average of 29 per cent (Ghana Statistical Service, 2007). But there are spatial variations, with the mangrove areas of the Gamenu area likely to have much higher poverty levels. Due to the lack of employment opportunities, the South Tongu District, like the Talensi-Nabdam District is an area of out-migration. The district's population growth rate reduced from 1.8 per cent per annum between 1970 and 1984 to 1.35 per cent between 1984 and 2000. This reduction has been attributed mainly to the out-migration of citizens, especially fishermen, to other fishing communities, and the migration of the youth to the cities (South Tongu District Assembly, 2003). This has resulted in a low sex ratio of 82.5 for the South Tongu District compared to the Volta Region ratio of 94.1 implying a dominance of females in the study area.

The Volta River provides the stimulus for livelihood activities in the study area which include mangrove harvesting, fishing, crab trapping, the production of crab traps made from palm fronds, and ropes and mat weaving and agriculture. However, the construction of the Akosombo Dam over the Volta in 1966 and later the Kpong Dam in 1982, to provide cheap electricity for rapid industrialisation, resulted in the cessation of seasonal flooding of the Volta's floodplain, thus changing dramatically the ecology and livelihood activities of communities located in the lower parts of the Volta River, which includes the study area. This resulted in the wholesale out-migration of Tongu fishermen and their families from the Lower Volta to the Volta Lake (Gordon et al. 1999; Tsikata 2004). In the Gamenu area, this has led to a restructuring of livelihoods with a focus on mangroves which were hitherto marginal to livelihoods, thus increasing their importance in the local economy.

Thus in both study areas, environmental changes have combined with economic liberalisation to add new economic pressures to the problems of already marginalised communities. This has led to the decline of traditional livelihood activities, thus setting the stage for the restructuring of livelihoods. It is within this context that the two case studies—small-scale gold mining into the Talensi-Nabdam District and mangrove exploitation in the South Tongu District—are examined.

Case 1: Small-scale gold mining in the Talensi-Nabdam District

Migration and mining settlement history

This section examines how the introduction of small-scale mining in the Talensi-Nabdam District in the early 1990s has affected the local economy, land use, tenurial arrangements, and gender and other social relations. It also examines the emerging hierarchies of participation in mining and the different labour relations and their implications for local participation in mining. The land tenure system of the area is discussed, focusing on the gender implications of the expansion of gold mining for farming and other livelihood activities.

Traditionally, the Upper East Region experiences high net out-migration, especially of males, but increasingly of females (Nabila 1975). Although the historical roots of migration lie in British colonial policy, out-migration has continued as a strategy for survival for many households in the region. The dominant form of migration in the area was seasonal and circulatory, with migrants returning to the area to farm at the beginning of the wet season and returning to southern Ghana at the beginning of the dry season after the harvests. With the discovery of gold, however, migration flows appear to have changed as miners came from all over Ghana as well as from neighbouring countries, such as Burkina Faso and Togo, and live in small temporary settlements in the Talensi- Nabdam District around Datoko and Sheaga (Figure 2). Table 1 shows the transient nature of the population in the mining communities. 42 per cent of respondents in the study area belonged to a household elsewhere. In the mining communities however almost three quarters (71.2 per cent) of residents belonged to a household elsewhere compared to only 13.3 percent in the farming communities. Almost 80 per cent of women in the mining communities were migrants compared to 63 per cent of men. Migrants in the mining communities come from diverse locations. Of the respondents, 43 per cent had come from areas outside the Talensi-Nabdam District. However, men had migrated longer distances, with only 33 per cent originating from

Table 1
Do you belong to a household elsewhere? By gender and community

Do you belong to a household elsewhere?	Mining Communities			Farming Communities			Total	
	M	F	T	M	F	T	N	%
Yes	63.3	79.3	71.2	14.3	12.5	13.3	50	41.7
No	36.7	20.7	28.8	85.7	87.5	86.7	69	57.5
Total	(30)	(29)	(59)	(28)	(32)	(60)	119	100.0

Source: Field work, 2004

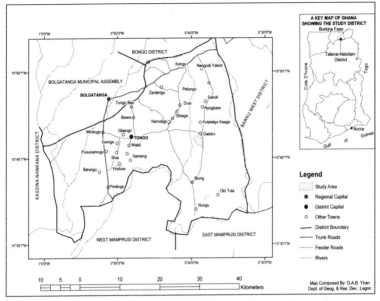

Figure 2 Map of Talensi-Nabdam District showing the study area

the Talensi-Nabdam District compared to 62 per cent of women. For example, whereas 33 per cent of men had come from Burkina Faso, Togo and from areas in southern Ghana, only 14 per cent of women came from these areas.

Mining settlements were named after either large towns, mining communities in southern Ghana or rich institutions. Thus settlements were given names such as Accra (the national capital), Kejetia, Bantama (large commercial centres in Kumasi, Ashanti Region), Obuasi, Tarkwa (well known large gold mining towns in the south), Gold Coast (former name of Ghana), World Bank and Croatia. Kejetia was the oldest community in this cluster. It was so crowded when mining started that it looked like Kejetia market, the largest market in Kumasi in the Ashanti Region and hence its name. Names of settlements appeared to convey the size and population of the new mining area when it opened. Each name also tried to outdo the one before it. There was rivalry among settlements as to which started first, which was larger in population size and which had the richest ore deposits. In-depth interviews revealed that although initially mining started in Croatia around 1995 for a brief period, Kejetia was the oldest settlement in terms of historical age and size of population. However, Tarkwa appeared to be the most important settlement at the time of the research because its central location had helped to make it the commercial centre of the cluster of settlements. The politics and rivalry in the naming as well as disagreements about the age of settlements was an illustration of aspirations and the potential promise of mining for improving the livelihoods of people in the district.

Changing livelihoods in the Talensi-Nabdam District

Before the introduction of small-scale mining into the district in the early 1990s, the main livelihood activities were farming, livestock-rearing and hunting for men, and farming, shea-nut picking and fuel wood gathering for women. Farming was the major livelihood activity and was centred on food crop (sorghum, cereal and legume) production. The influx of small-scale gold miners in the 1990s led to a restructuring of livelihoods around gold mining which was hitherto a marginal livelihood activity. Men came into the area and got involved in mining as sponsors, buyers, pit owners, different categories of mine workers, and as processors of ground ore. Women came in mainly as sievers of gold chippings and powder and as support service providers.

There were gender and community differences in the major livelihood activities in the area. For women in the mining communities, the main activities were gold processing (44.8 per cent), trading (31 per cent) and service provision to miners (17.2 per cent). Only 3.5 per cent of women mentioned farming while another 3.5 per cent mentioned gold mining as their main livelihood activity. For men, it was mainly gold mining (at 83.3 per cent). A few men mentioned farming (6.7 per cent) and gold processing (6.7 per cent). In the farming communities, farming was the main activity for both men and women. Even then, many more men than women mentioned farming as their main activity (93.4 per cent men to 74.2 per cent women). Of the women, 16.1 per cent said trading was their main activity while another 9.7 per cent mentioned gold processing. None of the men mentioned gold mining and only 3.3 per cent mentioned gold processing (Table 2).

The small-scale character of mining and its occurrence mainly in the dry season made its integration with other income generating activities—such as farming for men and women, and shea-nut picking for women—convenient. However, there were differences between locals and migrants with regard to the place of mining within their livelihood portfolios. For locals, mining was a dry season supplement to farming activities in the wet season. However, for the large group of migrants, it was the only activity they were engaged in and therefore more intensively pursued. For several decades, migration was an important avenue for the acquisition of household items, better housing and living standards in the Upper East Region. However, gold mining has become important for obtaining money for investment in other livelihood activities, improving living standards, and attracting people back to the area. In this sense, mining was perceived as being more important than farming by those in the mining communities. However, disappointments such as water-logged pits, the lack of capital and disputes over the distribution of earnings were leading to a reappraisal of the reliability of mining in certain communities.

Although small-scale mining could be integrated with farming, there were differences in men and women's approaches to this. Whereas men could start mining activities as soon as the rains ended and could continue until the beginning of the next rainy season, women had to finish with sowing and harvesting crops before they could join in the mining activities. In Zanlerigu, where a new surface mine had opened only weeks before the reconnaissance study, women arrived at the mine site late and therefore could only gain access to land abandoned by the men. This affected the quantities of gold and income women could earn from surface mining

In spite of the importance of mining, its impact on the economy of mining communities and the district as a whole was not clear, partly because there was a crisis in the industry. In many places, surface mines had given way to mining at depths below which miners could not work without technologies such as compressors and water pumps, thus requiring a higher outlay of resources. As many

Table 2
Main Livelihood Activity—by Gender and Community

| | Mining Communities | | | | | | Farming Communities | | | | | |
| | Male | | Female | | Total | | Male | | Female | | Total | |
	Freq.	%	Freq.	%	Freq.	%	Freq.	%	Freq.	%	Freq.	%
Gold mining	25	83.3	1	3.5	26	44	0	0	0	0	0	0
Gold processing	2	6.7	13	44.8	15	25.5	1	3.3	3	9.7	4	6.6
Service provision to miners	0	0	5	17.2	5	8.5	0	0	0	0	0	0
Farming	2	6.7	1	3.5	3	5.1	28	93.4	23	74.2	51	83.6
Trading	0	0	9	31	9	15.3	0	0	5	16.1	5	8.2
Artisanship	1	3.3	0	0	1	1.7	1	3.3	0	0	1	1.6
Total	30	100	29	100	59	100	30	100	31	100	61	100

Source: Field work, 2004.

locals had little access to such finance, they could only participate in mining as hired labour, while owners of mines tended to come from outside the district. The capital costs of establishing and working a mine and the fact that exploitation involved knowledge and technologies which were not local, also had implications for the nature of local participation in mining. In the village of Accra which was very actively mined in the mid to late 1990s, for example, many of the mines were no longer in service as a result of water logging. Many of the inhabitants had moved away to other mining areas. Only one group of miners seemed to have solved the problem of water logging, by purchasing the heavy equipment needed to pump out excess water. This group had external funding from a foreign national based in Accra. As a result, the group had purchased four Honda pumps, a generator for lighting, and a compressor. They operated three pits, employing 185 male workers, many of whom originated from various parts of Ghana and Burkina Faso.

Labour relations, new social identities and unchanging gender identities

Small-scale mining was highly segmented with emerging hierarchies of labour relations based on a combination of ethnicity, gender, migrant status and access to capital. Participants in small-scale mining included *sponsors* (financiers), buyers of gold (who were also often sponsors) *ghetto* owners (pit owners,), and the different classes of workers, made up of dynamiters, *moya men* or chisellers, *loco boys* (transporters of the blasted rock ore from the pit to the surface), *kaimen (*who pound the ore in metal mortars with metal pestles), and *shanking ladies* (who sift the pounded rock with a scarf to separate powder from chippings). Whereas *sponsors*, buyers, and to some extent *ghetto* owners tend to be migrants from outside the region and could include other nationals such as people from the Middle East and Burkina Faso, the workers at the lower scale (*loco boys, kaimen* and *shanking ladies*), tended to be locals. Even among the different categories of mine workers, the dynamiters and chisellers, who required some expertise in mining, tended to be from southern Ghana, while the *loco boys, kaimen* and *shanking ladies* requiring no specific training and earning the lowest returns, tended to be mainly locals. Women were mainly involved in processing as sievers of the ore powder (shanking), panners, and to a smaller extent, washing of gold. Migration had, therefore, resulted in technology transfer but had also reproduced certain patterns of labour relations which were disadvantageous to the locals and women.

Among the various categories of mine workers, the *shanking ladies*, who were women, were the lowest in the hierarchy and earned the lowest returns. Labour relations were unregulated and not predictable across the different mines. Relations between the sponsor, who had to be a licensed buyer or licensed services support agency, and the pit or *ghetto* owner were skewed in favour of the sponsor. Sponsoring was a pre-financing arrangement between a financier and the pit owner, where the sponsor loaned money or inputs to the *ghetto* owner and in return was paid with the gold produced from the pit at an agreed profit margin. The sponsor determined how much the ghetto owner was to pay back, apart from the initial capital costs. There were no laid down principles for sharing the profits and many ghetto owners felt exploited by sponsors. Some sponsors also financed buyers who went around buying gold from individuals. Similarly there appeared to be no laid down principles for the payment of the various categories of mine workers by the *ghetto* owner. The study found different types of sponsoring arrangements which included pre-financing in the form of money and or mining inputs; cooking food on regular basis for workers and the provision of credit facilities to miners by female traders to allow the former to purchase goods such as batteries, flashlights and Wellington boots on credit.

Sponsorship was a predominantly male activity, with only four female sponsors identified in the mining community. However, there were gender differences in the form of sponsorship. While men provided pre-financing in the form of cash and inputs, the common form of sponsorship by women was the provision of credit facilities, mining inputs and cooked meals for miners. The four female sponsors identified mainly provided credit facilities, inputs such as sacks, *loco* ropes, flashlights and batteries and gallons to miners, besides cooking food for them. However, the procurement of inputs for miners on credit by women sponsors was not recognised as sponsorship, but as a kind of informal arrangement. This tended to affect women's ability to recoup their investments. To minimise cheating from the miners, the male sponsors were also often buyers. They bought all the gold for which they had sponsored production, deducted the loan given as well as their profit margin, and gave the rest to the miner. Unlike male sponsors, women in informal sponsorship were not entitled to buy the gold and earn some profits. Even the few women recognised as sponsors were unable to keep an eye on the pit owners to see the quantities of rock ore they mined and the gold obtained after processing.

Interviews with *shanking ladies*[4] who were locals showed that they faced the same constraints as migrant *shanking* ladies. Once in the shanking business, the ability to obtain contracts and the amounts paid were dependent on the relationship between the ore owner and the *shanking lady*. Women with close relationships with ore owners, which were sexual in some cases, had the advantage of obtaining better payment terms as shown by the case of LA, the supervisor or *Mangazia*. This appeared to be at the root of female vulnerability in the mining area. Payment for services was unregulated and informalised, as there were no fixed payment terms for sieving a quantity of rock powder and women felt powerless to contest these payments for fear of not getting further contracts as there were hundreds of *shanking ladies*. This feeling of powerlessness was put forward by one of the local shanking ladies as *"You can't determine your pay because we are paid differently from day to day and between two shanking ladies. You don't complain because you do not know the relationship between the miner and the shanking girl. Some women sleep with the miners, but it is out of choice".* In addition to *shanking*, women dominated the service side of mining, supplying food, drink, washing clothes, providing public bath facilities and providing other general goods and services at the mines and in the mining community. Many also provided sexual services.

Table 3 shows that in the mining communities, it was sponsors and buyers of gold who were perceived to be the major beneficiaries of gold mining in the study communities. Out of the respondents in the mining communities, 47.2 per cent thought that buyers and sponsors gained the most from mining in the community. Male migrants were also seen to derive benefits from mining. At the bottom of the scale were local men (5.7 per cent), chiefs (5.7 per cent) and women migrants (7.5 per cent). Local women were not mentioned at all in the mining communities as beneficiaries. Not surprisingly, *ghetto* owners were ranked low as beneficiaries. It was often mentioned during the interviews that they felt cheated by sponsors. There were a few differences in the perceptions of male and female respondents as regards the major beneficiaries of mining. For example, 18.5 per cent of women identified ghetto owners as major beneficiaries while men did not mention them at all; 15.4 per cent of male respondents ranked female migrants as major beneficiaries while women did not mention them at all. In the farming communities, sponsors again scored very high as major beneficiaries, at 55.8 per cent of respondents. They were followed by male migrants (16.3 per cent). The rest of the respondents mentioned men from the local community (9.3 per cent) and chiefs and land owners (9.3 per cent). Both local women and female migrants scored the least, at 4.7 per cent each, in the farming communities. Men and women broadly agreed on these assessments except in one case. More men (13.6 per cent) than women (4.8 per cent) identified local men as major beneficiaries.

The participation of women in mining provided them with opportunities for income generation, but also had implications for gender relations. Many men in the area perceived the women in the mining communities, particularly the "shanking ladies", as being of low morals. Many men did not want their wives to live with them in the mining communities. This was related to the instability in sexual and marital relations in the mining communities which male respondents blamed on women. They were accused of being more clearly interested in what material benefits relationships offered than sustaining relationships. According to a prominent ghetto owner in Obuasi, "*Women are like chickens. They run towards where there is food*". Men from the locality especially felt that their wives would be "spoilt" by the more permissive climate in the mining communities. However, the absence of wives contributed to the cycle of marital instability.

Thus while mining brought opportunities for the development of new social identities for women, their gender identities often foregrounded the relationships that they could negotiate in their new

Table 3

Who Do You Consider To Be the Major Beneficiaries of Mining? By Gender and Community

Major beneficiaries	Farming Communities						Mining Communities					
	Male		Female		Total		Male		Female		Total	
	N	%	N	%	N	%	N	%	N	%	N	%
Local community (men)	3	13.6	1	4.8	4	9.3	1	3.8	2	7.4	3	5.7
Local community (women)	1	4.6	1	4.8	2	4.7	0	0	0	0	0	0
Chiefs and land owners	2	9.1	2	9.6	4	9.3	2	7.7	1	3.7	3	5.7
Male migrants	4	18.2	3	14.1	7	16.3	6	23.1	7	26.0	13	24.5
Female migrants	1	4.5	1	4.8	2	4.7	4	15.4	0	0	4	7.5
Sponsor (men)/ Buyers	11	50	13	62.0	24	55.8	13	50.0	12	44.4	25	47.2
Ghetto/pit owners	0	0	0	0	0	0	0	0	5	18.5	5	5.2
Total	22	100	21	100	43	100.	26	100	27	100	53	100

Source: fieldwork 2004.

roles, for example as sponsors. This appeared to be an important factor in women's sponsorship being seen as informal. In sum, struggles over resources and the emerging labour relations resulted in new social identities in mining areas which revealed an intersection of several social relations such as gender, migrant status, ethnicity and access to capital, with implications for the nature of local participation in mining. The new social identities did not necessarily translate into changes in women's gender identities.

Gender and changing land relations in the Datoko-Sheaga area

The importance of land as a resource for rural livelihoods and also as a source of social and political power and authority for those who control land and its resources makes it key to women's rights in the Talensi-Nabdam District as for most parts of rural Ghana. In the Talensi-Nabdam area, the land tenure system was characterised by communal ownership, with the allodial title vested in the Tendana or earth priest who gave out land to individual lineages and the lineage heads. As a result, men came to control access to the land (Kasanga 2002). This and other factors such as tenure arrangements, inheritance systems, marital status, the sexual division of labour and land use patterns operated to restrict the extent of control women could exercise over land. Whether for farming, mining or other livelihood activities, women had use rights but did not own land or control its use. Table 4 shows that in the farming community, while the major source of land for men was the family or lineage (96.9 per cent), for women access to land was either through their husbands (53.8 per cent) or their own lineage (38.6 per cent). In the mining communities, both men and women were using land belonging to other relations and friends (57.1 per cent of men and 69.2 per cent of women). Also, 23.8 per cent of men were able to use lineage land, something only 7.7 per cent of women were doing.

Division of labour in farm tasks as well as type of crops grown was gendered. Whereas women's labour was crucial for the production of millet, which was the staple crop on the household farm, traditionally they could not plant it on their own farms. Although women's labour was critical for household farm production, they were traditionally not obliged to weed although they could weed

Table 4
Who Owns the Land on Which You Are Farming/Mining? by gender and community

Major beneficiaries	Farming Community						Mining Community					
	Male		Female		Total		Male		Female		Total	
	N	%	N	%	N	%	N	%	N	%	N	%
Family/Lineage	31	96.9	10	38.6	41	70.8	5	23.8	1	7.7	6	17.6
Husband/Spouse	0	0	14	53.8	14	24.1	0	0	1	7.7	1	2.9
Myself	1	3.1	1	3.8	2	3.4	1	4.8	0	0	1	2.9
Purchased	0	0	0	0	0	0	2	9.5	1	7.7	3	8.8
Other relatives and friends	0	0	1	3.8	1	1.8	12	57.1	9	69.2	21	61.8
Chief	0	0	0	0	0	0	1	4.8	1	7.7	2	5.9
Total	32	100	26	100	58	100	21	100	13	100	34	100

Source: Fieldwork 2004

their own individual farms. Thus despite their heavy involvement in farm activities and their critical labour on household farms, there was a pervasive ideology that women were not farmers (See Benneh et al. 1995; Songsore 2001; Whitehead 1984 for similar findings). However, with migration of women away from their marital homes into mining settlements and further afield, and in the face of marital instability in the mining settlements, these gender divisions appeared to be changing:

> Women can also go to the bush such as in the mining areas and acquire a plot of land on their own from the land owners and plant any food crops they want on it. They can also hire labour to farm for them. In places far away from the home, such as in the bush, women can plant any crop they want including millet. This is especially so for women with no husbands. If you have no husband who will farm for you to eat? Married women can also plant millet on their own plots if they have the money for it (TS, miner and farmer, Datoko).

The relative abundance of land and the fact that the mining areas were in the outskirts of communities meant that there was as yet no sense of pressure on land or competition between farming and mining and no serious land use disputes as has occurred in mining communities in other parts of Ghana. Both men and women, migrant and non-migrant, could go to the *Tendana* or earth priest for land for farming or gold mining as explained below:

> To acquire farming land, the farmer is required to find his own site and the size of land needed. Only then would he inform the tendana or chief by giving him kola and two chickens. At the end of the harvest the farmer would give the tendana or chief any quantity of the harvest. For land for mining pits or *ghettoes*, the procedure is to allow *ghetto* owners to dig the pit and then after mining he gives the Tendana a quantity of rock ore for sacrifice to the gods. It is not mandatory to give the Tendana part of your harvest or rock ore, but the belief is that if you short-changed the Tendana or chief, the gods of the land would deal harshly with you (Chief of Digare and Tendana of Accra Lands)

The integration of mining with farming and other income generating activities was also a factor in the low incidence of land use conflicts. *"Farmers are the same as miners, so we understand one another"* as one informant pointed out. However, some informants noted that there were problems in the district between chiefs and the Tendana over land ownership as well as boundary disputes, especially in the gold mining areas. Examples were given of conflicts in the past between the Tendana in charge of Accra lands which was under the Chief of Digare and the Tarkwa Tendana, which land was under the Chief of Datoko. If the waterlogging problems of the mines should be solved and mining begins again in earnest, land conflicts may increase in the district.

These findings raise sustainability issues with regard to the impact of mining on the local economy. For example, the waterlogged state of several mines in the area points to the unsustainability of unsupervised mining. Another issue of sustainability was that the exploitation of gold involved knowledge and technologies which were not local. Furthermore, capital requirements for entry into small-scale mining were now much steeper as a result of water logging. This had implications for the future participation of locals in mining and the benefits they and the local economy could derive from this activity. Although mining offered women opportunities for improving their livelihoods, the labour segmentation, the less flexible gender division of labour and the persistence of certain gender norms limited the potential benefits of mining for them.

Case 2: Gender, Land Tenure and Livelihoods in the Gamenu Area of the Lower Volta

The changing contexts of livelihoods in the Gamenu Area: Volta River Project impacts

The Akosombo Dam, constructed over the Volta River in 1965, resulted in the cessation of the seasonal flooding of the Lower Volta. This reduction in the volume of water coming into the Lower Volta led to the drying up of the numerous creeks in the area and the proliferation of aquatic vegetation in the river. It has been conclusively established that both river and creek fishing, which used to be major economic activities in the area have been adversely affected (Gordon and Amatekpor 1999; Dankwah and Gordon 2002;

South Tongu District Plan 2002–04; Tsikata 2006). Before the dam, mangrove harvesting was integrally linked with the cycle of livelihood activities, dominated by fishing. With the decline in fishing, mangrove harvesting is now all year round, replacing fishing and trading in fish as the most popular livelihood activity.

The large mangrove forests used to have their water replenished by the seasonal floods. These days, the water underneath the mangroves can become too warm to support fish (SA, Hawui 2005). Informants have also reported the decline of mangrove forests and the near extinction of the white mangrove species as a result of more intensive harvesting and the increased commercialisation of the mangroves. Farming has been the most significant casualty of the floods. An informant explained,

> During the last flood we experienced, the Volta River burst its banks and inundated the whole land. After the water volume came down, the land became salty. We no longer could grow any crops again. Formerly, when there was regular flooding annually, the land was very fertile so we used

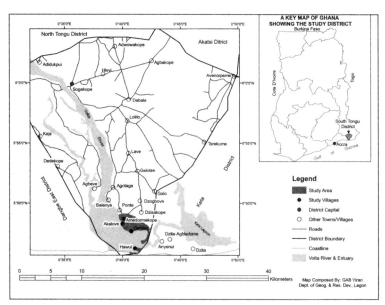

Figure 3 Map of south tongu district showing the study area

to grow crops such as cassava and maize, which thrived well here. These days we do not farm because crops will not survive (SA, Hawui, 2005).

The Tongu District Development Plan confirms this, identifying the scarcity of farmlands as an important problem of the district as a whole (South Tongu District Plan 2002–04). One of the impacts of the decline of livelihood activities in the Lower Volta was out-migration, mostly of men who went upstream to the Volta Lake to continue their fishing activities. In the study, only 26 (42.6 per cent) of men and 30 (50.8 per cent) of women had never lived outside the community, pointing to the widespread migration by both men and women. However, there were visibly more women in some communities than there were men. Of the respondents, 69.5 per cent were natives of the area while the others were from contiguous areas (Survey data 2005). This makes the area linguistically and culturally homogeneous.

From marginal resource to all-pervasive activity: the changing economic significance of mangroves

Mangrove harvesting was an old economic activity of the Gamenu area. However, before the Akosombo Dam, many of those involved in the harvesting were from the neighbouring Keta District, located on a narrow stretch of land between the sea and the Keta Lagoon. This area, home to fishing communities, did not support trees which could provide the fuel wood needs of the fishing industry. While mangroves were used for fuel wood at Gamenu, much more of it was sold in the market at Anyanui on the Volta Estuary, which fed the Keta District. After the Akosombo Dam and the decline of fishing, locals began to harvest mangroves more seriously. The result was that from being a marginal resource, mangroves assumed a new place of importance in the livelihood activities of people.

The mangroves cover between 50–75 per cent of Gamenu. Mangroves were used for firewood for fish processing, baking and the distillation of local gin. The boarding schools in the area were also important consumers of firewood. The current importance of mangroves to livelihood activities was confirmed by the study: 85 per cent of men and women in the mangrove communities of

Norsakope, Agorkpokope and Hawui said they were directly involved with mangrove harvesting (Table 5). This is in sharp contrast with Amedormekope, where mangroves play no part in livelihood activities in spite of its proximity to Gamenu. There, the majority, 67.7 per cent male and 44.8 per cent female, were engaged in farming; 12.9 per cent men were in fishing; 20.7 per cent women in trading, and 34.5 per cent in artisanship—mainly in the weaving of mats.

The situation in Amedormekope was more in keeping with the general situation in the Lower Volta, where farming has continued to be one of the main livelihood activities for both men and women. In the mangrove communities, 46.7 per cent of male respondents were engaged in mangrove harvesting, another 10 per cent were involved in servicing the mangrove industry while 6.7 per cent were fishing in the mangroves. On the part of women, 36.7 per cent were engaged in mangrove harvesting, 26.6 per cent were involved in harvesting crabs in the mangroves while 3.3 per cent described themselves as servicing the mangrove industry. Significantly, 20 per cent of female respondents were trading while 33.3 per cent of male respondents were engaged in river fishing (Table 6).

Apart from mangroves, other common livelihood activities in this area were fishing and the trapping of crabs. The crabs were caught in both the Volta and on land within the mangrove forests.[5] The production of crab traps from woven palm fronds was also popular, as was the weaving of mats from reeds growing in the area. Interestingly, a few people had small farms, but farming was never mentioned unless people were specifically asked. According to Togbe Norsa, there was farming on the land several years ago, but currently, there was no serious farming taking place. This was because the land was no longer fertile for farming.

Pre-dam livelihood activities for men were fishing, trapping river crabs, and mangroves in order of popularity. For women, it was crabs, fishing, mangroves and trading. In the post-dam situation, the order of importance of activities for men was now mangroves, fishing, crabs, making fish and crab traps and making ropes, and for women, it was mangrove crabs, tying and carrying mangroves, weaving ropes and small-scale trading in fried fish and other food items. Thus the livelihood activities in the area remained the same, although there

Table 5
Direct Involvement in Mangroves by Gender and Community

| Response | Norsakope / Agorkpokope / Havui | | | | | | Amedormekope | | | | | |
| | Male | | Female | | Total | | Male | | Female | | Total | |
	Freq.	%	Freq.	%	Freq.	%	Freq.	%	Freq.	%	Freq.	%
Yes	25	83.3	25	83.3	50	83.3	0	.0	3	10.3	3	0
No	5	16.7	5	16.7	10	16.7	30	100.0	26	89.7	56	6.6
Total	30	100	30	100	60	100.0	30	100	29	100	59	0

Source: Field work, 2005

Table 6
Main Source of Income—by Gender and Community

Response	Norsakope / Agorkpokope/Hauui						Amedormekope					
	Male		Female		Total		Male		Female		Total	
	Freq.	%	Freq.	%	Freq.	%	Freq.	%	Freq.	%	Freq.	%
River fishing	10	33.3	0	0	14	23.3	4	12.9	0	.0	4	6.7
Fishing in mangroves	2	6.7	8	26.6	6	10.0	–	–	–	–	–	–
Mangrove harvesting	14	46.7	11	36.7	25	41.7	–	–	–	–	–	–
Farming	0	.0	2	6.7	2	3.3	21	67.7	13	44.8	34	56.7
Trading	0	.0	6	20.0	6	10.0	0	.0	6	20.7	6	10.0
Artisanship	1	3.3	2	6.7	3	5.0	3	9.7	10	34.5	13	21.7
Servicing mangrove industry	3	10.0	1	3.3	4	6.7	3	9.7	0	.0	3	5.0
Total	30	50.0	30	50.0	60	100.0	31	51.7	29	48.3	60	100.0

Source: Field work, 2006

were shifts in their importance. These changes in the order were more a response to the decline in fishing than an expansion in the market for mangroves or a change in its economics.

Changes in Mangrove Tenure

Arising from the increased importance of mangrove harvesting, these changes were transforming the mangroves from a resource which once given out, could be used, exploited commercially, leased, exchanged and inherited to one which could now only be leased for a fixed duration at a fixed price (AA, retired, male informant, Norsakope, 2005). In the past, large tracts of mangroves were sold without measurement. A mangrove stand could be as large as half a mile square and its price was negotiable. The level of commercialisation now was such that mangroves were sold in smaller lots, in a measurement known as a rope.[6] The price of a rope depended on the size and age of the mangroves. The owners of the mangroves attributed their new measurements to the fact that people could not afford the prices of the larger tracts (Togbe Norsa, Norsakope, 2005).

The duration of the mangrove lease depended on the age of the stand. Mangroves were expected to mature in 12 years. Therefore, if a stand was two years old, it was given out for 10 years, if it was 10 years old, the duration of the lease would be two years to ensure that the mangroves would be harvested only when they reached maturity. Once harvested, the mangrove stand reverted to the land-owning lineage unless the lease was renewed or re-negotiated. Buyers who were unable to complete their harvesting within the time allotted risked losing their mangrove stands or being asked to pay some more money (K.A., Agama family elder, Norsakope, 2005; N.N., Hawui, 2005).

Several respondents considered it unjust that mangroves not harvested in time could be taken away from lessees. The land owners for their part felt that this was necessary for their control of the resource and to ensure its efficient and profitable use (K.A., Agama family elder, Norsakope, 2005). A device used by land owners to address the financial strains in the community was credit. It was possible to harvest and sell the mangroves before paying the land owners and there was no premium on the credit. This was a critical factor in people's ability to participate in mangrove harvesting.

Increasingly, it was becoming difficult to distinguish land tenure from mangrove tenure as much of the area, apart from the land on which the settlements have been constructed, had mangroves. However, mangrove land was distinguished from other land and even the use of mangrove land for other economic activities was distinguished from harvesting mangroves. Land for housing could be procured without much cost, although informants indicated that this was under review (AA, retired, male informant, Norsakope, 2005; KA, Agama family elder, Norsakope, 2005).[7]

Trapping crabs and fishing inside the mangroves was done at no cost and without having to go through any formalities. There had been attempts by the holders of mangrove leases to impose restrictions some time ago. However, the land owners insisted on maintaining the freedom to harvest crabs in another person's mangrove stands, arguing that the harvesting of crabs did not cause any harm to the mangroves (Togbe Norsa, Norsakope, 2005). The changes in mangrove tenure were a source of tension between the land owners and mangrove buyers and also between buyers (KA, Agama family elder, Norsakope, 2005; ANK, Hawui, 2005).

Mangroves are renewable and the technology for regeneration was well understood in the Gamenu area. However, the expansion in mangrove harvesting, the changing terms of mangrove tenure and the activities of the landlords were threatening the sustainable harvesting of the mangroves. Respondents argued that the terms of leases, threats of seizures of mangroves before harvesting was completed, the shorter harvesting time allocated to the activity and the boundary disputes were undermining the desire for conservation and sustainable management. Fewer people were now interested in replanting mangrove stands. Not surprisingly, the rate of mangrove depletion was high. According to Tutu (1998), the mangroves had depleted by 36 per cent within a period of 17 years (1973/74–1990/91). If this trend continued, it was likely to result in shortages in the future, given that mangrove harvesting was currently the most common livelihood activity in the area. Efforts to establish mangrove conservation projects through the provision of alternative economic activities were at the pilot stage (KA, Agama family elder, Norsakope, 2005).[8] Even more fundamentally, the changes in mangrove tenure which were implicated in the current state of the mangroves were not being considered by the project.

The gender implications of changing contexts and mangrove tenure and livelihoods in the Gamenu area

Mangrove ownership and tenure:

The majority of respondents involved in the exploitation of mangroves were not members of the lineage which owned the resources (Table 7). On the face of it, commercialisation of the mangroves would suggest that anyone with money could lease and harvest a stand of mangroves without discrimination. This supposition was explored in the survey through several questions about actual involvement in mangroves and the ease of acquisition of mangroves.

The majority of male and female respondents had purchased mangroves or were working as harvesters of mangroves. The responses to survey questions did not successfully differentiate between purchasers and their employees in spite of efforts to do so. This was partly on account of the fact that certain respondents were both purchasers and labourers in the industry. The majority of both male and female respondents said they had no difficulties with access to mangroves. However, 30.8 per cent of male respondents and 40 per cent of female respondents said they had problems. Their problems included the unavailability of mangrove plots, having to beg for a long time before being allocated the plots, the exorbitant

Table 7
Ownership of Mangroves Being Exploited by Gender

Who owns the mangrove you are exploiting	Sex					
	Male		Female		Total	
	Freq	*%*	*Freq*	*%*	*Freq*	*%*
My family/Lineage	4	17.4	4	15.4	8	16.3
Another family/Lineage	18	78.3	22	84.6	40	81.6
Spouse	1	4.3	0	.0	1	2.0
Total	23	46.9	26	53.1	49	100.0

Source: Field work, 2005.

demands of mangrove owners and not having enough money to buy mangroves.

The majority of respondents (96.3 per cent of male and 83.3 per cent of female) from the mangrove communities also were of the view that it was easy for women to acquire mangroves (Table 8). The minority who said that women had problems said that it was customary for men to be the ones who acquired the mangroves from the landowning groups. Others said it involved time consuming consultations and begging. The money issue was raised as a problem for many women (Survey interviews, 2005).

Informant interviews similarly disagreed about whether or not women could easily buy mangroves or even replant them. At least one female respondent reported that she had replanted mangroves (ANK, Hawui, 2005) while another had found it easy to buy mangroves. *"As a woman, it is easy for me to buy mangroves, unless I don't have money"* (NN, female informant, Hawui, 2005). This was contradicted by a male informant who argued that women could not plant mangroves because this was male activity (Interview with RY, male in his forties, 2005).

Beyond perceptions, there were questions about actual practice, designed to examine the responses to questions of perception. It became clear that there was not much difference in the modes of acquisition of mangroves. The majority had purchased them (100 per cent male and 86.4 per cent female respondents). In terms of the size of mangrove stands, a significant percentage of respondents (31 per cent male and 52.6 per cent female) had half an acre or less of mangrove resources they were using. Overall, the total area women were exploiting was significantly less than what men had, although women were represented among those with three acres and more of mangroves (Table 9). This qualifies the finding that both men and women were equally involved in exploitation of mangroves. Certainly, many women were involved in mangrove harvesting. While it may be that male out-migration had given them freer access to the mangroves, the terms of the access and the division of labour within the mangrove industry have reduced what they can realise from the mangrove resources. According to informants, women's mangrove stands tend to be smaller than those owned by men. *"While both*

Table 8
Is it easy for women to acquire mangrove resources? By gender and community

| Response | Norsakope / Agorkpokope / Havui | | | | | | Amedormekope | | | | | |
| | Male | | Female | | Total | | Male | | Female | | Total | |
	Freq.	%	Freq.	%	Freq.	%	Freq.	%	Freq.	%	Freq.	%
Yes	26	96.3	25	83.3	51	89.5	6	66.7	5	50.0	11	57.9
No	1	3.7	5	16.7	6	10.5	3	33.3	5	50.0	8	42.1
Total	27	100	30	100	57	100.0	9	100	10	100	19	100.0

Source: Field work, 2005.

Table 9
Size of Mangrove Resource—by Gender

What is the total size of mangrove resource you are using	Sex				Total	
	Male		Female			
	Freq	%	Freq	%	Freq	%
Half an acre or less	5	31.3	10	52.6	15	42.9
One acre	1	6.3	2	10.5	3	8.6
One and half acre	5	31.3	4	21.1	9	25.7
Two acres	3	18.8	1	5.3	4	11.4
Three acres and more	2	12.5	2	10.5	4	11.4
Total	16	100	19	100	35	100.0

Source: Field work, 2005.

men and women buy plots, men buy larger plots than women. They are also more heavily involved in harvesting mangroves" (Togbe Norsa, Norsakope, 2005).

Labour Relations within the Mangrove industry

The mangrove industry had a hierarchy of labour relations. It involved those who had leased the stands and the people they hired to execute the different activities involved in the harvesting. As a respondent explained, some locals and outsiders bought mangrove stands and gave these to people to harvest and market for them. The proceeds from the sale would be divided into two after the expenses were deducted—one part to the owner and the other part to the harvester. This was called *deme*, which means "farm and share", an indication that the practice had been adapted from farming. When stand owners were women, their labour costs were higher because they tended to hire people to do the cutting which was seen as men's work. Male owners were not under the same pressure and even when they hired labour, their own involvement in the process speeded things up and reduced their labour costs.[9] Thus women buyers made less from profit on their mangroves because of their higher labour costs.

More commonly, those who could not lease mangrove stands worked as labourers for those who could. The mangroves had to be cut and piled into mounds and left to dry. Pieces were then arranged according to size and tied in bundles. The bundles were then carried to the river. There, canoe owners ferried them to the Anyanui market to be sold. Mangrove labour was segmented by gender and age. Those who cut the mangroves were mostly men, with only about 20 per cent of them women. They worked between 8.00 am and 2.00 pm for a daily wage of 15,000 cedis. Women of all ages were predominantly involved in tying together the cut mangroves and conveying the bundles to the river front. Few men were involved in mangrove tying and conveyance. Those tying mangroves earned 25,000 cedis for 100 bundles. For those women who carried the wood to the riverside, the amount they were paid depended on the distance between the mangrove lot and the river. On an average, they charged about 20,000 cedis for carrying 100 bundles of firewood.

The canoe people who ferried the wood across the river charged about 30–40,000 cedis for every 100 bundles of wood. Some boats were powered with outboard motors and were large enough to carry 400 bundles in one trip. The smaller canoes had to make several trips before they were able to ferry 100 bundles across. Many of the canoe owners were from the mangrove communities. Those who did not own canoes sometimes hired them from the owners and after a day's work, they would pay for the use of the canoe. Depending on the size, they sometimes paid 10,000 cedis a day for a canoe.

It was clear that cutters had better conditions of service and pay in that they had a fixed daily wage and time of work, while the women who tied the mangroves were engaged in piece work (KA, Agama family elder, Norsakope, 2005). The cutters were more organised and at the time of the fieldwork, had recently increased their daily rates. The women were not similarly organised and had not been able to change their fees. Thus while women were paid less and were doing piece work, they also had more flexibility in relation to their time. However, the fact that the cutters were organised was helpful in terms of their negotiating power. Why the women did not have a similar organisation might also be because they tended to work alone, in pairs or in small groups, often composed of family members.

Both men and women were assisted by their children. Children were also heavily involved in working for others or for themselves in activities such as trapping crabs, fishing, cutting mangroves and carrying mangroves to the river front. Here again, there was gender division. The girls were involved in catching the crabs and carrying of mangroves while the boys were engaged in fishing, crabs, and cutting mangroves. The girls mostly caught their crabs on land in the mangroves while the boys caught their crabs from the river. The girls also had additional responsibilities of domestic work. The long hours the young people spent away from school, working, were certain to undermine their education and could result in their being trapped in marginal livelihoods.

Some implications of the case studies

The case studies have produced significant insights which confirm or extend many aspects of the gender and land literature.

The characteristics of a particular resource are determinants of its impacts on livelihoods

This concerns the nature of the natural resource in question, crucial to determining the impact of its exploitation on gender relations. It is what accounts for some of the differences between the mangrove and gold mining cases, as well as the differences between these and the agricultural land. Three areas of specificity were explored in the chapter. The first concerned tenure arrangements which were based on differences in the nature of the two resources and their implications for the participation of men and women in their exploitation. These two areas were both resource poor and environmentally fragile. In the case of north-eastern Ghana, this was a result of its history and continuing economic marginalisation and environmental deterioration, while for south-eastern Ghana, the construction of the Akosombo Dam was the single most significant trigger of its environmental and socio-economic decline. Thus for both areas, gold and mangroves grew in importance as the environments declined and increasingly could not support livelihood activities based on land and pre-existing natural resources. However, the differences in the nature of the two resources have been critical in shaping their impacts on livelihoods. The nature of the mangrove as a plant species which could be cultivated and the fact that its use and harvesting involved local knowledge made it easier for many more people to participate in its exploitation although women did it on terms different from men. Payments for mangrove stands could be made after the harvest and sale of the mangroves and this allowed more people to participate in the industry. The capital requirements were not so high so as to discourage the entry of women although there was evidence that they did not have access in the way men did. The result was that the involvement in mangroves was widespread within Gamenu. Mangrove supported other activities because of its use as fuel wood.

Gold, on the other hand, involved upfront capital expenditures before harvesting the ore or reaping the benefits. Locals needed sponsors—who were often from outside their communities—to enter to into gold mining, unless they sold their labour to others who had sponsorship. Gold was exploited with knowledge and technologies which were not local. Indeed, it was often remarked that technologies had been brought by people who had a long tradition of working in small-scale mining. Also, gold mining was quite distinct from agriculture and therefore there was not much knowledge transfer taking place. The capital requirements for entry were much steeper than those for mangroves and this excluded many people, especially women.

A second area of specificity concerned the linkages between global and local processes. These linkages were clearer in the mining industry than in mangrove exploitation, where the impact of long-term environmental change caused by land use changes and the damming of the Volta River at Akosombo and Kpong had resulted in the decline of traditional livelihood activities such as fishing and farming. An important difference between the two areas was the levels of capital injected into the local economy from outside. The gold mining area saw a large influx of Ghanaians and other West Africans, some of whom brought capital and gold mining technologies. However, this did not result in more economic benefits for local communities. The mangrove communities on the other hand did not see a similar scale of introduction of capital from outside. Mangrove technologies remained very basic and many of the people involved in the industry were locals or from neighbouring districts. In the case of gold mining, new communities, devoted mainly to this activity, were established, but were yet to be reflected on official maps. Mangrove harvesting relied on pre-existing settlements and socio-economic arrangements.

A related issue is the policy and conceptual importance of distinguishing between land tenure and the regimes of tenure relating to the resources found on the land. Legal scholars such as Okoth-Ogendo have long argued for distinguishing land from the rights in the fruits of the land such as tree crops, minerals and water bodies (Okoth-Ogendo, 1989). The case studies take this further by showing how the specificities of gold and mangroves as resources complicate the impacts of their intensified exploitation and commercialisation on women's land access. However, the distinction between resource and land tenures was not always clear cut. In the Lower Volta mangrove area, it was difficult to completely distinguish land tenure from mangrove tenure because the land was used for little else apart from mangroves. Also, the mangroves grew naturally although they could also be cultivated like an agricultural crop. However, land and mangrove tenures were connected because women's disadvantages in accessing and controlling land translated into their lack of control over mangrove resources. In the case of north-eastern Ghana, the distinctions were clearer. This had to do with the continuing importance of agriculture in the small-scale gold mining areas where access to land for agriculture was on very different terms from access to gold mining land.

Confirming the salience and persistence of social relations in resource control

The cases confirm the literature's conclusions as to the significance of social relations in the control of land and natural resources (Bortei-Doku Aryeetey 2002; Kotey and Tsikata 1998; Duncan 1997). Women's secondary land rights and interests in the Talensi-Nabdam District and their weak control over mangroves as a result of changing mangrove tenure in the South Tongu District have had direct implications for their access to mining rents and revenues and to control over the income generated from the commercialisation of mangroves. Thus the gender inequalities in access to and control over land and its resources, which are identified in the two case studies, can be deepened rather than reduced by reforms unless the reforms explicitly target this problem. The two case studies suggest the need for land tenure reforms to address the range of derived and informal interests in the light of the socio-economic and political changes in Ghana, as well as the growing commercialisation and commoditisation of land and resources over the years. Both resources had changed the structure of livelihood activities in the communities which had embraced their use. However, access to the mangroves and mines and their use was gendered, with unequal benefits accruing to women and men from their participation in these intensified livelihoods activities.

In addition to gender, there were other social relations which structured livelihoods and therefore the nature of participation in gold mining and mangrove exploitation. In the north-eastern Ghana study, there were differences between strangers and locals and those with and without capital in their ability to enjoy the fruits of mining. In the Lower Volta, the differences were also between the leaders of the land owning group and the rest. These differences intersected in various ways. In north-eastern Ghana, being identified as a local allowed men to combine mining with farming, something which was denied to the majority of miners from other communities, and to also women. The study on mining illustrates the modification and creation of social identities in the struggle over resources. The identities of *sponsor, ghetto owner, kaiman, shanking lady*, etc., were gendered and also linked with whether a person was a local or a migrant. While for men these identities were more permeable and easier to manipulate, for women, they were more fixed. Thus it was hard to come across a female pit owner. The women were largely trading in supplies and food, *shanking* (processing), or performing care activities such as washing clothes, cooking and sexual services. While some women could be described as sponsors in that they procured inputs for men on credit, they were not officially recognised as such. Thus in most spheres they tended to lose out to men.

The importance of labour in the structuring of land interests

Another finding was the importance of labour relations for land and resource tenures. In the literature, land and labour are often treated as separate resources that women often lack, which has a bearing on their livelihoods. The cases show the inextricable links between land and labour in the exploitation of land and natural resources by highlighting the different labour hierarchies in the exploitation of mangroves and gold mining. In the Talensi-Nabdam District, women participated in gold mining at the margins, mainly in support roles with payment terms unstructured and informalised, while being subject to social disapproval for their survival strategies in mining settlements. In the South Tongu District, the returns on female activities in mangrove harvesting tended to be lower than on male-dominated activities. Thus labour was segmented in both gold mining and mangrove harvesting, but was more flexible and therefore easier to breach in the latter. In both mining and mangrove communities, there were developing hierarchies of participation in mining and mangrove exploitation based on a combination of ethnicity, gender and access to capital. In the mining areas, labour relations were constructed along the lines of class, migrant status, and gender.

CONCLUSION

The study examined how the intensification of the use of the hitherto marginal resources—gold and mangroves—in two resource poor and ecologically fragile rural areas has affected livelihoods, land and resource tenures, and social relations. The chapter is based on the premise that globalisation, both as the context and as an economic process, has played a significant role in the restructuring of livelihoods and the emergence of new social identities linked to new livelihood activities. Social relations of gender, kinship, ethnicity, migrant status and access to capital were all implicated in the restructuring of livelihoods and changes in land and resource tenure relations as resources gained new or expanded economic significance. In north-eastern Ghana, gold mining resulted in the modification and creation of social identities in the struggle over resources, while in the mangrove area, the increasing commercialisation of mangroves resulted in more structured and formal mangrove tenure regimes plagued with contestations and conflicts. Access to mangroves and gold and the benefits from their exploitation were clearly gendered with labour relations constructed around a combination of social categories. These changes have had a differential impact on the livelihoods and welfare of men and women in the communities. While they offered opportunities for women, these did not translate into changed gender identities for them, which continued to be governed by social norms.

These findings have particular importance and relevance within the context of liberalisation and policies promoting the extensive development of land and resource markets. In north-eastern Ghana, the legalisation of small scale gold mining within a liberalised mining regime, and in the Lower Volta Basin, the impacts of economic liberalisation on an area already in decline, as dimensions of globalisation processes, brought about changes and transformations in gold mining and mangrove tenure. These transformations of customary norms of land and resource tenures fuelled tenure insecurities whose impacts were particularly severe for holders of derived interests—women, tenants, migrants and share croppers. For women in particular, their poorer access to resources exacerbated these insecurities and inequalities of customary tenancies.

The findings of the study have implications for Ghana's land tenure reform programme, the Land Administration Project (LAP), which is in the last year of a five-year pilot phase. The key thrusts of the reforms are the promotion of tenure security and orderly land markets through title registration, the adjudication of boundary disputes, the consolidation and harmonisation of land laws and the institutional reform of land tenure agencies. Questions have been raised about the capacity of the ongoing land reforms to address issues of gender equity in customary land and resource tenures. The current land tenure reforms need to recognise and address the gender inequalities in land and resource tenure systems in general, and in particular, address issues identified by the two case studies. Without explicit attention to these issues, gender and other inequalities in land and resource tenures are likely to be deepened rather than reduced in the long-term.

NOTES

1. The World Bank also asserts that there is a reduction in inequalities between countries
2. The Talensi-Nabdam District was a part of the Bolgatanga District at the beginning of the research study. Mid-way through the research in 2004, it was carved out as a district with its capital in Tongo. The rest of the Bolgatanga District became the Bolgatanga Municipality. As a result policy makers and stakeholders in land administration were interviewed in the then district capital of Bolgatanga rather than in Tongo.
3. Historically British colonial policy promoted the North largely as a labour reserve for the South. Consequently little investment in infrastructure or services was made in the north, while conscious efforts were made to develop the forest and coastal belts of the south for the production of minerals, cash crops and timber products for export facilitated by the creation of ports and harbours on the coast (Bening, 1975). The result has been high rates of migration from the North to the large towns and the cocoa growing areas of the South.
4. *Shanking ladies* is the term used to refer to the women who sift the pounded rock with a scarf to separate powder from the chippings.
5. The mangrove crabs are called ledzi and the river crabs are called torme gala.
6. A rope is 20 sq yards, but the owners of the mangroves are planning to reduce it to between 15 and 16 sq yards.
7. Land for building would now be given out on certain terms in order to preserve land for the use of people who wanted to set up infant industries.
8. Project activities included irrigation and fish farming
9. In many cases, all persons were paid only after the mangroves had been sold.

REFERENCES

Akabzaa, T., 2000, *Boom and Dislocation: Environmental Impacts of Mining in Wassa West District of Ghana*, Accra: Third World Network.

Awumbila, M., 1997, "Women, Environmental Change and Economic Crisis in Ghana", in E.A.Gyasi and J.I. Uitto (eds), *Environment, Biodiversity and Agricultural Change in West Africa: Perspectives from Ghana*, United Nations University Press, Tokyo, New York and Paris.

Awumbila, M. and Momsen, J.H., 1995, "Gender and the Environment: Women's Time Use as a Measure of Environmental Change", *Global Environmental Change* 5(5): 337–346.

Benneh, G., R.K. Kasanga, and D. Amoyaw, 1995, "Women's Access to Agricultural Land in the Household: A Case Study of three selected Districts in Ghana", Accra: FADEP.

Bortei-Doku Aryeetey, H., 2002, "Behind the Norms: Women's Access to Land in Ghana" in Toulmin, C. et al. (eds), *The Dynamics of Resource Tenure in West Africa*, London: IIED, pp. 86–97.

Butegwa, F., 1994, "Using the African Charter on Human and Peoples" Rights to Secure Women's Access to Land in Africa", in R. J. Cook (ed), *Human rights of women: national and international perspectives*, University of Pennsylvania Press.

Dankwah, H. and C. Gordon, 2002, "The Fish and Fisheries of the Lower Volta Mangrove Swamps in Ghana", *African Journal of Science and Technology (AJST)*, *Science and Engineering Series* 3(1): 25–32.

Duncan, B. (1997) *Women in Agriculture in Ghana*, Accra: Friedrich Ebert Stiftung.

Ghana Statistical Service, 2007, *Pattern and Trends of Poverty in Ghana, 1991–2006*. Ghana Statistical Service, April 2007.

Gordon, C. and J.K. Amatekpor, 1999, "Introduction", in Gordon, C. and J.K. Amatekpor, (eds), *The Sustainable Integrated Development of the Volta Basin in Ghana*. Volta Basin Research Project. Legon, University of Ghana.

Himonga, C.N. and M.L. Munachonga,. 1991, "Rural Women's Access to Agricultural Land in Settlement Schemes in Zambia: Law, Practice and Socio-Economic Constraints", *Third World Legal Studies* – Special Edition: 59–74.

Khor, M., 2000, *Globalization and the South: Some Critical Issues*, Penang: Third World Network.

Kotey, A.N. and D. Tsikata, 1998, "Gender Relations and Land in Ghana", in Kuenyehia, A. (ed), *Women and Law in West Africa: Situational Analysis of Some Key Issues Affecting Women*, Accra: WALWA.

Manji, A., 1998, "Gender and the Politics of the Land Reform Processes in Tanzania", *The Journal of Modern African Studies* 36(4): 645–667.

Mkandawire, T. and C. Soludo, 1999, *Our Continent, Our Future. Africa Perspective on Structural Adjustment*, Dakar, Council for the Development of Social Science Research in Africa.

Nabila, J., 1975, "Depopulation in Northern Ghana: Migration of the Frafra People", in A.S. David, E. Laing and N.O. Addo (eds), *Interdisciplinary Approaches to Population Studies*. Legon, University of Ghana, pp 70–83.

Okoth-Ogendo, H.W.O., 1989, "Some Issues of Theory in the Study of Land Tenure Relations in African Agriculture", *Africa* 59(1): 6–17.

Olukoshi, A.O., 1998, "The Elusive Prince of Denmark: Structural Adjustment and the Crisis of Governance in Africa", Uppsala: Nordiska Afrikainstitutet.

Rattray, R.S., 1932, *The Tribes of the Ashanti Hinterland*, Volume 1, Oxford: Clarendon Press.

Shivji, I., 1998, *Not Yet Democracy: Reforming Land Tenure in Tanzania*. London: IIED, HAKIARDHI, and the Faculty of Law, University of Dar es Salaam.

South Tongu District Assembly (2003). District Development Plan, South Tongu.

Tsikata, D., 2004, "The Volta River Project and Tongu Ewe Communities along the Volta Lake: A Case of Development's Unintended Consequences?" *Research Review*, NS 20.2 (2004) 33–51.

————, 2006, "Living in the Shadow of the Large Dams: Long Term Responses of Downstream and Lakeside Communities of Ghana's Volta River Project", Leiden: Brill.

Tsikata, I., K. Senah, and M. Awumbila, 1997, "Mangrove Resource Utilisation and Community Based Management in the Lower Volta: A Socio-Anthropological Study", *Lower Volta Mangrove Project Technical Report No.4.* 83p. Series Editor: Gordon, C., DFID/Ghana Wildlife Department/Ghana Environmental Protection Agency.

Tutu, K., 1998, "The Effects of the Volta Dam on Socio-Cultural Changes for People Living in the Mangrove Economy of the Lower Volta Basin", in Lauer, En (ed), *Changing Values, Changing Technologies*, Ghana Philosophical Studies II.

Wanyeki, L.M., 2003, "Introduction", in Wanyeki, L.M. (ed), *Gender and Land in Africa: Culture, Religion and Realizing Women" Rights,* London: Zed.

Whitehead, A. & Kabeer, N., 2001, "Living with uncertainty: Gender, livelihoods and pro-poor growth in rural Sub-Saharan Africa", *IDS Working Paper 134.*

Whitehead, A. and Tsikata, D., 2003, 'Policy Discourses on Women's Land Rights in Sub-Saharan Africa:', *Journal of Agrarian Change* 3(1 and 2; January and April).

Wily, L.A. and D. Hammond, 2001, "Land Security and the Poor in Ghana: Is there a Way Forward?" A Land Sector Scoping Study. Ghana's Rural Livelihood Programme. DFID.

UNDP, 1999, Human Development Report, New York: Oxford University Press.

World Bank, 2002, "Globalisation, Growth and Poverty, Building an Inclusive Economy", Policy Research Report, New York and Washington D.C.: Oxford University Press and the World Bank.

5 The Politics of Gender, Land and Compensation in Communities Traversed by the Chad-Cameroon Oil Pipeline Project in Cameroon

JOYCE B.M. ENDELEY

I fear that oil companies look to Africa for their resource and wealth without seeing the people. Resources-rich communities are dehumanized and the colour-line is ever present as the greatest profits flow steadily to wealthy white men who already control enormous wealth and power. [...] the next time you pull up to the pump, stop a moment and remember that the thick black crude is extracted from the earth's crust at great social, political and environmental cost. Then do whatever it is in your power to demand dignity and proper compensation for those whose land or sea may be cursed with the blessing of these natural resource. (Wood, 2006:1).

INTRODUCTION

This chapter examines how gender is implicated in the negotiation of land relations in the construction of the Chad-Cameroon Oil Pipeline project. The study critically examines the implications of gendered land relations with regard to compensation payments for destroyed land properties in selected communities that are traversed by the project in the Centre and South Regions of Cameroon. The Chad-Cameroon Oil Pipeline project is a US$4.2 billion project for the drilling of oil fields and the construction of 1,070 kilometres of pipeline to transport crude oil from fields in south-western Chad to a floating facility off Kribi on the Atlantic coast of Cameroon (News Release No. 2007/19/EXC).

Through a descriptive qualitative survey of selected communities, this chapter intends to examine how the dynamics of the gender and land tenure system unfolded during the process of allocating compensation to those affected by the project. It analyses the attributes given to men and women in relation to their access, use and control of land and related resources. To contextualise the study, gender relations to land are examined within the two main hegemonic land tenure systems in Cameroon: the traditional and the statutory. This analysis does not, however, ignore the fact that a multiplicity of tenure systems operate in Cameroon as a result of the huge diversity in ethnicity: over 240 groups and colonial legacies— German, French and English.

In essence, the study attempts to respond to the following pertinent questions: How has the common-sense understanding of men and women's land ownership and use impacted the compensation they received when farming land was affected by the laying of the pipeline? As a development project that is expected to positively impact poverty alleviation at local and national levels, what measures and precautions were taken by the management of the project to avoid the marginalisation of women, often associated with such projects? What new issues have emerged in the analysis of women's rights to land? It is imperative that we study the changes in land tenure from a gender perspective, paying attention to other social axes of differentiation. In Cameroon, women's land rights are often precarious, yet land is their primary resource to rural livelihoods, a cornerstone for their citizenship within a particular community, and the foundation for rural development. Land is a strategic resource for agriculture and the lifeline of most women in Cameroon (Endeley 1998). Since Cameroonian women constitute the majority of the poor and farm population, it is important to investigate how they were affected by this important globalising project.

Furthermore, the development dimension of the Chad-Cameroon Pipeline project merits that the compensation plan of the project be weighted against development realities of the affected communities/ population. How compensation relates to development realities not only highlights the project's contribution to the living conditions of affected people, but also enables an examination of the potential of oil extraction projects to eradicate poverty in rural areas and what it takes to do so. That the project, through land taxes, will provide Cameroon with additional capital to address its poverty situation and stimulate economic growth are the principal reasons for Cameroon's engagement in what has been the largest World Bank project ever.[1]

The discussions on compensation explore government or state responsibility and corporate social responsibility of companies in petroleum extraction projects. The profitability of the petroleum extraction business in comparison with the adverse impacts on communities has been the subject of several studies (Wood 2006; Fall 2001; FoEI/CED 2002; Ukeje 2005; Watts 1997, 2001; Pegg 2005). In the particular case of petroleum extraction, the male dominated character of the industry marginalises women, rendering them less visible as beneficiaries of opportunities from petroleum extraction projects (such as employment, consumption of technologies and human resource development) and more affected than men by the environmental damage resulting from such projects (e.g., water pollution, oil spillage, destroyed land, etc.) (*ibid.*)

Conceptualising the Chad-Cameroon oil pipeline project: land, gender and globalisation

Gender, land and the pipeline project

The key concepts that guided this study are gender, land and globalisation. It was clear that we needed to understand how gender relations are negotiated in the communities we studied. How have women and men made sense of their social relations and negotiated their positioning to land and to the project, especially as concerns compensation for destroyed landed property and resources, whether individually or communally owned? Throughout the study, we sought to analyse gender in relation to other variables such as education, social and political status and space (rural versus urban) in examining changes due to the Chad-Cameroon Oil Pipeline Construction project. It was especially important to use a gender perspective to analyse who was negotiating for whom in the project, and whose construction of land relations informed who received compensation for land. In essence, we observed that each of the project stakeholders (women and men in the different communities), the project management and the government of Cameroon, had a particular understanding of women and men's land relations which impacted on compensation decisions. These different actors influenced the production of gender relations of land tenure.

The researchers' approaches to research have also influenced how gendered systems of land tenure are discussed in the chapter. Who called the shots in land matters and compensation to land? Was it the communities? If so, were their considerations based on socio-cultural norms and structures? Was it the government? If so, which variable was instrumental in defining gendered land relations—customary or statutory law? If it was the project management, how did they conceive land relations? How did local and global discourses influence the notion of gendered land relations in the project? In the analysis, we observed the dynamics of power relations in the conceptualisation of gendered land relations and consequently on compensation for land. The history of gender inequality and infringements of women's rights to land necessitates that we pay attention to how gender discourses play out in the strategic concerns and interests of women and other vulnerable groups in the affected communities. We focussed on how those holding dominant power positions engaged in the debates about land and compensation in the context of the project.

The Chad-Cameroon Oil Pipeline project as economic globalisation

The Chad-Cameroon Oil Pipeline project is considered as an example of the activities of trans-national corporations in the service of economic globalisation. The size and costs of the project, its ownership by trans-national corporations, its financing mechanisms which involved international financial institutions and instruments, its complex range of technologies and expert skills and the large population of national and foreign participants involved in the project are all characteristics of projects which are an integral part of economic globalisation. These agents and processes of globalisation were brought to the doorsteps of rural Cameroon communities through which the pipeline passes. The oil pipeline construction project provided opportunities to experience the processes whereby economic, financial, technical and cultural transactions between different countries and communities throughout the world have become increasingly interconnected. The petroleum pipeline, (which is made up of 1070 kilometres of pipes, 30 inches in diameter, coated with an anti-corrosive layer, and buried about a metre deep, through farmlands, pristine forests and grasslands) transports crude petroleum from local South to global North.

A consortium of trans-national corporations owns the project and also has controlling shares in the project's two management companies: the Cameroon Oil Transport Company (COTCO) and the Chad Oil Transport Company (TOTCO). Exxon-Mobil Petronas of Malaysia and Chevron own 40 per cent, 35 per cent and 25 per cent of the project respectively. Chad holds minority interests in the two pipeline companies while Cameroon holds a minority interest in COTCO. On the basis that the project had the potential for improving Chad's development prospects and generating the much-needed revenues for Cameroon, the World Bank and the International Finance Corporation (IFC) provided loans to Cameroon and Chad to cover their shares in the two companies. COTCO and TOTCO oversaw the construction of the pipeline, and are responsible for assessing and paying compensation to people and communities whose crops or property were damaged by the pipeline. It is reported that the trans-national consortium will earn US$6.8 billion; the Government of Chad 1.7 billion, while about 0.5 billion will go to the Government of Cameroon (FoEI/CED 2002: 13).

The Chad-Cameroon compensation plan

The compensation plan is an important part of the project in Cameroon, because 80 per cent of the pipeline traverses that country, and therefore communities are more likely to experience its negative environmental impacts. Already, Cameroon has begun to experience oil spillages along the pipeline (News Release No. 2007/19/EXC). Private holdings/investments have been destroyed, necessitating compensation to affected individuals, families/ households and communities. This was anticipated and catered for in the Environmental Management Plan (EMP). The initiative was to mitigate possible agitation for destroyed farmlands and other investments owned

by either individuals, groups or persons and communities. The
Compensation Plan (for Cameroon) calls for a fair and adequate
compensation to adversely affected individuals and communities
(COTCO 1999). "The local population sees compensation as fair
and equitable based on local cultural values, people receiving what
is perceived as fair compensation as transparent and practicable;
the compensation processes treats people the same way wherever
practicable" (ibid. 1–4). The Compensation Plan expressed aims of
"fairness" and transparency. This was to be achieved by facilitating
effective participation and establishment of mutual relationships
between the affected populations, communities, the agencies of
COTCO (including local COTCO contact staff and contractors),
and government representatives to the project, especially those at
the community level. There was an understanding that project
management companies would make available adequate and relevant
information to local inhabitants to enable them to participate effectively in processes of compensation. Their voices were expected to
inform the determination of how the project affected their land and
community resources.

Of interest to this study is how land and gender were perceived
and used to establish, determine and distribute compensation to the
affected population and communities; and how gender played out
in the negotiations for compensation within the land law systems
employed by project management. The project compensation plan
allows for comparative analysis of realities in the field vis-à-vis
anticipated outcomes as reported in the plan. This allows readers to
assess management's obligations and corporate social responsibilities
to affected communities, the adequacy of the compensation plan,
and the role of the government of Cameroon in safeguarding the
interest of local inhabitants in the formulation of the compensation
packages.

The research methods

This chapter derives from a much larger empirical qualitative survey
research by Endeley and Sikod (2006) titled "The impact of the
Chad-Cameroon Oil Pipeline Operations on Gender Relations,
Land Tenure and Community Livelihoods in Selected Project Sites

in Cameroon."[2] The study area covered 27 communities in the South and Centre regions, two of the four regions through which the oil pipeline was constructed (see Table 1 and Figure 1). The sites were selected based on a defined set of criteria[3] and selection[4] procedures and in conjunction with the local Cameroon Oil Transport Company (COTCO) staff and community leaders in the research localities. The research lasted for about three years (from 2003 to 2006) and was carried out by a team of eight Cameroonians comprising two senior researchers[5] and six field research assistants.[6] In addition, other faculty members of the University of Buea (my home university) contributed to the organization of in one or more ways to two research methodology workshops to enhance the capacity of the research team in the areas of data collection, data analysis and dissemination of research results and to ascertain the validity and reliability of research instruments. All instruments were translated[7] and reviewed to ensure that the gender dimension of the study would not be lost. Occasionally, the team used "Pidgin English"[8] or a local language when respondents could not communicate in French or English. For such situations, local interpreters were hired. On the whole, communication between the research team and respondents posed no threat to the reliability of the study because members of the research team were fluent in at least French, English and Pidgin English languages.

The entire research was guided by several capacity building workshops[9] for members of the research team, and small meetings with communities through which the research subjects and team members were able to exchange ideas. This was one way to secure the commitment of the research subjects to the project. Research subjects also participated in the enlarged workshop to disseminate research results. Three representatives, with at least one woman, from each of the 27 research communities were invited to and participated in the workshop at which they contributed to a lively debate concerning their livelihoods and fate in the Chad-Cameroon Oil Pipeline project. It provided the first ever opportunity for communities affected by the Chad-Cameroon Oil Pipeline project to come together and exchange ideas, discuss problems and strategies for solutions. We witnessed a tremendous display of energy, which,

Table 1

Distribution of Study Sites by Administrative Units (Region, Division and Sub-division), Length of Laid Pipeline, Ecological Zones and Ethnic Group

Region	Division	Sub-division	Length of pipeline (km)	Study Sites	Ecological Zones	Ethnic group
South Region	Ocean	Kribi	42.9	Bidou		Fang
				Makoure 1		Ngumba
				Bandevouri		Fang
		Bipindi	35.8	Ndtoua	Atlantic, Littoral equatorial evergreen forest	Ngumba
				Bidjouka		Ngumba
		Lolodorf	39.5	Mbikiliki		Fang
				Saballi		Ngumba
				Bikoe 1		Ewondo
		Mvengue	27.6	Akom		Beti
				Akarobéllé		Beti

Region	Division	Sub-division	Length of pipeline (km)	Study Sites	Ecological Zones	Ethnic group
	Nyong and So'o	Ngomezap	16.2	Akongo III		Ewondo
		Ngoumou	15.5	Nyengue		Ewondo
				Nkongbibega		Ewondo
				Ngongmeyos		Ewondo
	Mefou and Akono	Mbankomo	25.2	Mbankomo village		Ewondo
				Zoatoupsi		Ewondo
				Leboudi		Eton
Centre Region	Lekie	Okala	18.7	Ebod		Beti
				Yegue	Equatorial evergreen rain-forest	Eton
	Mefou and Afamba	Soa	6.0	Esson Mintsang		Ewondo
		Esse	30.0	Ndzana		Beti
				Mvondoumba		Beti
		Mbandjock	23.8	Mbandjock plateau		Mixed settlement
	Upper sanaga			Ndjore II		Eton
				Nguinda		Nanga
		Nanga Eboko	49.6	Meyangue		Beti
				Mbongs'ol		Beti

Source : Environnemental Management Plan. Cameroon Portion.Vol .3

if built upon would definitely get the attention of government and project management. Participants were able to react to the research results, inform the public and government institutions on the realities of the Chad-Cameroon Oil Pipeline Construction project for their lives, do some advocacy and receive advice from human rights, legal and other experts on possibilities for redress.[10] The main findings of the research were corroborated by the information generated by the subjects during the workshop (presentation of the outcomes from the working session of the Chief of Akongo Village, HRH. Fouda Ndi Joseph Marie). The outcomes of the dissemination workshop were used to fine-tune the final research report.

In all, research subjects in 27 communities provided qualitative and quantitative data for this research through focus group and individual interviews. In all six categories of persons—chiefs/notables, women, men, the youth, service providers and individuals (men and women)—who received compensation were interviewed.[11] All these persons had lived the experience of the execution and realisation of the project from 2000 to 2003. The lack of gender parity in numerical terms did not marginalise women's participation or their voice in the study because of the multiplicity of research instruments. The different categories of subjects meant that we had to design differently structured interview guides.[12] However, the different instruments covered similar issues[13] as defined in the study objectives and research questions, though with different emphases.

Measures were taken to ensure that ethical standards were respected. The discussion of methodology remains incomplete without a discussion of some challenges encountered in the conduct of the study. The focus group discussions proved especially helpful in verifying evidence, establishing reality and bringing clarity to clouded issues. However, frequently, very lengthy discussions were necessary to address exaggerations, especially on emotional issues dealing with infringement of rights, humiliations, disregard and marginalisation, lack of basic entitlement, and poverty. The team found that it was important to work very closely with the chiefs of the different communities, especially as they served as liaison[14] between project management and the local community. It is no exaggeration to say that the research team experienced great difficulty in gaining the cooperation of project management and government officials and this created difficulties with interviews.[15] The foreign members of the project team were especially uncooperative. Often, the principal researchers had to be firm with project management to secure the needed information.

Despite these challenges, the study's findings exposed potentially, troublesome aspects of the project in need of the attention of all project stakeholders in order to avoid the conflicts and acts of sabotage, which characterise the petroleum regions of neighbouring Nigeria (Watts 1997; Turner and Brownhill 2004; Ukeje 2005).

Land tenure systems in Cameroon: Situating gender in the politics of land tenure and compensation to land

This section provides a brief overview of the evolution of land tenure in Cameroon in order to situate the context in which the Chad-Cameroon Oil Pipeline project operates. History reveals that Cameroon has been governed by three colonial powers—Germany, Britain and France. This has further complicated the land tenure systems of Cameroon. For example, in the conversion of collective or communal land to individual ownership, the Germans assumed that all unoccupied land was vacant land without an owner. Such land became "kronland", i.e., German land (Logo et al. 2003:48). Similarly, the 1938 Decree passed by the French named all unoccupied land as "Terre Vacant et sans Maitre" (land without owner). In this regard, many collective (customary) land rights were decisively transformed and registered as titled land with a new owner who was often not a native. While the British recognised natives as the sole owners of vacant land, such land was under the control of the state (see the Native Rights Ordinance of Northern Nigeria No.1 of 1916 and Southern Cameroon No. 1 of 1927 (Logo et al. 2003:48). There have been ongoing struggles over ownership of land and land resources between the State, the community and the individual. Within this project, we were especially concerned with the question of how individuals gain access to communal lands; and then consequently, what classification was given to unoccupied land in the Chad-Cameroon Oil Pipeline project. Was it a situation of "Terre Vacant et sans Maitre'? Who gained the entitlements to unoccupied land? Was it the government or the community? How did this impact on the communities and the population?

Citizenship and international[16] instruments, including conventions around land rights require that all members of a community enjoy secure access and rights to land. Thus, nations are expected to ensure that policies, practices and actions to land and related resources do not deprive men or women of their rights to access, use and control of land. Any contrary position is tantamount to infringement of the fundamental human rights of the individual. The Cameroon National Constitution of 1996 provides a legal framework for both men and women to enjoy equal access to, and control of land and other properties. It states that, "The human persons without distinction of race, religion, sex or belief possess inalienable rights". Where "ownership shall mean the right guaranteed to every person by law to use, enjoy and dispose of property. No person shall be deprived thereof, save for public purposes and subject to the payment of compensation under conditions determined by the law."

Samalang (2005:134) and Ngassa (1999) report that Cameroon's land tenure systems are guided by both national and international laws. Fisiy (1992:39) delineates two broad categories of land tenure in Cameroon based on the 1974 land ordinances: a) national land, which comprises land parcels that have not been registered as private property of legal persons, and b) state land which is the property of the State. The latter includes personal and real property acquired by the State without consideration or valuable consideration according to rules of ordinary law. Such property is intended or set aside for direct use by the public or for public services. The Cameroon Land Tenure Ordinance No. 74–1 of 6 July 1974, guarantees all persons and corporate bodies with landed property the right to freely enjoy and dispose of such lands. Article 9 of Decree No. 76–165 of April 1976, which modified the Ordinance of 1974, establishes the conditions for obtaining land certificates. It provides that customary communities and their members, or any other person of Cameroonian nationality, shall be eligible to apply for land certificates for national land, which they occupy and develop if they can show proof of effective occupation or exploration before 5 August 1974. Any land registered becomes unassailable (Art 1(2) of 76–165 of April 1976), thus making the occupant the landowner (Samalang, 2005: 134). By this article all members of any community, irrespective of gender, class or ethnicity have equal rights to access and own land. However, because of the high level of legal illiteracy and poor effort by government to inform its citizens, it is not clear if all the rural dwellers, the poor and women, are aware of these provisions or can afford the basic costs of obtaining land titles. Besides, how many women can withstand the cultural prejudices, which prevent them from pursuing their land rights?

The division between customary and private titles originated in the colonial era. Focusing on this colonial dichotomy, Mamdani (1996) argues that "the colonial state was 'bifurcated' not only spatially but also politically". It was not uncommon for rural colonial officials to assume vacant land as communal property, to be administered and controlled by the chiefs. Colonial administrators therefore granted chiefs enormous control over land.

The 1976 land legislation negates traditional (customary) land tenure systems, which while discriminatory, did provide women with some level of security to land. As the law's land tenure procedures are unknown to most women and the vast majority of the rural population, the traditional tenure system continues to be the de facto land tenure system in most rural locations in Cameroon. Samalang (2005) and Endeley (1998) have noted that although women are major land users, making up a substantive proportion (80 per cent) of the agricultural workforce and exploiting land and related resources to ensure their own growth and promote national development, men have hegemonic advantage in customary land tenure systems and practices. Not only is land perceived as an asset to be controlled by men, women too are perceived and referred to as "assets or chattels". Hence, they themselves cannot own and control land. In this connection, it is apparent that the 1976 land legislation is a double-edged sword. On the one hand, it enables rich and powerful individuals to own and register as much land as they can, while dismissing customary land tenure systems—the body of law that is most accessible to community members. In addition, it is clear that those who are able to obtain land title will be better placed to reap the most benefits from compensation paid to expropriated land owners due to the construction of the pipeline project, as against those who do not have land title.

In Cameroon, like in most African societies, the customary land tenure system prevails in spite of statutory laws. Governed by customary norms, practices and laws, the chiefs, traditional councils and family heads remain custodians of community and family land holdings. As we have already indicated, this system promotes male hegemony over land. That said, women's use rights are protected so they can grow food to feed their families. Equity is an important principle in the distribution of community land to families for redistribution to their members. Customary laws are also protective of communal resources such as watersheds, forests and quarries. Often, it is difficult for persons and families to have private ownership of communal land. However, this is possible with land carved out by chiefs for families. Private ownership under customary land tenure is tenable with or without formal titling. It is possible for both men and women to access land. In addition, in some communities, widows and unmarried women own land.

In the light of the above discussion, what were the implications in the Chad-Cameroon Oil Pipeline if the state is custodian of national land? Can one discuss acquisitions in terms of land expropriation? What were the implications for compensation to affected individuals and communities in general? What concept of private ownership prevailed in the communities studied? Did the project uphold and respect private ownership without land titling?

Laws governing compensation for land in Cameroon

Compensation for land is a fundamental issue in this study because all persons, either as individuals or as community members, suffered one or more forms of dispossession of private property and/or communal property due to the construction of the pipeline. A brief overview of the laws on compensation is in order. The project displaced as well as dispossessed the population, even if temporarily, of their rights to the exploitation of community resources. As stated in article 9 of the Ordinance No. 74–1 of 6 July 1974: "Subject to the laws and regulations relating to town planning, hygiene and policing, owners may on their lands exploit quarries as defined by mining regulations." This article is corroborated by Article 17 (3) concerning national lands, which states: "Subject to the regulations in force, hunting and fruit picking rights shall be granted to them [users of national lands] on lands in category (2) as defined in Article 15 [below], until such time as the State has assigned the said lands to a specific purpose."

Article 1(1) of Ordinance No. 74-3 of 6 July 1974, which concerns the procedure governing expropriation for a public purpose and the terms and conditions of compensation, states: "Expropriation for a public purpose shall be pronounced by decree on completion of the procedure defined by the present ordinance. By the said decree, existing titles over the land in question shall be extinguished and the land thus declared free shall be registered in the name of the State". However, it is stated that "expropriation for a public purpose shall only affect private property as defined in Article 2 of the Ordinance to establish rules governing land tenure" (says article 2 of Ordinance No. 74-3 of 6 July 1974).

This same ordinance regulates the compensation for dispossession of properties and identifies the types of compensation and what can be compensated, especially for the purpose of general interest as for the case of the Chad-Cameroon project. Article 13 (1) states: "The bodies on whose behalf expropriation is applied shall compensate the dispossessed persons from their budget." However, article 13 (2) states that "No compensation shall be payable for the destruction of dilapidated buildings liable to collapse, or buildings erected contrary to town planning regulations." The above-mentioned regulations do not apply to expropriation and compensation prior to the date on which the present ordinance enters into force (Article 13 (4)).

Under the ordinance, the government is expected to compensate those expropriated for the loss of resources and labour time and to protect and secure their welfare. Article 7 (1) of the Ordinance No. 74-3 of 6 July 1974 states: "expropriation shall confer the right to monetary compensation under the conditions defined by Article 9 below." Article 7 (2): "provided that the authority benefiting from the expropriation may replace monetary compensation for lands by compensation in kind of the same value." Article 8 states that "compensation for expropriation shall be related to the direct immediate and certain material damage caused by the eviction."

Article 13 (2) of the Ordinance, to establish rules governing compensation for expropriation, comprises the following: the value of the crops destroyed, calculated in accordance with the scale in force; the value of the buildings and other installations, calculated by the valuation commission referred to in Article 4; the value of the undeveloped land calculated as follows:

(a) in the case of urban lands officially allocated subject to payment, compensation may not exceed the official price of public lands in the particular town centre

(b) in the case of lands held by virtue of a normal transaction under ordinary law, compensation shall be the purchase price to which shall be added the ancillary costs of purchase and of obtaining title

(c) in the case of lands held by virtue of a customary tenure under which a land certificate has been issued, compensation may not exceed the amount of expenses incurred by the issuance of the said certificate.

However, several elements of the laws are problematic, particularly for poor rural people. One of these is the provision that no compensation is payable for dilapidated buildings liable to collapse, or buildings erected contrary to town planning regulations. Consequently, many people will not receive compensation for demolished homes. The status of unoccupied land in rural areas is another concern. For example, Article 11 of the Ordinance No. 77-2 of 10th January 1977, states that, "properties in rural areas which, for at least 10 years, have not been maintained or regenerated may, after due notice has remained ineffective, be incorporated in the private property of the State without compensation." Does this mean that the communities did not receive any compensation for such land when expropriated, because unoccupied land was transformed into the private property of the State? Do we also assume that the communities were not compensated because majority of the land under customary laws had no title? Article 10 demands that expropriation at the request of other public bodies requires negotiations with the owners concerned.

In the case of disputes, legislation demands that a commission be set up to hear and settle disputes. Article 11 of Ordinance No. 74-3 of 6 July 1974 states that "in the case of dispute over the amount of compensation fixed by decree, the dispossessed person shall send in a claim to the Prefect of the Division in which the expropriation took place; the latter shall submit the claim to the commission." In a context where the majority of the locals are illiterate, unexposed to forces of globalisation and not backed by people-centred civil society organisations, who speaks for the poor communities?

Gender, land and compensation in the communities affected by the Chad-Cameroon Oil Pipeline Project

Gender and land tenure systems in the selected communities

This section examines the perceptions of land and gender, which defined the determination and distribution of compensation for land. In two communities—Njore II and Mbanjock Camp—which are resettlement camps, the people said they were occupying land belonging to the government of Cameroon. The remaining 25 communities said their land was community land, land of their ancestors under the authority of their chiefs and managed according to their customs. In almost all communities, we noted that customary land laws and norms defined the mode of operation. This system informed access, use, control and transfer of land. The customs, irrespective of ethnicity, revealed that land is held in two main forms: community and family land. Community land is virgin land within the confines of the community or tribal geographical location. Family land is also managed collectively but under the custody of the head of the family. Acquisition of land through purchases or lease was atypical, perhaps because most communities had abundant land in relation to the size of their population. However, it was possible to acquire land through purchase and inheritance in two of the communities. In these communities, only about half of the men and women in the focus groups said that women could purchase land.

Contrary to customary laws on land inheritance, which do not favour women, the majority of men and women said that they owned parcels of land in which the pipeline had been buried.

The above responses warranted verification to determine if women could really own land. The overwhelming ruling from the focus groups was that both men and women could inherit land in their communities. A pertinent concern was whether women's rights to land would continue to be upheld with the increase in population and demand for land that has implications on land values. In the meantime, none of the persons interviewed in any of the communities complained about not having well established and respected use rights to land, even if men generally enjoyed more control over land than women and the youth. This was in spite of the existence of traditional barriers to female land inheritance. For the woman, access to land was primarily through her father, husband, family, or the chief.

Although individuals could own land in their communities, land title deeds were not yet known, particularly in areas where land was considered an abundant resource. Only in one community did some respondents indicate that people could own land and have land titles. It should be mentioned here that both men and women held similar views on women's relationships to land. Most of them reported that married women generally accessed land through marriage. As confirmed by most women and men in three quarters of the communities studied, single, divorced and widowed women could gain access to land either through their fathers or through their father's family. Buying land was not the norm in most communities, thus only a small minority of women in fewer than three—Saballi and Nkongbibega—communities said they could do so. It is worth noting that female chiefs head these communities but they differ in terms of their proximity to an urban location. Saballi is a peri-urban community, while Nkongbibega is not. Interestingly, divorced women in four communities said they were able to enjoy access rights over their former husbands' land through their children. Apparently, some women in five of the communities had no notion of the existing statutory laws governing land holding in Cameroon. The women did not think there was any rule regulating land ownership besides their customs.

Further analysis of the rights of men and women over individual land resources within the studied communities revealed that many more men than women perceived women as having control over land. Before rushing to any conclusion, it should be made clear that the control alluded to by the majority of men's focus groups (16 out of the 27 villages) is control over land resources on women's farms. According to most men, women have full (and equal) control while just about a third of women's groups said women had limited control over land resources. This means women have rights over what they produce from the farms. The predominant position of women and men interviewed in most communities is that community resources were unequally shared, with men enjoying more control over the resources than women. Women's limited access to resources, as noted by a woman in Saballi community is "because women move out of the family for marriage." She also said, "You can cultivate whatever you want on the land but you (woman) cannot sell the land." Furthermore, the majority of men in Saballi and Bidou communities confirmed that women's freedom to cultivate what they wanted was an uneasy freedom, since married women needed the consent of their husbands. Men, on the other hand, needed no one's consent to grow anything or to exploit any resource on the land in these two communities. In sum, in almost all of the affected communities, the traditional land tenure system was dominant, and it remained the de facto system operating in most of Cameroon. The findings revealed that although women, like men, were important users of land, their control over the land and timber resources were limited.

Gender, land and compensation (individual, community and regional compensation)

This section presents and compares field realities to those in the literature. An attempt is made to determine how gender is posited in the project and the implications thereof on land and in turn on compensation. The discussion underscores those who benefited and those who did not from the compensation scheme and how women fared in relation to men as beneficiaries and losers. The three main forms of compensation earmarked for the Chad-Cameroon Oil Pipeline construction project[17] were individual, community and regional. Individual compensation was for destroyed farmlands, crops and or other property such as buildings and economic trees, and expropriated land considered personal or private. The project upheld and compensated the labour time that individuals had invested on destroyed farmland(s), and not owners or other rights holders.

The position of women was somewhat interesting in cases where married women had invested labour on their husbands' farmland. In accordance with the Environmental Management Plan (EMP), both women and men, irrespective of class, ethnicity and age (mostly adult and aged) were recipients of this form of compensation. Of a total of 128 respondents who received individual compensation, the majority (61 per cent) were men. However, women formed a substantial proportion (39 per cent). This difference was not on account of the number of farmers, but because of the location of farms. The general pattern revealed that men's farms had the tendency to be located on the outskirts of communities, while women farmed much closer to home. The pipeline was more likely to destroy men's farms than women's farms, especially as deliberate efforts were made not to transverse human settlements. All communities confirmed that individual compensation was based on ownership rights of destroyed crops/farmland (labour invested for cultivation) and not on who has control rights to the land.

Generally, compensation rates were based on local market prices for the relevant commodities destroyed. Almost all the respondents, 98 per cent of the women and about 96 per cent of men, received a combination of cash and in-kind compensation for the destruction of their local food crops (cassava, maize, vegetables, and other tuber crops), cash crops (mainly tree crops such as cocoa and palm trees), fruit trees and medicinal plants. The cash value of compensation payments ranged from a minimum of 9,000 CFA[3] francs (about US$18) paid to a woman to a maximum of 12,000,000 CFA francs (US$24,000) paid to a man. The mean cash value for both men and women was 1,051,802 CFA francs (about US$2,103.00). Two women featured at the upper end of compensation received cash values of 2 million CFA (US$4,000) francs and 4,000,000 CFA francs (US$8,000) respectively.

Respondents—men, women, chiefs, government, COTCO and other companies—all attributed the gender differences in paid compensation to differences in the market prices for crops produced by women and men. The traditional division in crop cultivation and farming activities by gender was observed in this study. Men, more than women, were involved in the cultivation of highly valued export crops such as cocoa and palm oil trees, while women were more into food production, primarily for home consumption and the local market. The differences in global market prices for traditional export crops and local market prices for food crops explain the enormous differences in compensations.

The study found that while the relations between men and women were largely unequal and land tenure arrangements favoured men, it was not unusual to hear men talk of the retribution they might suffer if women's concerns were neglected in sharing community or regional compensation. Under the project, women, as active farmers in their own right under customary systems, were protective of their use rights. They were informed by civil society organisations of global debates on gender equality. It was therefore not surprising that they resisted any attempts from any quarters to dispossess them of their land resources without some form of compensation.

There were no striking differences between men and women in their use of their compensation money. It was difficult to locate anyone—woman or man—who had invested their compensation in the expansion of their land holdings. Both said they spent a larger proportion of their money on non-food items—consumables that they were unable to produce. Individual compensation for expropriated land remained an outstanding issue for many people in the affected communities. In the absence of a landowner, some respondents said the family head designated a family member to collect compensation on the owner's behalf.

In relation to community compensation, there were payments made to local communities to compensate them for the pipeline passing through community land or other community common property, and causing some environmental damage such as damaged communal resources, or environmental disturbances or inconveniences such as noise, obstruction during construction and general disturbance of community peace. Similarly, regional compensation was paid to communities sharing a common ecosystem affected by the pipe-line. Both community and regional compensation was paid in kind and not in cash. Forms of community compensation included cartons of fungicide, corrugated iron sheets for roofing, classrooms, community hall, wells, football fields, palm seedlings, classroom furniture, grinding machines, spraying machines, wheel-barrows, moulding machines for making bricks, equipment for community halls and sports outfits. Regional compensation included classrooms, grinding machines, zinc and wells. While all affected communities received community compensation, not all of them received regional compensation.

Members of affected communities showed more interest in the decision-making processes around community compensation than in the case of regional compensation. The majority of men, women and youth in two-thirds of the communities indicated that they participated in deciding their community compensation. In general, the majority of respondents—men and women alike—said they favoured the "in-kind" approach to community and regional compensation. Respondents, however, had some concerns regarding both regional and community compensation schemes. The majority of the people were unhappy with the items given to their communities. Women in these communities were very bitter about the choice of community compensation, as they would have preferred farming tools.

Some of the communities affected by the project were home to ethnic minority groups such as the Bakola and Bagyeli pygmies. The government of Cameroon, over the years, has made efforts to address the developmental problems of such communities. For example, there have been efforts to resettle pygmy communities on more accessible locations away from enclave sites deep in the forests. In addition, there have been measures to provide them with basic services such as healthcare, education, shelter and citizenship identity cards. Whether these measures have improved their lives is a matter of debate, which is beyond the scope of this essay. Within the context of the project, the Environmental Management Plan had a special action plan, which made provisions for both the Bakola and Bagyeli pygmies, considered the primary users of forest resources. Such provisions were not without controversy, since other ethnic groups such as the Ngumba have not benefited from similar arrangements.

The intersection between gender and ethnicity has given rise to differences in compensation. Bantu groups are more diverse and differentiated by the intersections of gender, ethnicity, class and land tenure systems, all of which have affected compensation and control over compensation. Both women and men within Bantu communities benefited from compensation given to members of communities or regions sharing the same resources. Yet, obvious differences existed between women who were farmers and experienced the destruction of their farms or other land properties, and those who did not farm. While almost all Bantu communities were settled farm communities, the indigenous pygmies were typically hunters and gatherers. There were more similarities in how men and women in indigenous groups exploit land, and therefore they received similar compensations. In contrast, compensations to men and women in Bantu groups differed in terms of their use of land.

A review of the Environmental Management Plan (1999) and the field research illustrated that statutory laws such as the 1974 and 1976 Ordinances primarily guided matters of compensation on land ownership, although there was some reference to customary norms. The statutory laws categorise all land, even that effectively occupied by customary communities as national land. For example, Ss. 1 (2) and 16 (2) of Ordinance No. 74-1 of 1974 states that, "The State shall be the guardian of all lands." Few persons, mainly the male elite, had title to their land; no community land was titled under the ordinance. Instead, the majority of local inhabitants, men and women alike, had usufruct rights under customary tenure systems. Only statutory rights in land were considered to be capable of expropriation and compensation under the ordinance. Therefore, while individuals and communities were denied the use of occupied land for close to three years, they received compensation only for destroyed assets and not for loss of use of land. At the time of the study, many people had not been able to re-occupy their land.

The majority of men as well as women did not have a sense of the importance of formal land titling, particularly in the context of the project. At no time during field data collection did the researchers sense that the population fully understood how their land rights were positioned in the project. While the majority knew they would receive compensation for destroyed crops and not land, they had received no explanation as to why this was the case. Why the communities were not informed and assisted to establish titles for land they occupied remains unknown. This was a shortcoming in a project expected to alleviate poverty, given that titled land gives the owner greater leverage during negotiations for compensation. It is uncertain whether the government of Cameroon and the management deliberately kept vital information from the locals, information that would have informed them in making better choices. However, by paying individuals awarded compensation, the management reduced the effects of unequal power relations in traditional society. Regardless of gender, age, education and class, control was vested to the individual beneficiary. This explains why male hegemony, that is embedded in customary land tenure systems, which tends to negate women's control, was greatly minimised and not very visible in the project. However, what communities received relative to the profits from oil did not bridge the unequal relations between communities and the company. This issue is discussed in more detail in the next section.

Community preparedness, participation and satisfaction with Project Plan: viewpoints and tensions

Viewpoints about preparedness, participation and satisfaction

This section discusses the viewpoints of the chiefs on conduct of the project. The Environmental Management Plan stressed that the communities and persons likely to be affected be informed and educated about the activities of the upcoming project. The chiefs (notables) played a central role in preparing the communities, acting as intermediaries between the populations and the consortium/ government. They were well aware of the implementation of EMP, what transpired in the affected communities and the preparedness of the communities to participate effectively in opportunities created by the project, as well as the challenges deemed inappropriate for their welfare.

We investigated whether the communities participated in establishing compensation entitlements as defined by the EMP. All chiefs, either on their own or in partnership with COTCO staff, consulting NGOs and other companies reported that they organised several meetings to prepare and sensitise their communities about the project and its implications for community welfare and poverty alleviation. For example, the chief of Leboudi informed his people about possible job opportunities in the project, while at Meyang and Essong Mintsang, the chiefs stressed the importance of the project and its possible benefits for the local communities. Women, men, youth, beneficiaries and service providers attest to the efforts of chiefs and COTCO agents to educate them on the project. Many people remembered receiving information on compensation (procedures for receiving compensation), resources to be provided by the project (the project will bring much money), employment opportunities and safety, security and health (STD and HIV/AIDS). In general, the population expressed satisfaction with the information they received before the construction of the pipeline. That said, it is important to question the quality of information that was given to the affected persons and communities. It is clear that the information was inadequate, given that it was mainly propaganda with very little said about the disadvantages of the project. Consequently, the affected population was not empowered to secure and protect their rights and entitlements.

Most chiefs had complaints about the poor quality or quantity of compensation and delays in payment. The research team found evidence of most complaints—poorly completed buildings, poor quality hoes and other farm implements and differences in selected and received in-kind compensation.[18] In some cases, communities had their requests rejected. This was the case of Mvondoumba Village, which had requested electricity supply and this had not been provided at the time of the study. While the choice of compensation was a function of the financial allocation per community, chiefs confirmed that communities were restricted in the choice of compensation allowed in that they had to choose from a catalogue prepared by COTCO.

Nevertheless, across all communities, the chiefs set up committees composed of men and women to manage the community and/or regional compensation. To cite a few examples, of the 20 members of the committee in Njore II, 5 were women. Each of the committees in Makoure and Meyang had 4 men and 2 women, while in Okarobelle and Bandewouri, each committee had 3 men and 2 women. There were 5 men 3 women in the Nkongbibega committee.

However, the chiefs complained that the level of community participation in the activities of the pipeline, concerning livelihoods and welfare, was minimal. This was because the population at large, and most chiefs, were not informed about strategic matters and this made them vulnerable to accusations of bribery and corruption. Some chiefs were accused by COTCO staff and members of their communities of acts of corruption in relation to compensation matters. A broad spectrum of women respondents was in agreement with the chiefs that communities—men, women and youth—were informed on the implications of the upcoming project. For example, the women noted that chiefs, COTCO and government officials closely worked with the men in some communities to identify the parcels of land and their owners, defined boundaries of land in the path of the pipeline and determined forms of community and regional compensation. To illustrate the passive role of women in the preparatory process, most women in Leboudi community reported that "COTCO agents simply asked the women about their worries but no further information was given them about the project." In particular, they commented that the value of community compensation and the paucity of employment and business opportunities under the project were not exposed to them. This was a clear indication of the limitations of the participatory processes and consultations and how women's access to land and compensation is mediated by men at crucial points in the project.

The researchers observed that women, men and youth were informed about the process of compensation. However, there were variations in the level of awareness and participation across communities and segments of the population. It was not unusual to hear women in some communities express their lack of knowledge of how the choice of community compensation was done. Across communities, women decried the lack of uniformity in compensation given to the population, a reflection of lack of transparency in the distribution of compensation and differences in the depth of understanding about the project by different categories of the population.

Some early tensions

The study found examples of tensions in the research communities in relation to certain aspects of the construction of the pipeline. Some of these tensions are discussed here, paying attention to the nature of women's participation in activism around these issues. A recurring issue was the question of local recruitments for the project. In Okarobelle for example, the youth protested against the recruitment of persons from outside the community to work on a segment of the pipeline in the community. At Meyang, where women took part in a strike action as defenders of their husbands' and children's rights to employment in the project, the road was blocked with tree trunks and stones. These demonstrations resulted in the employment of more youth by the projects. In Essong Mintsang, the youth employed on the project went on strike because they were not paid on time, and the problem was resolved. However, a positive outcome was not always the case. In Nkongbibega—another affected community— youth protests resulted in the detention and imprisonment of some of the protesters.

The pollution of streams and water bodies was another source of tension. In Mbikiliki, there were protests against the pollution of streams in the village. According to the chief, these protests, which involved the entire population (men, women and youth), did not yield positive responses from the project. In Leboudi, where water wells were destroyed by machines, people formed a human barrier at the construction site and work had to be stopped until a solution was found. The company concerned gave money to repair other wells. The chief reported that women did not participate in this action.

While these struggles in the communities affected by the Chad-Cameroon project are not on the scale of conflicts around oil exploration regions in Sub-Saharan Africa, they are pointers to future tensions. News reports of local people and gangs kidnapping foreign oil workers and sabotaging oil pipelines and transportation facilities are quite common in the Niger Delta and other places. There have also been numerous reports of sit-down strikes and legal efforts to demand reparation for environmental damage following decades of oil spills and constant burning/gas flares. Examples of such damage include farmlands rendered useless, polluted rivers and waterways with depleting marine life. Communities have also demanded attention to problems such as the lack of jobs and basic social services.

While governments are quick at protecting oil ventures and company workers, especially foreigners, they have been quite poor at negotiating the plight and rights of citizens who have been downtrodden. In the case of the pipeline project, the Chief of Akongo said, "there was a lot of disdain from COTCO towards the local population and this seemed to be encouraged by our own government. Each time the population came up to defend their rights it was the Sub-Divisional Officer who sent policemen to disperse the population. As a result, the human factor was not taken into consideration in this project." The use of law enforcement agencies to resolve civil unrest is normal in Cameroon and other African countries. In Nigeria, military force has been used to provide security and protection for the oil companies against sabotage by the locals. Young men have been arrested, beaten, tortured and imprisoned without regard for their basic entitlements. Women have been present and active in these struggles because of the strategic nature of land to welfare and survival of their families, themselves and their communities.

CONCLUSION

We have discussed the implications of the Cameroon Oil Pipeline project for land tenure and gender relations in 27 affected communities in Cameroon. The study on which this chapter is based found that although there were gender inequalities in land ownership and inheritance in the study communities, women's use rights in land were reasonably secure. The project's decision to adopt three categories of compensation and to compensate individual land users for their crop and labour losses ensured that women were beneficiaries of compensation. However, it was also the case that more men than women enjoyed compensation and that the former's payments were, on average, higher than what women received. This was because of the differences in the nature of the crops they grew and the location of their farms. Men's export crops had a higher market value than women's food crops. In addition, men had much larger farms, which were located further away from dwellings, closer to the pipeline that was located as far away from settlements as was possible.

Whereas the global debates on the need to promote gender equality and prevent further exploitation and discrimination of women informed the project's compensation strategy, rural communities were not sufficiently protected, not even by the government of Cameroon that was best placed to do this. Through the principle of "fairness", the project was able to ensure gender equity to some extent even though interviews and project literature revealed that gender equality was not a principal concern. However, the compensation strategy helped to reposition gender in the social dimensions of the project. In other respects, women remained marginalised in the Chad-Cameroon Oil Pipeline project, which was largely a male dominated undertaking.

With respect to the situation of local communities as a whole, it was difficult to talk about "fairness". Unprotected and uninformed about the forces of globalisation, local communities found themselves at the mercy of the global and national elites. In this regard, women were the most marginalised. With the exception of a few national elites, men and women in rural communities did not have titles to their land. This exposed them to being dispossessed of their land without compensation. The implications of not having land title are many. According to the statutory legal provisions indicated in the "Regime Foncier et Domanial—Land Tenure and State Lands" (1983), land is owned by individuals only when they have title. Without title, the government pays compensation only for the development on the land and not the land itself. Government and civil society groups failed to sensitise and educate the population on their position under Cameroon land law, thus making it difficult for communities and their members to protect their land interests.

For a project that was meant to eradicate poverty, the pittance given to people as compensation was in no way commensurate with their long-term losses. Like other petroleum regions of Nigeria and other African countries (Wood 2006), the study communities were relatively poor and lacking in basic services such as potable water, health centres, schools and infrastructure such as accessible roads, markets and electricity. They also lacked the human capacity to exploit their environment and to advocate for fair compensation. The majority of the people lived in houses constructed with mud or mud plastered with cement. No hospital was found in any of the communities. Only a few settlements such as Saballi and Nanga-Eboko, which enjoyed proximity to a Divisional headquarters, were able to access Divisional hospitals. This explains why many communities expected that the pipeline project would provide them with substantive compensation needed to boost their local economies and generate social transformation and development. Many were disillusioned by what the Chad-Cameroon Oil Pipeline project offered them.

The disappointment of the communities that housed the pipeline project is not atypical of the outcomes and impacts experienced by the rural poor in the processes of globalisation. As Pegg (2005) and Woods (2006) have argued, the Chad-Cameroon Oil Pipeline project is unlikely to lead to poverty alleviation. That said, some important lessons could be drawn from the project. Within a context of insecure rights to land and where land titling is not the practice, the re-definition of gender on the basis of invested labour on occupied land has helped to protect the rights of women and men to land. Existing land laws need to be revisited and reformed where it is found that their provisions do not benefit the poor, rural dwellers and women. Government and civil society need to prepare adequately the population, through sensitisation and education, on strategic issues such as the nature and likely consequences and outcomes of processes of globalisation on land tenure. To enhance the policy implications of the study, on which the chapter is based, further research should be carried out on gender and land tenure in the socio-culturally and economically diverse areas traversed by the project in Northern Cameroon and Chad. An issue of interest would be the fate of women who do not own farm but exploit land resources through extractive activities. An overarching question would be how research could strengthen citizenship rights and corporate social responsibility in the Chad-Cameroon Oil pipeline project.

NOTES

1. As already indicated, the project is estimated at US$4.2 billion.
2. IDRC Project number 101176–007.
3. The duration of project construction in a community, communities known to have agitated or resisted the project, communities with female leadership, communities with construction camps and other pipeline installations and the number of persons who received compensation.
4. The selection was based on the advice from the Cameroon oil transport company (COTCO), the local community contacts (LCC) officers responsible for the management and administration of the project in the field and on the research team's observations and experiences during the pre-site visits and the pre-tests of the research instruments in selected villages.
5. A female principal investigator and male co-investigator; their areas of specialisation include agriculture, women/gender studies, economics and environmental issues.
6. Two male and four female undergraduate and postgraduate students in the women and gender studies, geography and sociology-anthropology degree programmes in the University of Buea.
7. This translation was done by trained staff of the Department of Bilingual Studies and the Advance School for Translation and Interpretation (ASTI) of the University of Buea from English to French, the official lingua franca in the area of study.
8. Pidgin English is an important local but unofficial lingua franca spoken by many Cameroonians, both literate and illiterate. Cameroon has over 240 ethnic languages.
9. Two international workshops organised by IDRC in Ottawa; two small local workshops held in the University of Buea for members of the research team.
10. Some workshop participants questioned the non-participation of the World Bank, the government and COTCO in open workshops organised by members of the civil society to defend the rights of the local populations along the pipeline (Presentation of the outcomes from the working session of the Chief of Akongo Village, HRH. Fouda Ndi Joseph Marie).
11. The sample included: 27 key informants made up of chiefs/notables (2 women and 25 men), 27 all women focus groups (totalling about 159 women), 27 all men focus groups (totalling about 165 men), 27 youth focus groups (totalling about 111 men and 64 women), 81 service providers (69 men and 12 women) and 128 beneficiaries of individual compensation (78 men and 50 women). Chiefs/notables (the liaison person between project management and community), women, men, youth in separate focus groups (important segments of the population who lived through the construction of the project and benefited from one or more form of compensation given to each community), service providers (men and women who were employed or made

use of opportunities presented by the project to engage in gainful services
to earn money) and individuals (men and women) who received individual
compensation (for destroyed personal land or related properties during the
construction of the pipeline).

12. The instrument comprised two semi-structured questionnaires that generated
data from individual recipients of compensation and service providers (those
with formal contracts, daily paid workers, and suppliers), and one interview
guide each collected information from three respective groups, namely, a
community key informant (preferably the village chief or notable), women's
and men's focus groups and the youth group).

13. The research issues included land resources, tenure systems, compensation
(nature, utility, and sustainability), livelihood practices, social structure,
participation in the construction of the pipeline project, impacts of the project
on gender relations and social behaviour; community and environmental
change, and demographics characteristics. Measures were taken to ensure that
ethical concerns were respected. No data was gathered without the consent of
respondents.

14. They proved invaluable for identifying those individuals who received
compensation, and in establishing the forms, types, amount and procedures of
compensation.

15. They were unfriendly if critically questioned, aloof if they did not want to
respond to questions and had a superiority complex due to their belief that
they are more knowledgeable about oil construction and other technical issues
than the researchers. The controversies around the project made it very difficult
for project management to divulge relevant information to the research team.
The team sought information on the following aspects of the project: a list
of those who received individual compensation, gender disaggregated data by
compensation, indications of daily or monthly wages by employers, types of
work or services by community and the list of service providers. Only three top
ranking COTCO management staff and one international partner accepted to
speak to us. The sealed lips stance of COTCO officials was quite frustrating
for a public project.

16. The Universal Declaration of Human Rights (UDHRs) 1948, article 17 states
that, "Everyone has the rights to own property alone as well as in association
with others". It further states that, "...no one shall arbitrarily be deprived
of his property"; the United Nations Charter in its preamble on human
rights demands equal rights for men and women. The African Charter on
Human and People's Rights 1984, Article 18 (3) is no different. It states
that, "The State shall ensure the elimination of every discrimination against
women and the protection of the rights of the women and child as stipulated
in the International declarations and conventions"; the Convention on the
Elimination of all forms of Discrimination Against Women (CEDAW) in
Articles 2 clearly calls for condemnation of discrimination against women; the
need for national constitutions to promote the principle of equality of and

to enact legislative measures and sanctions to prohibit discrimination against women.
17. The Environmental Management Plan, Volume 3, 1999.
18. For example, a village might have requested a dry grinding machine and instead, a wet grinding machine is supplied.

REFERENCES

Agarwal, B., 1994, "Gender, Resistance and Land: Interlinked Struggles Over Resources and Meanings in South Asia". London: Frank CASS. *The Journal of Peasant Studies*, Vol. 22, No. 1.

COTCO, 1999, *Chad Export Project Environnemental Document : Environnemental Management Plan, Cameroon Portion,* Volumes 1, 2, 3, 4 Base Documents.

Endeley, J. B., 1998, "Structural Adjustment and the Cameroonian Women's Lifeline: 1986 to 1995", in Carla Risseeuw and Kamala Ganesh (eds), *Negotiation and social space: a gendered analysis of changing kin and security networks in South Asia and Sub-Saharan Africa,* New Delhi: Sage Publications India Pvt Ltd.

Fall, Yassine, 2001, "Gender and Social Implications of Globalization: An African Perspective", in Rita M. Kelly, Jane Bayes, Mary Hawkesworth and Brigitte Young (eds), *Gender, Globalisation, and Democratization.* New York: Rowman & Littlefield Publishers, Inc. pp. 49–74.

Fig, D., 2005, "Manufacturing amnesia: Corporate Social Responsibility in South Africa", *International Affairs* 81(3): 599–617.

Fisiy, Cyprian F., 1992, *Power and Privilege in the Administration of Law: Land Law Reforms and Social Differentiation in Cameroon.* Research Reports 1992/48, Leiden: African Studies Center.

Fonchingong Charles, C., 1999, "Structural adjustment, Women and Agriculture in Cameroon", *Gender and Development* 7(3) Oxford.

Fonchingong, C. and L. Fonjong, 2002, "The Concept of Self-Reliance in Community Development Initiatives in the Cameroon Grassfileds", *GeoJournal* 57(1–2).

FoEI/CED, 2002, "Traversing Peoples Lives: how the World Bank finances Community disruption in Cameroon". Cameroon: FoEI/CED. (September 2002).

Henn, J.K., 1986, "Intra-household dynamics and state policies as constraints on food production: Results of a 1985 agroeconomic survey in Cameroon", paper presented at conference on Gender Issues in Farming Systems research and Extension. Gainsville: University of Florida.

Kevane, M. and L.C. Gray, 1999, "A woman's field is made at night: gendered land rights and norms in Burkina Faso", *Feminist Economics* 5: 1–26.

Logo, P et al.. "Women and Law in Cameroon: Questioning Women's Land Status and Claims for Change" in Wanyeki, L. M. (2003) *Women and land in Africa: culture, religion and realizing women's right's,* London: Zed Books.

McGrew, Anthony, 2000, "Sustainable Globalization and the Global Politics of Development and Exclusion in the New World Order", in Tim Allen and Alan Thomas (eds), *Poverty and Development into the 21ˢᵗ Century*, Oxford: Oxford University Press.

Mackenzie, F., 1998, *Land, Ecology and Resistance in Kenya, 1880–1952,* International African Institute, Edinburgh: Edinburgh University Press.

Margaret, A. Rugadya, 2003, *"Consent or Co-Ownership: Policy and Legal Responses around the Matrimonial Home in Uganda"*, a paper presented at Jurists Conference, Kenyan section of the International Commission of Jurists, 19th–23rd August 2003, White Sands Hotel, Mombasa.

Mamdani, M., 1996, *Citizen and Subject: Contemporary Africa and the Legacy of Late Colonialism*. Princeton: Princeton University Press.

News Release No. 2007/19/EXC; Cameroon Oil Spill Update, January 30, 2007.

Ngassa Vera, 1999, *Gender Approach to Court Actions*. Cameroon: Friedrich-Ebert-Stiftung.

Pegg, Scott, 2005, "Can Policy Intervention beat the Resource Curse? Evidence from the Chad-Cameroon Pipeline Project". *African Affairs*. 105/418, 1–25. New York: Oxford University Press.

Republic of Cameroon, 2003, Poverty Reduction Strategy Paper. Yaoundé: Government of Cameroon.

———, 1983, Regime Foncier et Domanial; Land Thenure and state lands. Yaounde: Imprimerie National.

Samalang, Irene., 2005, "The Customary Land and Marginalisation of Women: Impediments to the Rural Woman's Access to Land in Anglophone Cameroon", in O. Oyediran, *Tropical Focus: The International Journal Series on Tropical Issues*, Vol 5.

Tantoh, William. and Yenshu, Emmanuel, V., 2005, Gender and rural Economy in the Wimbum Society, Cameroon: a study in perceptions and Practices with particular reference to the land question.. University of Buea, Cameroon (unpublished).

The Chad Cameroon Project, 1999, *Environmental Management Plan*. Cameroon portion, Vol. 1 and 2.

Turner, Terisa. E. and Brownhill, Leign. S. 2004, "The Curse of Nakedness: Nigerian Women in the Oil War", in Luciana Ricciutelli, Angela Miles and Margaret H. Mcfadden (eds), *Feminist politicts, Activism and Vison: local and Global Challenges*, pp. 169–191.

Ukeje, Charles. 2005, "From Aba to Ugborodo: Gender Identity and Alternative Discourse of the Social Protest Among Women in the Oil Delta of Nigeria", in Signe Arnfred, et.al. *Gender Activism and Studies in Africa*. CODESRIA Gender Series 3. Senegal: CODERIA, pp. 67–87.

Watts, M., 1997, "Black Gold, White Heat. State Violence, Local Resistance and the National Question in Nigeria", in Pile S. and M. Keith (eds), *Geography of Resistance*, London: Routledge.

Watts, M., 2001, "Petro-Violence: Community, Extraction, and political Ecology of a Mythic Commodity", in Nancy Lee Peluso and Michael watts (eds), *Violent Environments,* Ithaca: Cornell University Press.

Woods, Emire, 2006, "The Politics of Oil and Poverty". *Pambazuka News 272,* www.pambazuka.org

World Bank, 2006, Today's Challenges on the Chad-Cameroon Pipeline: An Interview with Ali Mahamoud Khadr, World Bank Country Director for Chad. Visit the Chad-Cameroon Oil Pipeline official website.

Yngstrom, Ingrid, 2002, "Women, Wives and Land Rights in Africa: Situating Gender Beyond the Household in the Debate Over Land Policy in Changing Tenure Systems", *Development Studies* 30(1) 2002, *Oxford.*

———, 1999, Gender, land and development in Tanzania: Rural Dodoma, 1920–1996, DPhil Dissertation, University of Oxford.

WEBSITE

http://web.worldbank.org

6

Facing Globalisation
Gender and Land at Stake in the Amazonian Forests of Bolivia, Brazil and Peru

NOEMI MIYASAKA PORRO, LUCIENE DIAS
FIGUEIREDO, ELDA VERA GONZALEZ,
SISSY BELLO NAKASHIMA AND
ALFREDO WAGNER B. DE ALMEIDA

INTRODUCTION

This chapter is about gender relations among people who live in the Amazonian lands of Peru, Bolivia and Brazil, and their experiences in dealing with the impacts of neo-liberal policies on their ways of life. We will particularly examine the connections between gender and land, exploring the workings of global capital on international nuts and vegetable oil markets, and the interactions of people working on extraction of brazil nuts and babaçu kernels. The objective of this chapter is to understand how gender has been negotiated in situations of change in land tenure, and how these negotiations are inter-related to processes of neo-liberalisation of international markets operating globally.

Women, who identify themselves as *castanheiras* and *peladoras,* and *quebradeiras de coco*, gather and peel brazil nuts and break open babaçu fruits, respectively. These identities, embraced by peoples who have endured slavery, de-tribalisation and forced migration, are intrinsically founded on ways of life based on a specific form of labour which they call *trabalho livre*—free labour or work without a boss. *Trabalho livre,* which integrates agriculture and extractive activities, is performed through specific gender relations lived in complex social and natural environments (Kainer and Duryea 1992; Campbell 1996a; Porro 1997 and 2002).

Brazil-nut trees (*Bertholletia excelsa*) are found in the Amazon basin uplands, as emergent trees in species-rich forests, especially in areas managed by indigenous people. Mostly men collect the fruits in the forests to bring them home or take them to processing plants, where mostly women peel the seeds. Brazil nuts are marketed as a sustainable sound rainforest product (Mori 1992). Babaçu palms (*Attalea speciosa*, previously known as *Orbignya phalerata*) constitute 20 million hectares (ha) of equilibrated, continuous secondary growth forests (MIC/STI 1982, Anderson et al. 1991). Babaçu fruits are gathered and kernels are extracted by women and children, who sell the kernels to be used in the oil industry for the production of soap and margarine, among other things. In both cases, men and women work in shifting cultivation, managing agricultural and extractive resources in the forests of their territories. In Peru, Bolivia and Brazil, there were no laws explicitly discriminating against women regarding access to land. Instead, laws and programmes are increasingly incorporating rules related to gender equality. However, as institutionally and culturally most women were perceived as in supporting roles in running their farms, men were still considered by governmental agents and communities as the primary subject entitled to land. While women might have relative control over their own extractive production, men were viewed as the main decision-makers over land in a household perceived as a monolithic unit.

These apparently simple gender divisions of labour and differences in access to, control of and benefits from land were reflections of historically and culturally constructed arrangements, sustaining complex relations within and between social groups with different powers, and between them and nature (Belaunde 1994; Balée 1989; Ingold 1992). In each and every studied situation, groups of women were struggling against gender inequalities, looking for improved social arrangements, within their communities and between them and dominant segments.

Through their struggles, local people have managed to conserve large areas of forests with brazil nut trees (Allegretti 1995; Clay 1997), and extensive babaçu palm forests (Anderson et al. 1991; May 1990) in the Amazon basin, sustaining an estimated number of 500,000 families. Despite these undeniable social, economic and environmental

achievements, forest peoples have been excluded by major agrarian
and economic policies favouring logging, cattle ranching and agri-
business for international commodities production. These policies,
which have been driven by the imperatives of globalisation, and
which have failed to take into account the interests of forest dwellers,
have resulted in wealth and land concentration and environmental
degradation. They have provoked the mobilisation of forest dwellers
in defence of their lands and forest resources (Almeida 1990;
Schmink and Wood 1992; Schmink 1992; Allegretti 1995; Kainer
et al. 2003). Women extracting brazil nuts and babaçu kernels have
actively participated in these collective actions of resistance (Wolf
1999; Lanao 1998; Campbell 1996b; Arnold and Spedding 2005;
Porro 2002.)

Effective access to public resources is quantitatively and quali-
tatively unequal in terms of class and gender in Latin America.
Although in agrarian reforms and settlement projects rules for land
distribution and titling are becoming more equitable in terms of
gender, the actual control and ownership of land by women continues
to be far away from their current legal land rights (Deere and Leon
2001), making them more vulnerable to market uncertainties in
international and national contexts (Kabeer 1994). The increasing
effects of neo-liberal policies on nut and vegetable oil markets has
brought further challenges to gender relations for people living on
extractive activities (Almeida 2001, Shiraishi 2001).

In these situations of changes in land tenure, how has gender been
negotiated? How have these negotiations affected their interactions
in processes of neo-liberalisation of markets operating globally?
Through case studies located in Amazonian forests of Brazil, Bolivia,
and Peru, this chapter intends to trace the relationship between gender
and land, making evident both the specificities of the workings of
global capital and of people's interactions with it.

RESEARCH METHODOLOGY

This research is part of the process launched by the IDRC Gender
Unit's 2001 "Gender, Land and Globalization" call for research
projects. The findings presented in this chapter are based on research

in five sites in three countries, in discontinuous periods of fieldwork, during rainy and dry seasons, between April 2003 and December 2004. The research team consisted of four female researchers (a Peruvian brazil nut gatherer leader, a Bolivian biologist, a Brazilian educator and a Brazilian agronomist-anthropologist) working part-time, with support of a male Brazilian anthropologist consultant.

The site selection was based on a partnership promoted by Women in Informal Employment Globalizing and Organizing (WIEGO) in Bolivia and Peru and by the principal investigator and author in Brazil. It involved several institutions. Each institution chose one co-researcher and one or two sites for this research-action, process, depending on the variation of issues regarding our main themes: gender, land, and globalisation. In Bolivia, in the depart-ment of Pando, the NGO Herencia selected four villages within the Manuripi National Environmental Reserve for Wildlife; and in the department of Beni, the NGO OMED—Organization of Women in Development and the Federation of Factory Workers of Riberalta, selected two brazil-nut processing plants: a brazil-nut alternative cooperative and a large conventional factory. In Peru, in the department of Madre de Dios, the NGO Candela-Peru selected a brazil-nut processing factory and three villages of brazil-nut gatherers, along the dirt road connecting the Peruvian town of Puerto Maldonado to Assis Brasil in Brasil, and three villages along the rivers. In Brazil, the grassroots organisation MIQCB—Inter-state Movement of the Babaçu Breaker Women—selected four villages in the states of Maranhão and Pará. The Rural Workers' Union of Brasiléia, in the state of Acre, selected three communities—one in the Chico Mendes Extractive Reserve, another in Pão de Açucar, a conventional Settlement Project, and the third among squatters in Pindamonhangaba, a village in public land.

The research team carried out data collection through interviews, surveys, participant and direct observation, exchange programmes and international and local workshops. In our research design, a con-sideration was that the authors' own interests and engagement with the research issues would affect the definition and implementation of the research. This brought a specific perspective to the analysis of the results. Warned by the critique about the problems regarding the authoritarian representation of the "other" (Marcus and Fischer 1986) and the risks and contradictions of imperial translations of "other's" narratives (Fine 1994), we applied to ourselves—as researchers and practitioners—the constant exercise of asking the questions proposed by Foucault (1972: 50–55): Who is writing? What kinds of qualifications do we, as authors, have? From which kind of social relations does our enunciation emerge? What are the institutions from which we write? What tools do these institutions provide to us? We offer, therefore, our selection and our reading of field narratives, while positioning our authorship (and, sometimes, translations) as women, married and single mothers, Brazilian, Peruvian, and Bolivian leaders, grassroots practitioners and scholars.

Our research design also integrated research and collective action. Crossing national borders, groups of women babaçu breakers and brazil-nut peelers exchanged simple but concrete experiences of dealing with alternative products and markets, trying to establish partnerships and disseminate information, and lobbying for policy change. Through an exercise designated as "One Hand Washes the Other," men and women shared their knowledge about medicinal plants and soap making. The objective of this and other exercises was to establish an interactive process among Bolivian, Peruvian and Brazilian women participating in this project, aimed at a collective understanding of their diverse situations. Our participation in collective actions carried out by grassroots organisations was designed as part of the methods of data collection, to refine our listening, and to inform our analysis and facilitate devolution of results.

Qualitative data on people's perceptions of research issues were gathered through 128 informal interviews and 12 life histories. The resulting narratives and excerpts of life trajectories were examined not as representations or synthesis of cultural types, but as allegories spelled out by the subjects (Clifford and Marcus 1986:19) "to tell a story" about ways of life, and from these stories, the authors extracted theoretical and practical findings for this research. We also applied quantitative surveys and participant observation and engagement in collective actions as a means to fine-tune and continuously adapt our original research design and data analysis.

Through inception and ending international workshops, and an international exchange field trip among leaders, we aimed to contribute to public policies. The closure of the project activities, in December 2004, occurred at the V Inter-state Meeting of the Quebradeiras de Coco Babaçu, where approximately 260 representatives of women babaçu breakers welcomed eight women Peruvian, Bolivian and Brazilian brazil-nut gatherers. Through a workshop conducted by the leaders participating in the project, the results of the research were shared, discussed in a public space, and presented to authorities and policy makers (MIQCB 2005).

CONCEPTUAL FRAMEWORK

At a start-up workshop at IDRC in Canada, in 2002, which provided the opportunity to engage with conceptual and methodological insights from European, North and Latin American, African and Asian researchers, we were excited by the diversity of approaches and views. We felt we were prepared to take into account the diversity, expect the unexpected, and to listen to differences in the field. We did encounter many diversities. However, we were also shocked to hear women in distinct social movements at different sites in the Amazon, in Bolivia, Peru and Brazil, repeating the exact same words we had read in our books: "Sex is a biological construction! Gender is a social construction! Without gender, no sustainable development!" How was it that a descendant of the Takana Indians in the Manuripi Reserve was saying in Spanish exactly the same words as the black Brazilian babaçu-breaking woman was saying in Portuguese, in Maranhão?

What social construction is gender after all, to be spoken of so uniformly everywhere? How was this "common" discourse formed, broadcast, germinated and intertwined at certain points with notions of sustainable development in the histories of so many peoples? What pre-suppositions did this involve? From which positions and by whom was this first and continuously spelled out, impregnating a homogenising language and history of gender relations in every space to be developed? (Foucault 1972). Do the reverberating slogans and jargons on gender carry the same meanings, goals and effects everywhere, to everyone? Or do they collide with other equally powerful discourses of development being restricted to certain places, certain social groups, and hierarchies of interest? And above all, what local discursive and non-discursive practices do these global discourses of development supplant and displace?

Going to the villages and listening to women at each site, we could observe situations in which women have created the option to really get into the gender discourses of conventionally recognised social movements and the world of NGOs. This option seemed a means to find new ways to deal with relations between men and women, both in domestic and public domains. But there were also situations in which women wanted less intervention and control in the way they were struggling against men, and more support for their struggles against the obstacles to survive with their men. In either case, the uniform discourses on gender as a solution for the malady of under-development somehow superseded any discontinuous or dissonant discourse, presenting all women as a same "Third World woman" speaking about the same gender. These uniform discourses were not present in daily life within the forests and extractive industries. The question here is not whether these discourses are legitimate or not; it is how women are deploying discourses learned from these NGOs, to negotiate their relations with men and other dominant social categories. Furthermore, how have these negotiations interacted with their relations to land in the context of globalisation?

We became aware of the danger of establishing a common language, terminology and concepts of gender for peoples in different situations, in the diverse places of the Amazon. Through our interviews, we realised that much of these uniform discourses had been diffused through the NGOs from the "manuals" of the UN, World Bank and agencies of development and cooperation. Certainly, we all have benefited from insightful concepts and accumulated knowledge emerging from these domains (Moser 1993 and Moser et al. 1999; Overholt et al. 1984). However, to understand how gender relations in the study sites have been negotiated in situations of change in land tenure, we sought a research approach that did not reproduce these discourses as truths. Rather, we recognised them, and identified the genesis and the use of related notions and concepts, analysing them in the light of what we observed in the field. Studies of other situations in Latin America (Alvarez 1990; Alvarez et al. 1998; Caldera 1990) and discussions on gender and global changes (Rakowski 1995; Thomas-Slayter and Rocheleau 1995; Escobar 1995 and 2001) supported our analysis.

In each social situation, interviewees elicited specific social identities and contexts in which gender issues were intertwined with their relationship with lands and forests. This study then became concerned with these gendered social identities, their positioning in the political arena and perceptions of globalisation processes affecting their territories. Gender inequality and exclusion of women from rights to land have been relevant factors in the emergence of these social identities. As we will see in this chapter, these identities will help us to understand how gender has been negotiated in situations of change in land tenure.

NARRATIVES FROM WESTERN RESEARCH SITES

This section focuses on livelihoods in forest-rich environments, where brazil-nut trees abound as emergent trees in primary rainforests. These research sites are located in the western-most extreme of the arc of deforestation (Wood 2002), where Amazonian forests are cut by Peruvian, Bolivian and Brazilian national frontiers. In the context of globalisation, these rich landscapes have been increasingly challenged by cattle ranching and logging, which have been pushed upwards and westwards in the last years by the expansion of soybean plantations (Pacheco 2002; Soares Filho et al. 2006).

These pressures have been intensified by the paving of the Trans-Oceanic highway, planned to connect the Bolivian, Peruvian, and Brazilian Amazonian resources to Asian markets through the Pacific (Brown et al. 2002). Commodities for global markets, such as soybeans, beef and timber—produced in the Amazonian lands and forests—are the main stakes in this expression of globalisation. In all three countries, land markets have been affected along this highway project, and along other interconnected roads. Government investments have mainly focused on integrating markets (IPAM-ISA 2000), thus intensifying competition among forest users.

Researchers have warned that the negative social and environmental effects of economic competition are more far-reaching than the often ineffective social investments, policies and programmes designed to mitigate them (Brown et al. 2002).

In this context, brazil-nut gatherers continue to struggle for their way of life, trying to protect their forests and lands. In addition to threats to their rights to land and forest resources, having to abide by new international regulations and standards has been debilitating for those brazil-nut processing industries which are less prepared for the rigours of the international market. The workings of global capital have pushed people to resistance. In these interactions, their social identities have acquired new meanings.

From rural and urban settings in Brazil, Bolivia and Peru, local people have presented their identities according to their work in the forests: *castañeras, seringueiras, extrativistas* and *zafreras,*[1] and in the factories, *peladoras* and *fabriles,*[2] and also according to their relationship with land, *colonas, concessionárias, comunárias,* and *assentadas.*[3] In the following sections, we examine how each of these identities has been deployed in negotiating gender while struggling for land to resist globalisation. For example, a woman who is a rubber tapper and a colonist with legal rights to agrarian reform lands and access to rubber and brazil-nut trees in a Brazilian Extractive Reserve has more opportunities to participate in grassroots organisations and negotiate gender rights in public spaces. In contrast, a landless *zafrera,* who works as a rural labourer hired to gather brazil nuts during the harvesting season in Bolivia, and then to compete to be hired as a blue-collar nut peeler, has relatively fewer chances to negotiate fairer gender relations. Even so, in either situation, resistance to gender inequalities has manifested itself in women's agency, irrespective of their assumed number of identities.

COMUNÁRIAS: BRAZIL-NUT GATHERERS IN THE MANURIPI WILDLIFE RESERVE, BOLIVIA

Mrs. Roca is sewing a dress for her daughter, who is actually one of the grand-daughters she raises as a daughter, while she tells her history:

...Five years ago ...we had no land to live; the place where we were was a place that our son-in-law had allowed us to stay in and take care of. But then my son came here and told us he had found a land for us, so we left the place of our son-in-law and here we are...My husband still gathers brazil nuts and we work on our chaco[4] together. When I was younger, we used to work together, gathering brazil nuts as zafreros. We went to the forests to gather and bring heavy loads of nuts home and put them out to dry in the sun. We had to work for barraqueros all the time. My son died on this land because of an accident with gunfire. But before dying, he was the one to first come here and find this land for us... Now I am a comunária... When my son died, my husband wanted to leave this land, but I said no, because it cost too much to our son to reach this land and there was too much of his work here, and I will never abandon this land. ... My 14–year-old daughter wants to marry, and I do not agree, but my husband says it is better for her to marry before she gets pregnant. She may escape once, but...so he says; this is his opinion. I want my daughter to study, she is still a girl! But my husband gave his permission for her to marry; I had no alternative but to accept... When my son was shot, I was in the forests. At that time, we lived in the forests, but now we live closer to the village because of our daughters' studies. (Maria Gomez Roca, 52 years old, interviewed by Sissy Bello, biologist co-researcher, 8 April 2003)

Mrs Roca identifies herself as one of the so-called *comunárias* in the Manuripi National Reserve for Wildlife[5]. Her identity as *comunária* reaffirms her free access to land and her hard earned freedom against the *barraqueros*, who have exploited her family in their past as *zafreros*. However, unlike her husband, she still does not have formal rights to the 500 ha assigned by the government to those associated with the OTB.[6] She lives on the extraction of brazil nuts and slash-and-burn shifting cultivation, through *chacos*. These shifting gaps opened in the forests are typically used by *campesinos*, peasants, in contrast with the pastures permanently opened by *barraqueros*, who although no longer have legal rights to land and forests, still dominate large public areas, using their seasonal labourers, the *zafreros*.[7]

However, even as a *comunária*, in her current situation, price instability and dependency on unfair commercial practices by *barraqueros* threaten the only source of maintenance for Mrs Roca's family during the months in-between the agricultural harvests. Every year, for three and a half months, entire families leave the village to gather nuts in their *centros castañeros* (lands with brazil-nut trees assigned to each family.) Then, they transport the nuts by mules to the roads, delivering these to the *barraqueros*, who send them to the processing plants by boats and trucks.[8]

Mrs Roca's narrative was illustrative of three important aspects of this study on gender and land, which were recurrent in the systematic data collection of observed social situations in all the other research sites. First, the subject of the narrative, the social actor relating the history of the family was a grandmother. At all sites, we observed a significant number of women in charge of coordinating three or four generations of their extended household units.[9] To these women, who have in situations of resource scarcity and land deprivation taken command of the family, relations with husbands may be as relevant as those with their eldest sons. Therefore, unlike most western feminist studies which focus on husband-wife relations, gender relations along inter-generational, vertical lines can be as significant as along matrimonial, horizontal lines.

Secondly, the narrative confirms that there is a breaking away from the conventional notion of the household as a unit, perceiving and accessing land in a monolithic fashion. Social situations in which men and women have different perceptions and practices towards land were registered at all sites. Mrs Roca established her connection to the land on the basis of how much work was done on it, and not necessarily as per the legal rights or conditions of land markets. The recognition of these differences is important because it may open doors to new changes. By standing against her husband, to fight for that specific land acquired by her son, Mrs Roca was breaking the established cultural norms regulating decision-making power over land. Would legal rights to land for Mrs Roca help her in her struggle to raise her daughter as she wants? Would actual rights to land empower women to better negotiate new forms of gender relations for their daughters and sons, breaking the prevalent notion that women *"can escape once"*, but not always? According to Datta (2007), the answer is yes. Although there is no biological determination on it, women have presented a rational and strategic attachment to their places, as a response to "the patriarchal, unequal and conflict-ridden world in which women find themselves". Therefore, "joint property rights increase women's participation in decision making, their access to knowledge and information about public matters, their sense of security, self-esteem, and also the respect they receive from their spouses" (2007:288,293). The answers by women living in Bolivian forests and lands are still a work-in-progress, but one must recognise that the step Mrs Roca took, to reconstruct her identity from *zafrera* to that of *comunária*, was a step closer to achieving further rights, including rights to fairness in gender relations in her way of life.

Third, Mrs Roca expressed her perception of land not only in material terms. By recalling their son's journey to find and work the land, thus transforming it into their land, she was restating the concept of the social construction of land, that is, land understood as territory. As a background scenario for her narrative, there is a whole set of political struggles for land between *campesinos* and *barraqueros*. Her son accessed that land in a context dominated by powerful *barraqueros* and weak governments. In this scenario, access to land by lower rated *zafreros* was viewed as a political achievement, celebrating their freedom against the patron. Therefore, when Mrs. Roca left her identity as *zafrera* and built her new identity as *comunária* by struggling for her territory, both at family and societal levels, she gave political meaning to land and to her own gender. She was no longer a *zafrero's* wife. She carried out a process that led to the emergence of a new woman, a woman who wanted new gender relations and who, being a member of a community, stands for her land. In this sense, although Mrs Roca had attended some meetings for women's groups promoted by NGOs, their discourses were far removed from her own life and her struggles with her husband's decisions over their land and daughter's future. In spite her efforts to provide formal education for her children, schooling as offered by the government has not been effective in changing gender relations for the future generation. Therefore, gender has been negotiated quite apart from non-governmental and governmental efforts to change gender inequalities. Instead, attachment to land as a *comunária* is what has provided new basis for the construction of the woman she is becoming and gender relations she is establishing.

All the three above mentioned aspects are enmeshed in contexts where gender and land are central elements of new social, political and gendered identities. However, gender justice is not an automatic and direct by-product of women's access to land, as these identities have been gestated along a troubled trajectory and were born to face resilient contexts of domination. In lands and forests such as those of the Manuripi reserve, starting still in the 19th century, as rubber trees became an attraction for national and international investors,[10] family-owned enterprises named *Casas* (Houses), established a powerful and extensive system of extractive production and commercialisation. These entrepreneurs established numerous posts for the recollection of rubber and trade in food and supplies, the so-called *barracas*, throughout the lowland forests of Bolivian Amazon. There were similar developments in the Peruvian and Brazilian forests.

The patriarchs of these Houses sent immigrant labourers to extract latex from the rubber trees spread throughout the forests of Pando, all immobilised by a chain of credit and debt. As the Houses defined the prices of supplies and the amount paid for the extracted rubber (and later brazil nuts), the labourers were consistently in debt. The term slavery, referring to this situation, is used even today, as permanent oppression and even violence have been applied to keep the order imposed even in far-off places throughout the forest.

> He [barraquero] used to say: You, do this. I am going to pay you this or that. And that was it. We were slaves. (Don Firmino, 52 years old)

> Because, in past years … and even in the last year, we, the peasants, were like when one presses something with an iron, like ironing a dough, shattering it completely… that was how we were, because they [barraqueros] spoke more and louder than we did, because we were placed at the margins. (Don David, 45 years old)

In the early 1980s, hunger and the weight of debt led to a decade-long process of mobilisation among *campesinos* of different origins and ethnicities brought to the area. By 1986, in the final stages of the last rubber crisis, the *barraqueros* had their economic power increasingly weakened. Concurrently, peasants' mobilisation also reached a peak.

As a result, the National Colonization Institute and the Agrarian Reform National Council finally recognised *campesinos"* rights and expropriated *barraqueros* of their domains. On this occasion, the government resumed, more than a decade later, the matters of Manuripi as a protected area. Peasants hoped that *"the time of slavery had finally ended,"* and each *campesino* family attained the right to access 500 ha of land.

The *barraqueros,* however, did not leave the land. Instead, they promptly replaced rubber with brazil nuts as a means to maintain their domains and create new forms of labour relations termed by *campesinos* as slavery. Although by law *barraqueros* were no longer supposed to have access to any land in the reserve, they remained in the area. At each and every harvesting season, these former bosses would recruit landless *zafreros* to gather brazil nuts for them. This provoked conflicts between *zafreros* and *comunários*, as the bosses of the former ordered invasions of the latter's lands. Although NGOs and agencies of cooperation have invested in some economic initiatives aimed at biodiversity, environmental conservation and social progress, the results have been far from satisfactory. In spite of all the battles fought over decades, *comunários* found that they still had to face corrupt governments, unlawful private sector activities and weak communities. *Barraqueros* were able to maintain their access to forest resources through their control of social, political and financial capital.

> Last year, he (a peasant) was expelled by Alvarado (a barraquero), threatened with firearms. At the beginning of this year, he again entered the same area, very trustful this time because the government had placed stones as landmarks to define the boundaries of the community's land. But the Alvarados just uprooted the stones and threw them away, saying they were worth nothing. The barraqueros are invading the community's lands like always. We made a complaint about this to the authorities, but without results. They (Alvarados) put the money on the table and nothing happens to them. This is because, in Chivé, if one of us has problems, nobody cares. (Don Juán, 66 years old)

Today, struggles like those of Mrs Roca and Don Juán face new challenges set by globalisation. They know that the construction of the Trans-Oceanic highway has intensified changes in land markets in the entire region. This highway was planned to connect Amazonian lands and forest resources in Brazil, Peru and Bolivia to the Peruvian port of Ica and, from there, to Asian markets, through the Pacific. On the one hand, an intense process of privatisation of lands cut by inter-connecting roads has been put in motion. On the other, the awkward, old-fashioned *barraca* system co-exists with and is sustained today by modern processing industries linked to the international market.

One emblematic example, the modern all-computerised, export-oriented Tahuamano industry, located in the town of Cobija, had its raw material produced through labour relations referred by the interviewees as similar to those of the "time of slavery", in contexts where 95 per cent of the *campesinos* were below the poverty line. Alvarado also sold brazil nuts to the Tahuamano[11] industry. This exceptional, 12–year-old factory, located in the city of Cobija, had the most advanced technology in terms of nut processing. Tahuamano did not intend to get land ownership, but instead financed trucks or tractors and capital for both *barraqueros* and producers in exchange for the promised nuts. They preferred to focus on processing, delegating extraction and collection to producers and middlemen. Also, high technology allowed the processing of 4,000 hectolitres into high export quality nuts with only 300 direct employees. According to its engineer, interviewed in 2003, Tahuamano processed 25 per cent of the entire Bolivian production, and dominated 75 per cent of the world market for processed nuts. This champion in the global market managed to do all these without any land claims or agrarian conflicts. However, they sustained situations like Alvarados in the reserve.

The engineer affirmed: "*I can control each and every part of this processing plant with the touch of my finger.*" Fingers clean of earth. All the modernity, efficiency, detachment from land and sense of free and clean competition in an impartial market were, however, contradicted by the backwardness of the situation narrated by Don Juan. Sustaining the entire productive chain, a combination of inefficient state, outlaw entrepreneurship, careless consumers and weak communities fed an international "green" market avid for "ecological" products. It is interesting to note how these ecological products have become an integral part of the same global market ruled by commodities such as soy, timber and beef, which were destroying the forests and peoples where they came from. Even the production of brazil nuts in the current intensity and scale of extraction, and agrarian conditions may become unsustainable (Peres et al. 2003; Mori 1992). Therefore, the globalising Trans-Oceanic highway, now crossing either privatised or reserved Amazonian lands, intensified tensions among stakeholders with very unequal powers. These tensions constrained progress towards gender justice and were intensified where competition for resources was greater, exposing differences between *comunárias* and landless peelers,[12] as described in the next narrative. Although Mrs. Roca had not been able to better negotiate gender with her husband, for her daughter's sake, the fact that she was a *comunária* gave her more grounded opportunities as compared to landless women who were economically more vulnerable.

PELADORAS: LANDLESS BRAZIL-NUT PEELERS IN AN ALTERNATIVE TRADE ORGANISATION, PERU

Sarah, a former homeless street dweller child and now a single mother of three, talks about life as a brazil-nut peeler in Peru, stating her identity up front:

> I speak as a peladora, nut peeler. I am from Cusco and arrived at Puerto Maldonado when I was 11 years old. I remained for three months with a local family and after that, I left [that family,] and was alone. When I was 16 years old, I began to have a family myself. I have been peeling nuts since very early in my life. First, I worked at Exporter La Selva and learned to peel nuts. We had social benefits at that time. Then, I worked at Protesa factory. We were organised in a union, and we began to earn benefits as we all deserve. We underwent a hunger strike. The police came and we all ran in fear…We detained the factory administrator as a prisoner. We attained some benefits, but only until the year of 1989… When Fujimori won elections, they no longer wanted to pay for our benefits…I went to the Ministry of Labour, I went to the police and

nothing…For four years, when the factories began to close down, we left [the factory, the city] to work together with the zafreros [nut gatherers in the forests], …Then, Candela [an alternative trade organisation] showed up, and it has lasted for eight years… We did not have benefits when it started. Many women were single mothers, out of 120 women, 40 did not have a husband. For eight years at Candela, we did not have benefits. Only this year, with the fair trade, they are paying social security. They need better quality nuts, and this demands more work, and that is why they improved our gains. (Sarah M, interviewed by the first author in collaboration with Peruvian co-researcher Elda Vera Gonzalez)

Like many families and individuals with their lives disrupted by the fragmentation of family farms in the Highlands, Sarah was sent to the Amazonian Lowlands. By the time she arrived, the Land Reform launched in 1969 by President Velasco Alvarado had already divided up those large brazil-nut concessions of 10,000 ha and more into 10 parts, distributing them to small producers. However, *"very few women benefited directly through the agrarian reform, primarily because beneficiaries were required to be household heads over eighteen years of age with dependents"* (Deere and Leon 2001: 90). In addition, single women without dependents, and teenagers like Sarah, without male partners who could transport brazil nuts on their backs, were not able to access *habilito*, credit. Without it, they were not only excluded from rights to land, but it was impossible for them to access forest resources through a concession. Therefore, the only opportunity for single women, teenagers and children was in the processing stages of this economy.

The period in which unions were strong, as narrated by Sarah, corresponds to the period in which president Alan Garcia had intended to decentralise the government. The Women Brazil-nut Shellers Union, once representing 400 women, was so important at that time that its leader was one of the representatives of the Inka section, one of the 11 regional governments (Lanao 1998). When Fujimori assumed his mandate, the Peruvian economy as a whole was in crisis for several reasons. As neo-liberal policies impacted the brazil-nut economy, the workers' strikes described by Sarah just catalysed the end of the brazil-nut businesses, as they were known until the early 1990s.

In the following years, medium and small enterprises and the Alternative Trade Organization Candela resumed part of the business in Puerto Maldonado, trying to adjust themselves to international market demands (Collinson et al. 2000). Among these demands, the enforcement of international quality standards has had a significant impact on the lives of brazil-nut peelers (EC 2003). Ever since the European Union determined the maximum level of *aflatoxin* in brazil nuts as 4 ppb,[13] brazil-nut processing factories in the three producing countries began to invest on procedures to meet the standards. However, much of the burden of these quality improvements has fallen on the peelers as they now have to take care of quality and not the quantity, while still being paid according to the quantity of nuts they process.

In addition to the challenges of meeting new international quality standards, the collection stage of the brazil-nut productive chain has been affected by critical problems of land use conflicts (GRADE 1998). Agrarian titles have been granted by the Peruvian government to *campesinos* working on agriculture, on the same lands previously granted as brazil-nut concessions to *castañeros*. After 10, 20 or even 40 years gathering nuts in the same concession, *castañeros* have begun to lose their rights, since titling is a stronger legal instrument than a concession. Logging and agriculture have displaced extractive activities and more than 500 brazil-nut concession holders are facing the loss of their access to land and forests due to the weaknesses of their land stakes and allocation of their land to other users (Leguia 2004).

Consequently, the entire brazil-nut productive chain in Peru has been affected, changing the scenarios for both men and women. Regarding the landless women peelers who live in urban neighbourhoods around the processing factories, Sarah's narrative illustrates their fragile relation to land:

> I rent a small piece of land where I plant beans, maize and many other things. I rent this land from the Peruvian Air Force. They have this land, where they do not do anything. I plant all my things and then I pay them back with my products.

Ironically, this former street dweller child, stranded wife, single mother and low-income nut peeler not only feeds her family, but also makes a contribution to the table of the Peruvian Air Force. Raising chickens, pigs, and vegetables in their yards, exchanging services and goods with landowners, share-cropping or renting land, these women peelers have managed to informally access some of the benefits of the land. However, it is notorious how macro policies have increased the fragility of their connection to the land, and made this group highly vulnerable to the impacts of globalisation.

In these situations in which land is at stake, identities founded on relations to land and forests are reaffirmed, but gender has been negotiated with little bargaining power within the household and between the women and society. *Peladoras, concessionárias, colonas,* and *castañeras* present themselves as women in charge of reproductive and productive spheres and continue to fight for their rights to land.

Another important point to recall is that resistance based on these identities, besides being expressed through mobilisation by formal organisations, may also be expressed at family and community levels. Sarah's invisible achievements on her little piece of rented land, multiplied by the achievements of thousands of women just like her, should not be minimised. The terms of land renting were informal and unstable, the payment through a percentage of produced vegetables was negotiated at each harvest, yet, it was this production that complemented her earnings at the brazil-nut processing plant to secure her livelihood. While her achievements might have been irrelevant in terms of statistics, they were what fed her children and made her the woman, the *peladora*, she had become. In the context of globalisation, these achievements have not been accomplished either by governments or by the brazil-nut industrials. Therefore, her identity as *peladora* did not only mean that she was an employee of a brazil-nut factory, but reaffirmed her achievements and her future struggles.

NARRATIVES FROM EASTERN SITES

In this section, we will leave the forest-rich environments of the western sites at the tri-national frontiers of the previous sections and focus on the eastern extreme of the Amazon, where forest-poor sites with babaçu palm secondary forests abound. We will learn about the so-called *quebradeiras de coco*, women babaçu breakers. Babaçu palm forests constitute 20 million ha of secondary growth. In many areas now covered by babaçu palm forests, the devastated primary forests were previously composed of populations of brazil nut as emergent trees. Therefore, several of the women babaçu breakers in the state of Pará had gathered brazil nuts when they were younger.

In these landscapes, where primary forest resources have been depleted, a process beginning in the colonial times and intensifying in the last few decades imposed changes in land cover and tenure. Although highly homogeneous, the babaçu palm forests were in an equilibrated second climax and are home to traditional communities of babaçu breakers. However, currently, in spite of this second chance offered by nature, these forests named by biologists as "the subsidy of nature" (Anderson et al. 1991), have been threatened by pastures and plantations owned by cattle ranchers and entrepreneurs.

The low diversity and scarce forest resources have not been attractive to environmentalists and donors focused on biodiversity. However, these secondary forests provide the basis for the livelihoods of a peasantry formed by the descendants of enslaved Africans, de-tribalised Indians, and displaced migrants. More than 300,000 families in the states of Maranhão, Pará, Tocantins and Piauí live on babaçu. Babaçu fruits are gathered and kernels extracted by children and women, who sell the kernels to be used in the oil industry for production of soap and margarine, among other things. Men direct as well as work in agricultural activities of slash-and-burn shifting cultivation, together with women and children.

These gendered labour relations assure the material and symbolic significance of *roça*, the agricultural fields planted in patches of slashed forests as a foundation of this agro-extractive system of production. Similar to *chaco* in Bolivia, a successful *roça* expresses the freedom and autonomy of the household as a unit of production and consumption within a context dominated by powerful landlords. *Roça* is also the result of good social relations within the community, as certain stages demand inter-family collective work.

Most of the social mobilisation carried out by *quebradeiras* was around the defence of the babaçu palms and the right to plant a *roça*. Among these families, the nexus between gender and land varied tremendously, and in this section we will contrast two situations. The first was a site in the central portion of the state of Maranhão, in the Mearim valley, where a set of grassroots associations and unions from eight municipalities come together to form a common association named ASSEMA—Association in Settlement Areas in the State of Maranhão. Since 1989, ASSEMA has been one of the most vocal and visible forms of social organisations in the State. The second situation was in the southeast of the state of Pará, where landless women babaçu breakers survived on degraded lands, extracting kernels from scattered palms. After an effervescent period of political struggles and mobilisation in the 1980s and early 1990s, these women were now apparently facing a prolonged period of social demobilisation. The two sites were linked through the Inter-state Movement of the Women Babaçu Breakers—MIQCB.

In the study situation, highlighting the differences and commonalities between these two eastern site cases has provided insights into how gender has been negotiated in diverse situations of change in land tenure. The expression of globalisation observed in this case is the impact of the expansion of deforestation-based commodities such as beef and soy beans and palm oil, the latter nationally produced in large plantations of oil palm (*Elaeis guineensis*), in addition to the competition imposed by the import of palm oil from Malaysia.

QUEBRADEIRAS, BABAÇU BREAKER WOMEN: COLLECTIVE STRUGGLES FOR LAND FACE NEW CHALLENGES IN THE GLOBAL MARKET, STATE OF MARANHÃO, BRAZIL

> I began to break babaçu nuts at age of ten…At that time, we had plenty of chickens and pigs and our crops were enough for us to eat and to sell. There were lands for all. Today, we cannot raise our animals because there is no longer wood to make fences. Before, it took eight years to plant a crop again in the same place, and today, just after two years we have to slash the same place….who first had the right to Centrinho

village's land was a woman named Alice. However, she granted her right to a son. Now all her sons are big men. And she still takes care of four grandchildren, all of them break babaçu. …

When my great-grandfather arrived at Centrinho, the land was free and the babaçu palms were available to all. However, at a certain point in time, Luís Vieira [cattle rancher] began to plant pastures inside the village's land, and João Horesta [another cattle rancher] began to say that the babaçu palms were his own property. They became fazendeiros [owners of a cattle ranch or landlords; in this case, land grabbers]. These and other men started to claim ownership of the land and forests. They even forced people to return babaçu kernels extracted from the lands they claimed as theirs. Many of our men left for gold mining.

In the beginning of this struggle, we were forced to share half of the kernels produced with the people who claimed to be landlords. Women were prohibited from making charcoal-holes to burn babaçu husks. They supervised us all the time. They start to slash the palms to plant pastures, saying there were too many palms. Everything [resistance in defence of land and forests] started because of babaçu palms. It was either in 1983 or 1984. I remember it was in the dry season, at a time when they would slash the palms and plant pastures. The former "owner" had sold our land to a new landlord.

We sent a letter to this new landlord saying that we did not want them to slash our palms. He came to talk, but we did not reach an agreement with him. Then, his brother came with gunmen and humiliated our men. He was like on drugs, like a devil. Their cowboy was also very mean, and did not allow women to make charcoal on the lands the landlord claimed as his. One day, Felé [a woman babaçu breaker from that village] entered the forest to get babaçu and make charcoal. The cowboy found her and told her to move and make charcoal in another place.

She told him that she did not know where she could do that. [Later she told us that] she did not know whether it was the devil, or whether it was the beast which had made her say unusual things, but she got mad and yelled at him that if he did not allow her to make the charcoal-hole in that place, he was to open his ass hole because she would burn the charcoal right inside his ass. The cowboy got so scared that he left and no longer prohibited women from making charcoal. That land still belongs [legally] to that owner, but babaçu gathering in these lands is free for all, and we managed to obtain another land for ourselves. (Sebastiana Siqueira, babaçu breaker woman from Centrinho village)

Centrinho was one of many peasant villages throughout the state of Maranhão that had experienced conflicts between peasants and powerful land grabbers who wanted to expropriate their labour, land and forest resources, which constitute the foundations of their way of life. Centrinho was a centre-piece for awakening more than 15 villages and changing power relations in the municipality of Lago do Junco. As a result of this social movement, local associations and cooperatives were founded. Joining with other grassroots organisations, they formed regional and even inter-state organisations such as ASSEMA and MIQCB. The Agro-extractive Cooperative of Lago do Junco is a successful example, completing 16 years of uninterrupted activities with monetary and social benefits for its members. Another example is the Association of Rural Women Workers of Lago do Junco, which has completed 19 years of intense work on social mobilisation. After regaining access to land, they experimented with organic, unburned *roças*, and carried out projects with essential oils and medicinal plants. They were commercialising babaçu oil, starch, and handcrafted soaps and paper, in the national and international markets, through alternative fair trade partners such as AVEDA, the Body Shop, and Pacific Sensuals, thus occupying a "green" visibility niche.

In terms of political representation, there were visible advances in this example from the municipality of Lago do Junco. The movement that emerged from the villages managed to elect six city commissioners in the last three governments (among them one woman), and successfully put forward a municipal secretary of agriculture. A massive presence of the movement in the City Hall also forced changes in the municipal organic law regarding environmental regulations, protecting the babaçu palm and allowing free access to babaçu even on private properties, the so called "Free Babaçu Law" (municipal law number 005/97).[14]

The visibility of these movements has fomented further changes, both formal and informal. As every public position and every public job was contested in the party politics space, the movement challenged the monopoly of formal public employment by the dominant local elites. This confrontation was especially important in the case of the employment of elementary school teachers, and women played an active role in the selection of those they believed were better for their children.

In addition, the spreading of the "Free *Babaçu* Law," an informal practice of free access to *babaçu,* even on private property, has benefited people beyond the boundaries of the local social movement.[15] The same happened with *empates,* a pacifist practice of stopping the devastation of the palms. The Ministry of Environment called them to make a video of their movement in defence of the palm forests, and its coverage in the media increased considerably. In the last few years, this movement has been on three major TV channels, and has been the subject of articles in magazines of national circulation such as Marie Claire, Veja, Globo Rural, and Cláudia among others, as well as in the main national newspapers. Changes were indeed underway, although not as per the quality and speed desired by the women and men involved, who have opted to further foment these transformations.

These struggles for gender equality and rights to land and forests were facing new challenges related to globalisation. As one of the most relevant expressions of globalisation affecting babaçu economy, the entrance of the Malaysian palm oil in the Brazilian market for vegetable oils provoked profound changes in the babaçu oil productive chain. Most of the babaçu palm oil processing industries in the states of Pará, Tocantins and Piauí had to close their doors, and only a few, more competitive ones remained in the state of Maranhão.

On the one hand, the reduction in the number of industries had interrupted babaçu gathering in large areas, affecting thousands of families who were left without economic alternatives. On the other, for those who had reached a level of mobilisation and integration into markets, especially "green" markets, business intensified. However, even these niches of "green" visibility were not exempt from the broader impacts of globalisation.

Our research among the *quebradeiras* made us aware that, similar to the situation of the brazil-nut gatherers in Bolivia, in addition to the modern transnational entrepreneurs of the oil markets, the same old antagonistic actors such as *fazendeiros,* cattle ranchers and land grabbers were at large. In the context of globalisation, these external threats have impacts and provoke ruptures within social categories. This phenomenon may be expressed by the way members of communities adopt new forms of consumerism and imported systems of production, disrupting the dynamics of their own trajectories as a people. Sebastiana from Centrinho illustrates these through the effects of the global demand for beef on the negotiations over gender relations within her community. She continues her narrative:

> Today, our problem is not so much with landlords, but with ourselves. That land, for which we struggled so much, which was so hard to get… There was a meeting in our local village association, to discuss what to do with our land. Some wanted to slash everything and plant pastures to breed cattle on it, because the income would be greater than waiting [the forest to grow again and slash] to plant a roça. In the meeting, this was the idea that prevailed. But João [interviewee's husband] did not accept it. After the meeting, he convinced Antonio Leite [leader who was not present at the meeting]. Among the women who are associated, but who have husbands, only Antonia always attends the meetings. Curta, Maroquinha, Antonia and Dominga [women] were against cattle. But Felé [the same woman who faced the cowboy] stood by her husband Doquinha; and Doquinha wanted to slash everything and plant pastures [and had threatened to leave her otherwise]. Women who were not in the meeting were against the planting of pasture. They wanted to plant roça there. Our argument was that we had fought for the land to plant roça and, all in a sudden, people came with this proposal of everything turning into pastures? In the end, the opinion of letting everything remain as it was prevailed, to let the bushes grow again, to plant roça later. But, until today, João has problems, because he was the one against the first proposal that had won at that meeting.
>
> In the beginning of everything, our fight started because of the babaçu nuts, but today, the men are slashing too many palms. In the last roças they planted, they slashed so many palms. My father-in-law slashes too many palms, all men do… When the women complain, they say that

we do not know what we are saying. Zezinho e Luis Preto are the ones who slash more palms, but the women will not denounce them [to the governmental environment defence office]. They fight at home. Zezé's husband does not slash as many palms as before, because she turns into a beast when she knows her husband has slashed palms.

This is something that is very hard. We [women who participated in the social movements] are working our ways to not burning the forests to plant our roças. We are studying and making experiments on how to plant in a way that we can save the palms, but they say this [planting without burning] is a madman's story. This idea does not enter their heads. The women babaçu breakers will not disappear because there are palms throughout the pastures. Now, on the cattle ranchers' pastures are the places where we can still find palms. But in places where we plant roças, palms are disappearing.

In the neighbouring village of Centro dos Aguiar, Doninha, wife of Lata's landlord, began to hire outsider labourers to gather all the babaçu for her, and she wanted to dominate all the forests up to Aguiar. And she ordered the hired men to transport the babaçu on a truck to the town of Lago do Junco. Then, our people started to make a movement and made a blockade to stop the truck. They prohibited the truck to pass and the women ordered the hired men to drop the whole load on the road. The landlord complained to the police and a meeting was called. During the meeting, he argued that in the places where our husbands plant roças, the land is becoming like a field, clean of palms. In this moment, we lost our strength and spirit. (Sebastiana Siqueira, woman babaçu breaker and leader, 2003).

Beef has been one of the most significant of commodities ruled by the global market, affecting Amazonian lands (Margulis 2004). Both big cattle ranchers and small beef farmers have been engaged in unsustainable practices that changed local people's relations to land and forest resources and threatened their ways of life based on *roça* and babaçu breaking. By slashing the palms, "the mother of the people", men were destroying not only the physical, but also the social means of their reproduction as a unique people. And as Sebastiana alerts, "*in this moment, we lost our strength and spirit.*" At moments like these, when land has been at stake, gender is negotiated, not between biologically defined sexes, but between socially constructed men and women. In this negotiation, the socially constructed woman assumed a specific identity, the *quebradeira*, a politically constructed identity imbued with the strength and spirit of her people's history of relations with their lands, forests and territory.

This strength and spirit, which gave origin to so many formal grassroots organisations and recognised social movements, was present when women introduced themselves as *quebradeiras de coco babaçu* to the public at large. However, as Sebastiana noted, this identity, that had been assumed at TV shows, in their demands to authorities, in public spaces, must also be present in community and domestic spaces. The lesson learned from Sebastiana's narrative is that, in the context of globalisation, the results of negotiations of gender depend on struggles carried out simultaneously in both public and domestic arenas. The success of such negotiations depends on how well both dimensions are integrated.

Therefore, although both Mrs Roca in Bolivia and Sebastiana in Brazil had access to land, their negotiations of gender presented clear differences. Sebastiana, as part of her social mobilisation, brought gender issues to the public table, in contrast with Mrs Roca, who had kept the issues at the domestic level. Sebastiana's daughter was likely to have more opportunities to make better choices than Mrs. Roca's daughter. This pattern, however, should not lead us to disregard the interaction between agency and social conditions. In addition to the need to integrate the public and domestic dimensions, there is a third aspect to consider. At this point of the social movements' trajectories, it is necessary to keep one eye focused on the visible and the expected, both in the public and domestic spheres and also to look for what has been made invisible to us. Are there struggles, either public or private, aimed at new constructions of gender that are still invisible to us; accounts made invisible to us not only by the *fazendeiros*, industrials and governments associated with globalisation efforts, but also by the recognised organisations and movements?

Our fieldwork allowed us to observe many strategies at family and community levels that were clearly effective in terms of progress towards equity in gender relations and access to land. However, these were not being recognised either by the supporters of the social movements or the public in general. The social construction of a *quebradeira* might occur in struggles in daily life, at family and community levels, therefore, the identity of *quebradeira* cannot be erased by the general label of "poor" only because they do not participate in recognised social movements such as MIQCB, ASSEMA and others. Although invisible to us, they defined the spirit and the strength with which gender was negotiated. And though this kind of social mobilisation and negotiations were not recognised yet, their existence was clear. People were struggling each year for their *roças* and practising *trabalho livre* (free labour, work without a boss, peasant type of labour relations) according to ways of life that confronted the dominant modes. The census numbers (IBGE 2006) show that their existence is not a given, but a struggle against landlessness, insecure relations to the means of production, and socially and environmentally unfavourable conditions.

The large numbers of people outside the recognised social movements are by no means disqualified by this. Rather, their desperate conditions reinforce the legitimacy of their invisible social movements. In the context of globalisation, in which land tenure is at stake, gender has been negotiated at community and family levels through a myriad counteractions that are still invisible to us. Women are leading these invisible struggles in the margins of the recognised movements. Our fieldwork in the villages taught us that a multiplicity of trajectories are lived by protagonists with defined identities, in accordance with unique ways of life based on *trabalho livre*, and daily battles to access rights to land, demarcating a territory of tremendous resistance.

In the next section, we will describe the trajectory of Mariana Lino, who lives in the southeast part of the state of Pará, who did not belong to any recognised, formal social organisation or movement. Her conditions of existence and her struggles validate family-based forms of mobilisation and resistance which might not be visible to the public eye.

MARIANA LINO, AN UNCONCEALED FIGHTER FOR THE *QUEBRADEIRAS*, STATE OF PARÁ, BRAZIL

Walking around the dusty outskirts of the urban perimeter of Palestina, one can be surprised by a rich grove of trees right at the end of its last dirt street. The little town of Palestina is located in the basin of the Araguaia River, south of the Brazilian state of Pará. The region was once an important site for brazil-nut production. Actually, throughout the last century, most of the brazil-nut consumed in the world came from these lands. However, road construction, a sequence of economic cycles involving cattle ranching, mining, logging and slash-and-burn agriculture, high wealth and land concentration and the deforestation that followed, put an end to the brazil-nut business in the region[16] (Schmink and Wood 1992; Guerra 2001).

After primary forests were slashed, babaçu palms emerged as part of the secondary growth, often constituting extensive, homogenous, but ecologically stable palm forests. However, in southern Pará, not even "the mother of the people" has been spared. The palm forests that emerged have been continuously slashed; and remaining tracts of palm forests are under threat. Today, extensive, poorly managed pastures with scattered palms dominate the landscape. The few sawmills here keep processing the logs brought in from increasingly distant primary forests. Hopelessness, as a result of economic, environmental, and social degradation was consistently encountered in observations and interviews in Palestina.

So, approaching this oasis on the edge of this town surrounded by pastures, one was intrigued by a gracious, newly painted little Catholic chapel in honour of Saint Francis of Assis. As an additional surprise, right beside it, another neat, colourful little construction stands by. It is a temple in honour of Saint Barbara, one of the most important deities of *terecô*, one of the expressions of a religious syncretism of African origin in Brazil. While observing the birds attracted by palms, fruit trees, and fresh water from a surprisingly clean water stream, one may have the chance to meet dona Mariana Lino. She is a descendant of slaves brought to work on cotton and, later, sugarcane plantations in the neighbouring state of Maranhão. After abolition of slavery, her family joined waves of former slaves and Northeastern migrants, composing a unique peasantry, who spread southward and westward, in search of lands and work free of landlords (Droulers and Maury 1980).

Dona Mariana has survived the diverse whirlwinds of policies that periodically sweep Amazonian societies and economies. One after the other, rubber, brazil nuts, cattle, timber, babaçu, among others, were economic cycles which formed an integral part of her saga. In the 1970s, when mobilisation against the military dictatorship in Brazil was being crushed in urban settings in southern states, the Communist Party chose the region to promote the famous "Guerrilla of Araguaia" (Schmink and Wood 1992). Dona Mariana recalls the "people of the forest," as the peasants named the guerrilla activists who once lived among them and, when the military persecution started, needed to hide in the forests. (In contrast, peasants often refer to themselves as "people of the *roça,*" in reference to their shifting cultivation.) These party activists and many peasants who joined or simply helped them, were summarily assassinated by the military. Years of development investments that followed the massacre could not erase these military actions and suspicion against the government. Terrifying remembrances emerged in the interviews. Dona Mariana Lino's ways of living survived all these. The military were gone and she and her family were still right on their land.

In the 1980s and early 1990s, dona Mariana watched the Catholic Church link to the Theology of Liberation, agencies of cooperation, NGOs, and professionals linked to the University, investing in social organisation and mobilisation among peasants. An intensive and vast mobilisation resulted in several struggles for agrarian reform and implementation of settlement projects. Research and development projects, aiming at better production, conservation and political mobilisation, involved several communities in the region (Guerra 2001; Cruz Neto and Maia Neto 2002). In the early 1990s, women mobilised at a regional level, and some representatives began to participate in the Inter-state Movement of Women Babaçu Breakers, joining leaders from four Brazilian states in their struggles for land reform and conservation of babaçu palms. A cooperative and a special system of rural education were implemented, in addition to promoting women's groups and greater participation in party politics.

However, in the context of globalisation, interviewees stated that the land which was subject to agrarian reform became islands in a sea of landlessness, forced to absorb outsiders and structural problems. In these situations, most of the economic alternatives proved ineffective, in spite of investments by NGOs and agencies of cooperation. Pressured by national programmes driven by international market forces, even the beneficiaries of land reforms adopted cattle as an economic strategy, slashing palms to plant pastures. Dona Mariana remembered how she raised all her children, going to the palm forests everyday, to gather and break open the babaçu fruits, extracting the kernels and selling them to buy food.

> Today it is much harder for the mothers-of-families, because there are no jobs for them. It is a sin to cut a palm, but those who have access to land… their own husbands are forced to slash palms. Otherwise, how will they eat, if there is no land to plant [rice]?

In this region, for those without access to land and forests, economic conditions were even worse. Landless men had to travel far away, looking for uncertain daily jobs, especially in pasture clearing and more recently, also to collect babaçu fruits for charcoal for the iron industry. Women had to struggle against these collector men and cattle ranchers to access babaçu fruits in order to make oil to sell, because the trade in kernels had ceased in the region. Dona Mariana lived through all these changes which transformed her social and economic environment. She faced the devastation of primary forests and elimination of brazil nuts, the emergence and degradation of the babaçu palm forests, and the encroachment by cattle ranchers. Overall, she saw entire communities disappear once their lands were taken by land grabbers. Although not formally involved in recognised social movements, she also had her share of battles and engagements in strategies to mobilise people around her family and community goals. From her narratives, it was possible to see how she negotiated her views on gender, taking into account class and race.

For many years, the rich cattle rancher Frazão tried to grab her land, using numerous strategies, from attempts to buy her land to threats against her life, without success. "*So, here I am. I had to struggle to keep this land of mine. Frazão persecuted me for years, threatening to kill me, but I was always here to face him. Once, he dared to threaten me in public. Now, he is dead and here I am, still on my very own land. He thought I was alone, but I am not.*"

Dona Mariana was never a member of a recognised social movement. She was neither a formal leader nor participant in the regular meetings promoted by the Catholic Church, workers' party and the NGOs. Even so, certainly Saint Francis and Saint Barbara did not leave her alone and surely did not let her down. But neither did the Catholic authorities, whom she managed to attract with her neat chapel and numerous followers; nor the politicians interested in the votes of the large black community gathered together under Saint Barbara's protection. In the context of globalisation, as many recognised formal organisations succumb to the challenges of development, sacred lands and relations have flourished in the hands of women such as Mariana Lino. Her stated identity of *quebradeira de coco* is also present in these unconcealed forms of resistance.

GLOBALISATION PROCESSES AND THEIR IMPLICATIONS FOR LAND AND GENDER

Through narratives by brazil-nut gatherers and peelers, and women babaçu breakers, we have learned of specific social identities in which gender was intertwined with relations with land and forests. This chapter, concerned with these social identities, examined their positioning in contexts affected by globalisation. Gender inequality and exclusion from rights to land have been relevant factors in the emergence and renewal of these social identities. In contexts marked by expressions of globalisation, these identities will help us to understand how gender has been negotiated in situations of change in land tenure.

Globalisation in the Amazon

In our fieldwork, we identified several developments which in our view best illustrated how globalisation was affecting the livelihoods of people working on extractive activities in Amazonian forests and lands. These were: a) the construction of the Trans-Oceanic highway connecting Amazonian lands and forest resources to Asian markets through the Pacific; b) the enforcement of international standards of quality on brazil nuts; c) the impacts of competition from imported Malaysian palm oil on Amazonian babaçu palm oil in the Brazilian market for the vegetable oils; and d) the expansion of the production of commodities such as beef and soybeans on Amazonian lands. These investments, policies and policy outcomes are mainly focused on integrating markets (IPAM-ISA 2000), and will further intensify competition among forest users. They are occurring in contexts dominated by the effects of market-oriented structural reforms and neo-liberal policies undertaken by the respective national governments. Pressured by international agencies, Brazil, Peru and Bolivia underwent IMF-oriented reforms mostly since the 1990s (Chossudovsky 1997, Loaysa et al. 2002, IMF 2000). To become recipients of aid for poverty alleviation, the adoption of specific forms of governance and policies compatible with economic globalisation are a requirement (Dollar and Levin 2004). National and local governments and societies were led to deal with the incisive demands from global markets, agencies and donors. Resulting policies have been expressed through new infrastructure such as highways and power plants, imposed rules, standards and practices, resulting in profound changes in natural and social environments in the Amazon.

TRANS-NATIONAL ROADS INTERCONNECTING FORESTS AND MARKETS

The Trans-Oceanic highway will connect the Bolivian, Peruvian, and Brazilian Western Amazon to Asian markets, through the Pacific. Commodities such as soybeans, beef and timber, and more recently, products related to bio-fuels, are the main stakes. As Mrs Roca's narrative in section 2 implies, governmental decrees defining Bolivian protected areas are necessary, but not sufficient for securing environmental conservation and local people's rights to land and forest resources in this context of globalisation (Hall 2000). As shown in our case study in the Manuripi reserve, laws and residents' rights are disrespected and overruled by *barraqueros* and other social actors that are more adapted to globalised contexts.

The same can be seen in the Peruvian narratives, where land-use zoning established by the Peruvian Ministry of Agriculture has not responded to the problems provoked by the re-designation of brazil-nut concessions as agricultural lands by the very same Ministry. This has also affected the processing industry and the lives of the brazil-nut peelers. Policies and programmes to prevent or mitigate social and environmental negative impacts have been insignificant. Researchers have warned that effects of economic competition progress faster than social investments (Brown et al. 2002.). In Brazil, the Agrarian Reform settlement projects, and even more, participatory processes such as the creation of the Extractive Reserves, have not being enough to contain expansion of cattle ranching. The heavy investments in the construction of the road BR 317, the Brazilian part of the Trans-Oceanic highway, has had and will continue to have a profound impact on peoples and forests. In all three countries, the land market and, consequently, people's lives have been deeply affected along these roads.

ENFORCEMENT OF INTERNATIONAL QUALITY STANDARDS FOR BRAZIL NUTS

Demands to comply with international quality standards have affected the brazil-nut economy in all three countries. For example, shelled brazil-nut loads imported by the European Union from Brazil were halted beginning July 2003. As of May 1, 2004, exports to the European Union were still prohibited because Brazilian exporters surpassed the regulatory tolerated amounts of aflatoxins (EC 2003). All agree that higher food quality is an important goal. Therefore, the question is not whether or not quality standards should be improved. Rather, the questions are: under what conditions will local producers manage to reach better standards; who will pay for the quality improvements; and who will benefit from the improvements? Sarah's life showed that she was already paying too high a price for her contribution to improving the quality standards of this export food, but was getting too little return for her efforts.

Equally pertinent in this regard is the fact that the acceptable level of *aflatoxins* has yet to be scientifically determined, and the norm is a precautionary measure (Newing and Harrop 2000). What, therefore, may appear to be a matter of meeting norms and regulations is actually a question of political-economic negotiations. As an interviewee peeler stated: "*To be sick is bad, so they worry about a disease they may get, but they do not worry about diseases we already have.*" Although workers have been trained for and keep repeating "*not quantity, but quality*," they are still paid by quantity, and earnings have not yet compensated for the extra time and attention that goes into pursuing better quality. Dealing with these regulations unilaterally may take more time and investments than this already vulnerable industry can afford.

PALM OIL IMPORTS FROM SOUTHEAST ASIA

When the government reduced and later eliminated the import taxes on vegetable oils, in the early 1990s, numerous babaçu oil processing industries closed down. Palm oil from Malaysia, which is similar to babaçu oil in composition, entered Brazilian markets through very aggressive marketing. By the mid-1990s, the Malaysian government and entrepreneurs had intentions to access Amazonian lands through joint ventures between Malaysian and Brazilian enterprises to establish extensive palm plantations. However, a strong social mobilisation prevented these projects from taking off. Even so, national and trans-national industries such as Unilever, which use these lauric oils, decreased their purchases of babaçu oil and increased their consumption of Malaysian palm oil. These industries began to stock this oil imported from the other side of the globe at competitive prices, and took control of prices for other similar oils.

Since the Northern and North-eastern elites running Brazilian industries based on babaçu kernels were used to governmental subsidies and tax exemptions, most of them succumbed to the competition. In the states of Piauí, Pará and Tocantins, most industries closed down and the commercialisation of kernels was practically eliminated. In the state of Maranhão, many industries shut down, and those that managed to survive were restructured. The latter benefited from the decreased local competition for kernels. However, once a significant number of local industries and the traditional channels of collection of kernels were disrupted, production never reached the same levels as of the 1980s (IBGE 2006). By the end of 2003, the price of Malaysian oil was similar to that of babaçu oil, and demand for the latter increased, but not to the point of attracting industries to resume the processing of kernels.

INVESTMENTS IN THE PRODUCTION OF COMMODITIES

Public investments in commodities such as beef and soybeans have affected the livelihoods of women babaçu breakers and brazil-nut gatherers, besides other traditional communities. As a result, the production of babaçu kernels and brazil nuts is decreasing while the expansion of commodities like beef and soybeans has intensified (IBGE 2006). The trend of increasing demand for beef in the international market, which motivated further expansion of pastures in the Amazon (IBGE 2006), has revived warnings made by Mayers in the 1980s, known as the "hamburger connection". There is a direct relation between the devastation of tropical forests and consumption of beef by rich countries (Kaimovitz et al. 2004). In addition, the increasing significance of Brazilian soybeans in the international market and the expansion of its fields in the Amazon have pushed cattle ranching and logging to new frontiers, provoking further devastation of extensive forested areas (Homma and Carvalho 1998; Nepstad et al. 2002 and 2006).

During the years of this research, the demand for soybeans by China was alleged to be a great pushing factor for the paving of the Trans-Oceanic Highway. When soybean prices fell in 2004–05, coupled with government efforts to restrain corruption and illegal logging, there was a reduction on deforestation rates. However, there was no evidence that the fall observed in those years indicated a trend for the next decade. Social mobilisation by international environmental NGOs such as Greenpeace and grassroots coalitions have been involved in negotiations aimed at greater governance, with relative success (Souza 2006), but deforestation rates increased again in 2007/2008.

Another example of commodity expansion in the state of Pará is oil palm, especially by the Agropalma entrepreneurial group. This group has expanded its plantations and has obtained ISO 9001 and 14001, and OHSAS 18001 quality certificates. The group also has invested in the so-called "green" market, including IBD organic certification, especially in the United States, Germany and Holland (Agropalma 2009). Although they displaced entire peasant villages in the 1980s, they are now investing in the welfare of their labourers, and marketing the social aspects of their endeavours. Therefore, grassroots organisations will have to compete with Agropalma in the "green" market. Agropalma managed to clear entire forested areas and plant palms prior to the laws and the collective mobilisation by civil society and environmentalist groups that prevented Malaysian entrepreneurs from doing the same.

GENDER AND LAND IN THE CONTEXT OF GLOBALISATION

In contexts marked by these expressions of globalisation, how has gender been negotiated in situations of development driving changes in land tenure? As we have seen in our fieldwork, as land is at stake, men and women have participated in diverse forms of social mobilisation, either recognised, public forms of mobilisation at local, regional and national level or invisible, but effective forms of resistance at family and community levels. We learned that these processes of resistance in development contexts have thrown up new meanings to their social identities. Each of these identities is shaped by specificities of ethnic background, nature of access to land and public resources, religion, historical trajectories and gendered relations to forest products. Assuming the identities of *comunárias, assentadas, landless peladoras, quebradeiras, seringueiras* and *castanheiras*, women were also emphasising the need for struggles for gender equality.

These social identities emerged from processes of resistance against imposing forms of development and were related to negotiations of gender in situations of change in land tenure. These processes are, therefore, mutually constituted. To understand them, we were led to search for more plural conceptualisations of gender, which reflected locally-based forms of living. According to the interviewees, the experience of struggles for their land as a territory was an integral part of the construction of a woman's gender. As one of the participants in this project noted:

> My experience as a woman... I don't know. I never think too much about what is to be a woman. But I always think that as women, we have some difficulties. Yes, we have, but we do not spend much time thinking about them. But one of the good things that happened to me, I believe it was my participation [in the social movements] that began through the conflict. Sometimes, I say that until 1985 [the year when she and other villagers fought for their land], I was another person. I was a person of the female sex, but I was not really a woman, and now I am. (Maria Adelina Chagas, leader of the Movement of the Babaçu Breaker Women, interviewed by Brazilian co-researcher educator Luciene Dias Figueiredo)

Therefore, we can see that being the women they were had emerged from a specific construction, one that involved the struggle for the land and the defence of forests of babaçu, the "mother of the people," and the brazil-nut trees. Their identity as women was intrinsically linked to how they identified themselves in relation to specific processes of political struggles for their places and lands in the context of globalisation.

An important element of women's gender identity was its heterogeneity in terms of ethnicity, economic conditions, access to land, religion, and migration trajectory, among other things. This resulted in forms of political mobilisation that often displaced conventional categories such as class, parties, and formal institutions. This heterogeneity was also expressed in the different stages of both the biological and social life cycles.

Recalling the trajectory of Felé, that tiny black woman who so bravely faced the cowboy to defend her rights as a woman, we can see one stage, followed by a u-turn when later, in fear of losing the love of her life, she stood by him, opposing her women's group. At that point, the women of her village wanted to protect "the mother of the people's" palms from husbands who wanted to slash them, and her husband was one of them. Years later, in January of 2007, I attended the annual meeting of their Agro-extractive Cooperative in one of the villages of Lago do Junco. There was Felé, as always, actively participating in the activities and discussions about how to use the exportation profits they had made last year. Together, we recalled the first manifestation of the women babaçu breakers, sixteen years ago, when more than 200 women left their babaçu forests to arrive noisily at the capital to demand their rights from the government. They took over the central plaza, filled the streets with their songs, and shook the governor's palace with the sounds of their machetes breaking babaçu. There was Felé then, happily whirling with her friends, taking over the streets with the spinning of the "babaçu-nut dance." Our gendered lives have had so many turns and returns since then. Felé is single now. "He wanted to find his own way. Life will take care of him." The sadness and conviction in her eyes confirmed the rightness of her words: "it doesn't need to be this way."

In globalised contexts as lived by Felé, gender has been negotiated in many complex, insecure, and convoluted ways, resulting in much success but also much loss and pain. The certainty is that it does not need to be the way it is now. Another world is possible. As the journey is far from over, there is hope for a much more inclusive agenda of negotiations over gender and land, which is intrinsically inter-connected with the ways of life built by women and men.

CONCLUSION

In the context of globalisation, gender has been negotiated through exceedingly unequal power relations between men and women in a multitude of social situations. In those situations in which land is at stake, gender issues have emerged from the most disenfranchised stakeholders: forest-dweller grandmothers burdened by unaided childcare, landless peeler single mothers in charge of assuring family social security, displaced teenagers dealing with undesired pregnancies, concessionaires struggling against the re-designation of their lands, minorities facing consequences of commodity production, and many others.

These protagonists, however, have negotiated gender through unique social and political identities forged through struggles for their ways of life, which intertwine the *trabalho livre*, work without a boss, with their lands and forests to establish a territory. These identities and their mobilisation are not always visible to governments and international agencies of development, and sometimes not even to the recognised social movements and organisations. Nonetheless, these protagonists have negotiated new forms of gender relations, and women have led, in domestic and public domains, practices of resistance for the continuous construction of their territories and ways of life.

In our research sites, the authorities and promoters of neo-liberal policies, as discussed by Mackenzie in our theoretical chapter, were also "deeply engaged in the double practice of describing as inevitable ... something which they are at the same time trying to produce" (Massey 200:283). "It is that tendentially totalising imagination of a necessary future, which enables the imposition of strategies of structural adjustment ..." (*ibid.*). This sense of unavoidability, also denounced by Bourdieu (1998) in his proposals to resist the neo-liberal invasion, permeated the realm of the struggles faced by the protagonists of this study.

By the end of our journeys through Bolivian, Peruvian and Brazilian lands, our team was saturated by the acts put in motion by neo-liberal policies. It was, however, even more overwhelmed by the daily counteracts lived by local people. Contesting them with their own ways of life, the interviewees' discourses and practices confirm what the babaçu breaker Felé affirmed: "it does not need to be this way." It does not.

NOTES

1. *Castañeras* are those women who gather brazil nuts mostly on their own lands; *seringueiras* are female rubber tappers; *extrativistas* are those who work on any extractive activity; and *zafreras* are landless labourers hired seasonally by *barraqueros,* who are former owners or leaseholders of rubber tapping areas. Currently, most of the barraqueros run brazil-nut, cattle ranching, gold and/ or logging businesses. Many of them do not have formal rights to land, but manage to remain in business through their connections with industry owners, governmental officers, and also by maintaining their symbolic power over the peasantry.

2. *Peladoras* are women who peel the brazil-nut seeds in processing plants in Peru. They are known as *fabriles* in Bolivia, where the Federation and unions for brazil-nut peelers have been relatively stronger than in Brazil and Peru.

3. *Colonas* are colonists. *Concessionárias* are concessionaires to whom the Peruvian government grants permits to use forested areas with brazil-nut trees (~ 1000 ha). *Comunárias* are members of a Grassroots Territorial Organization—OTB in Bolivia; and *assentadas* are settlers within Agrarian Reform programmes in Brazil.

4. *Chaco* is a small agricultural field with rice, corn, beans and other vegetables planted in gaps within the forest, through the slash-and-burn shifting cultivation system. Analogous to the Brazilian *roça*, it is also the physical expression of unique and complex social relations. In the studied communities, these relations build a system of production that sustains the reproduction of a social group as a peasant community. For further discussion on the conceptualisation of the peasantry in other current contexts, see Kearney 1996.

5. This National Reserve is located between the Manuripi and Madre de Dios rivers, in the southwest region of the Pando Department. It was created in 1973, initially with 1,773,000 ha. After several changes in the agrarian and environmental political settings, by the time of our research, it had 747,000 ha. Since 1999, the Protected Areas National Service (SERNAP) administers the reserve (Herencia and Dirección de la Reserva Manuripi 2003). Bolivia had 70 protected areas under federal, departmental or municipal protection. Among them, 28 national protected areas, or approximately 17 per cent of Bolivia's territory, are linked to the National Service of Protected Areas (SERNAP). (http://www.sernap.gov.bo/areasprotegidas/man.htm).

6. There was relative progress from the 1953 Law of Agrarian Reform in which contradictory articles excluded women as beneficiaries, to the 1996 INRA Law, which formally stated its intent to promote gender equality. In practice, however, the INRA Law does not present mechanisms to prevent gender inequality (Deere and Leon 2001:176). Ten years after the INRA Law, and with the election of Evo Morales, even those women associated with Grassroots Territorial Organizations are still uncertain of their rights. See also Urioste and Baldomar 2003.

7. See Helbingen (2003) and Henkemans (2003) for a view on the interactions among these stakeholders and Herencia (2001 and 2003) for the specifics of the Manuripi National Reserve.

8. Most of the brazil-nut processing plants in Bolivia are located in Riberalta, a city in the neighbouring department of Beni. However, the most modern and largest processing plant, the Tahuamano industry, is located in the city of Cobija, in the department of Pando.

9. Few studies have examined the connection between gender and inter-generational relations. In an interesting study about the "grandmother effect" reported at Science, the authors showed that family assistance provided by grandmothers positively affected the mortality and longevity of descendants, and this was not due to any social security support for the elderly (Lahdenperä et al. 2004).

10. Between mid-1800s and 1920, agreements between rich national entre-preneurs and enterprises sustained by foreign capital set the rules of the rubber economy.

11. Tahuamano played an important role in buying nuts from Brazil during the period of this research, as in 2003 and 2004 the Brazilian Cooperatives in Acre failed to process the nuts coming from the diverse affiliated associations, due to administrative and technological difficulties. This export of unshelled nuts to Bolivia affected the most famous Brazilian exporter, the Mutran family, located in the state of Pará.

12. For the situation of landless peeler in Bolivia, see PDA 1992.

13. Aflatoxins are toxins secreted by mould *Aspergillus flavus and A. parasiticus*, found in high-protein nuts such as peanuts and brazil nuts. The European Authority for Food Security determined maximum amounts of tolerated *aflatoxin* through regulation CE 493/2002. There are studies linking aflatoxins and cancer (Bommakanti and Waliyar 2000.)

14. Shiraishi points out that this legal achievement at municipal level has reinforced the free access and common use of the palms, suggesting, however, that it was necessary to change the juridical system in which the property was still viewed as an absolute right. Otherwise, this municipal law would be an easy target for debates over its constitutionality (2001:53).

15. By 2006, the movement of the babaçu breaker women had managed to pass municipal laws in defence of their palms in 14 municipalities (Shiraishi 2006).

16. Similar to the large "Houses" in Bolivia and Peru, the Mutran was a clan of Syrian-Lebanese descent who arrived in Brazil in the 19th century as merchants, and grew their fortune by extending credit to brazil-nut gatherers. In a couple of decades, they became landlords of vast forested areas, assigning family members the roles of mayors and legislators who protected the family's expanding business. The Mutran established a monopoly on the brazil-nut productive chain, mostly on public lands that were initially leased to them through political deals. While many blame the Mutran family for the failure of Brazil-nut business in Brazil, Benedito Mutran, the president of the Brazilian Association of Nut Growers, says that the fall from 19,000 tonnes production in 2000, to 7,000 tonnes in 2003, had nothing to do with them (Rohter 2004).

REFERENCES ▰▰▰▰▰▰▰▰▰▰▰▰▰▰▰▰▰▰▰▰▰▰▰▰▰▰▰▰▰

Agropalma, 2009, Accessed on 10–12–2009. http://www.agropalma.com.br/default.aspx?pagid=DPJCPLTO

Allegretti, M.H., 1995, "The Amazon and extracting activities", in M.Clussener-Godt and I. Sachs, (eds), *Brazilian perspectives on sustainable development of the Amazon region*, pp. 157–174. Paris and New York: UNESCO/Parthenon Publishing Group.

Almeida, A.W.B., 1990, "The State and land conflicts in Amazonia: from 1964 to 1988", in Goodman, D. and A. Hall (eds), *The Future of Amazonia: Destruction or Sustainable Development?* London: Macmillan Press.

————, 2001, Preços e possibilidades: a organização das Quebradeiras de coco babaçu face à segmentação dos mercados. In Economia do Babaçu: levantamento preliminar de dados, pp. 27–46. MIQCB, São Luís, Maranhão.

Alvarez, S., 1990. *Engendering Democracy in Brazil. Women's Movements in Transition Politics.* Princeton, NJ: Princeton University Press.

Alvarez, S., E. Dagnino, and A. Escobar (eds), 1998, "Introduction: the Cultural and the Political in Latin American Social Movements", in *Cultures of Politics and Politics of Cultures: Re-visioning Latin American Social Movements*, Boulder: Westview Press.

Anderson, A.B., P.H. May, and M.J. Balick, 1991, *The Subsidy from Nature: Palm Forests, Peasantry, and Development on an Amazon Frontier.* New York: Columbia University Press.

Arnold, D. and A. Spedding, 2005, *Mujeres en los Movimientos Sociales en Bolivia 2000–2003*. La Paz, Bolivia: ILCA and CIDEM.

Balee, W., 1989, "The Culture of Amazonian Forests", in Posey, D.A. and W. Balee, (eds), *Resource Management in Amazonia: Indigenous and Folk Strategies*. New York: New York Botanical Garden.

Belaunde, L.E., 1994, "Parrots and Oropendolas: the Aesthetics of Gender Relations among the Airo-Pai of the Peruvian Amazon", *Journal de la Societé des Américanistes de Paris* 80: 95–111.

Bommakanti, A.S. and F.Waliyar, 2000, Importance of Aflatoxins in human and livestock health. http://www.aflatoxin.info/health.asp. International Crops Research Institute for the Semi-Arid Tropics.

Brown, I.F., S.H.C. Brilhante, E. Mendoza, and I.R.Oliveira, 2002, Estrada de Rio Branco, Acre, Brasil aos portos do Pacífico: como maximizar os benefícios e minimizar os prejuízos para o desenvolvimento sustentável da Amazônia sul-ocidental. In La Integración regional entre Bolívia, Brasil y Peru. eds. Tizón, A.W. and Duarte, R.S.G. Série Seminarios, mesas redondas y conferencias no. 25, pp. 281–296. ISSN 1017–51211. Lima, Peru: Editora CEPEI.

Campbell, C.E., 1996, Forest, field and factory: changing livelihood strategies in two extractive reserves in the Brazilian Amazon. Ph.D. dissertation at University of Florida, Gainesville.

Campbell, C.E., "Out on the front lines, but still struggling for voice: women in the rubber tappers" defense of the forest in Xapuri, Acre, Brazil", in Rocheleau, D., B. Thomas-Slayter and E. Wangari, (eds), *Feminist Political Ecology: Global Issues and Local Experiences,* New York: Routledge, pp. 27–61.

Caldeira, T., 1990, "Women, daily life and politics", in Jelin, E. (ed) *Women and Social Change in Latin America,* London: UNRISD/Zed Books, pp. 47–78

Chossudovsky, M., 1997, The Globalization of poverty: impacts of IMF and World Bank reforms. Third World Network, Penang, Malaysia.

Clay, J., 1997, "Brazil nuts, the use of a keystone species for conservation and development", in Freese, C. (ed), *Harvesting wild species,* The John Hopkins University Press, pp. 246–282.

Clifford, J. and G. Marcus, (eds), 1986, *Writing Culture: the Poetics and Politics of Ethnography.* A School of American Research Advanced Seminar. Berkeley: University of California Press.

Collinson, C., D. Burnett, and V. Agreda, 2000, "Economic Viability of Brazil Nut Trading in Peru", Report 2520. Natural Resources and Ethical Trade Programme. Natural Resources Institute. University of Greenwich, UK.

Cruz Neto, R. and Maia Neto, B., 2002, Em busca do Desenvolvimento Sustentável. Cepasp—FASE, Pará.

Datta, N., 2007, "Joint Titling—a WinWin Policy? Gender and Property Rights in Urban Informal Settlements in Chandigarh, India", in Deere, C.D., and D.R. Doss, (eds), *Women and the Distribution of Wealth: Feminist Economics,* London: Routledge, pp. 271–298.

Deere, C. and M. León, 2001, *Empowering Women: Land and Property Rights in Latin America.* Pittsburgh, Pa: University of Pittsburgh Press.

Dollar, D. and V.Levin, 2004, The Increasing Selectivity of Foreign Aid, 1984–2002. World Bank Working Paper no. 3299. World Bank, Washington D.C.

Droulers, M. and P. Maury, 1980, "Colonização da Amazônia Maranhense", *Ciência e Cultura* 33(8): 1033–1050.

EC, 2003, Decision of the European Commission of 4/7/2003: special conditions to import of shelled Brazil nuts, originally or coming from Brazil. 2003/493/CE. Official Journal of European Union.

Escobar, A., 1995, *Encountering Development: the Making and Unmaking of the Third World.* Princeton, NJ: Princeton University Press.

Escobar, A., 2001, "Place, Economy, and Culture in a Post-Development Era", in Prazniak, R., and A. Dirlik, (eds), *Places and Politics in an Age of Globalization,* Boulder: Rowman & Littlefield Publishers, Inc, pp. 193–218.

Fine, M., 1994, *Working the Hyphens: Reinventing Self and Other in Qualitative Research. Handbook of Qualitative Research,* in Norman Denzin and Yvonne Lincoln, eds. Thousand Oaks, London: Sage Publications.

Foucault, M., 1972, *The Archaeology of Knowledge.* New York: Pantheon Books.

GRADE, 1998, Derechos de propiedad, regulacion de concesiones y uso optimo de los recursos naturals: criterios para regular a los extractores de castaña en la Provincia de Tambopata en la Selva de Peru. Proyecto de investigacion presentado por el Grupo de Análisis para el Desarollo (GRADE). http://www. rimisp.org/webpage.php?webid=469.

Guerra, G.A.D., 2001, O posseiro da fronteira: campesinato e sindicalismo no sudeste paraense. UFPA/NAEA, Belém, Pará.

Hall, A., 2000, "Environment and Development in Brazilian Amazonia: from protectionism to productive conservation", in Hall, A. (ed), *Amazonia at the crossroads: the challenge of sustainable development,* London: Institute of Latin American Studies, University of London, pp. 99–114.

Helbingen, A.J.B., 2003, El Balance es lo hermoso: desarrollo sustentable y los bosques de la Amazonia Boliviana. PROMAB Serie Científica no. 8, Riberalta, Bolivia.

Henkemans, A.B., 2003, Tranqulidad y sufrimiento en el bosque: los medios de vida y percepciones de los Cambas en el bosque de la Amazonía boliviana. PROMAB Serie Científica no. 7, Riberalta, Bolivia.

Herencia, 2001, Informacion General de Barracas y Comunidades en la Reserva Manuripi. Annex 1. Elaboración propria con base a registros y entrevistas comunales, consulta a la Dirección de la Reserva y datos parciales proporcionados por AARENARMAPA, PANFOR e INRA. Unpublished Manuscript. Cobija, Bolivia.

Herencia y Dirección de la Reserva Manuripi, 2003, reserva Nacional de Vida Silvestre Amazônica Manuripi: Plan de Manejo. Unpublished report. Cobija, Bolívia.

Homma, A.K.O., Carvalho, R.A., 1998, "A expansão do monocultivo da soja na Amazônia: início de um novo ciclo e as conseqüências ambientais", *Congresso de Ecologia do Brasil* 4: 348–349. Belém, Brazil: FCAP.

IMF. 2000. Debt relief, globalization, and IMF reform: some questions and answers. http://www.imf.org/external/np/exr/ib/2000/041200b.htm#III

Ingold, T., 1992, "Culture and the Perception of the Environment", in Croll, E., and D. Parkin, (eds), *Bush Base, Forest Farm: Culture, Environment, and Development.* New York: Routledge.

IPAM-ISA, 2000, Avança Brasil: os custos ambientais para a Amazônia. Instituto de Pesquisa Ambiental na Amazônia—Instituto Socio-Ambiental, Belém.

Kabeer, N., 1994, *Reversed Realities: Gender Hierarchies in Development Thought.* New York: Verso.

Kaimowitz, D., B. Mertens, S. Wunder, and P. Pacheco, 2004, "Hamburger Connection Fuels Amazon Destruction: cattle ranching and deforestation in Brazil's Amazon". Bogor: Center for International Forestry Research.

Kainer, K.A. and M.L. Duryea, 1992, Tapping women's knowledge: plant resource use in extractive reserves, Acre, Brazil. *Economic Botany* 46(4): 408–425.

Kainer, K.A., M. Schmink, A.C. Leite, and M.J. Fadell, 2003, Experiments in Forest-Based Development in Western Amazonia. *Society & Natural Resources* 16(10/November–December 2003): 869–886. Taylor & Francis.

Kearney, M., 1996, *Reconceptualizing the peasantry: anthropology in global perspective.* Boulder: Westview Press.

Lahdenperä, M., V. Lummaa, S. Helle, M. Tremblay, and A.F. Russell, 2004, Nature. 2004 Mar 11; 428(6979): 178–81.

Lanao, M., 1998, Gendered political ecology of Brazil nuts in Madre de Dios Peru: "No chorea, pero gotea." Master thesis at University of Florida, Gainesville.

Leguia, B., 2004, Informe numero 15–2004-AG-PETT-DCR del director de Proyecto Special Titulacion de Terras y Catastro Rural. Exclusión de areas agrícolas en concesiones forestales. Lima, 11 febrero 2004.

Loayza, N., P. Fajnzylber, and C. Calderón, 2002, Economic Growth in Latin America and the Caribbean: Stylized facts, explanations and forecasts. Washington, D.C.: World Bank.

Marcus, G. and M.M.J. Fischer, 1986, *Anthropology as Cultural Critique: an Experimental Moment in the Human Sciences.* Chicago: University of Chicago Press.

Margulis, S., 2004, Causes of Deforestation of the Brazilian Amazon. World Bank Working Report, No 22. World Bank, Washington, D.C.

May, P., 1990, Palmeiras em Chamas: Transformação Agrária e Justiça Social na Zona do Babaçu. EMAPA/FINEP/Fundação Ford, São Luís.

MIC/STI, 1982, Secretaria de Tecnologia Industrial do Ministério de Indústria e Comércio. Mapeamento e Levantamento do Potencial das Ocorrências de Babaçuais. Estado do Maranhão, Piauí, Mato Grosso e Goiás. Brasília: Núcleo de Comunicação Social da Secretaria de Tecnologia Industrial do MIC.

MIQCB, 2005, Carta das quebradeiras de coco babaçu, elaborada em 10 de dezembro de 2004, durante o V Encontro do Movimento Interestadual das Quebradeiras de Coco Babaçu. Flavia Moura, ed. Manuscript. coordenacao@miqcb.org.br. São Luís, Brazil: Institutional Document.

Mori, S.A., 1992, "The Brazil nut industry: past, present and future", in Plotkin, M. and L. Famolare, (eds), *Sustainable harvest and marketing of rain forest products,* Conservation International, Island Press, pp. 241–251.

Moser, C., 1993, *Gender Planning and Development: Theory, Practice and Training.* New York: Routledge.

Moser, C., A. Tornqvist, and B. van Bronkhorst, 1999, Mainstreaming Gender and Development in the World Bank: Progress and Recommendations. Washington, D.C.: World Bank.

D. Nepstad, D. McGrath, A. Alencar, A. C. Barros, G. Carvalho, M. Santilli, M. del C. Vera Diaz, 2002, Environment Enhanced: Frontier Governance in Amazonia. Science 25 January 2002, 295(5555): 629–631.

Nepstad, D., M.C. Diaz, J. Carter, D. McGrath, P. Pacheco, O. Almeida, and D. Kaimowitz, 2006, Risks and opportunities of Amazon cattle ranching and agro-industry. Manuscript submitted to Science. For related information see http://www.whrc.org/southamerica/agric_expans.htm.

Newing, H., and S. Harrop, 2000, European Health Regulations and Brazil Nuts: Implications for Biodiversity Conservation and Sustainable Rural Livelihoods in the Amazon. *Journal of International Wildlife Law & Policy,* June 22, 2000.

Overholt, C., M. Anderson, K. Cloud, and J. Austin, 1984, *Gender Roles in Development.* West Hartford, Connecticut: Kumarian Press.

Pacheco, P., 2002, "Deforestation and Forest Degradation in Lowland Bolivia", in Wood, C.H., and R. Porro, (eds), *Deforestation and Land Use in the Amazon,* Gainesville: University of Florida Press, pp. 66–94..

PDA—Programa de Desarollo de Agro-Exportaciones, 1992, La Situation Socio-economica de la Mujer en el Area de la Castana (Amazonia Boliviana). Manuscript. Riberalta, Bolivia: PDA.

Peres, C.A., C. Baider, P.A. Zuidema, L. Wadt, K. Kainer, D. Gomes-Silva, R. Salomão, L.Simões, E. Franciosi, F. Valverde, R. Gribel, G. Shepard, M. Kanashiro, P. Coventry, D. Yu, A.Watkinson, and R. Freckleton, Demographic Threats to the Sustainability of Brazil Nut Exploitation. *Science* 19 December 2003, 302(5653): 2112–2114.

Porro, N., 1997, Changes in Peasant Perceptions of Development and Conservation. Master's Thesis. Gainesville, FL: University of Florida.

————, 2002, Rupture and resistance: gender relations and life trajectories in the babaçu palm forests of Brazil. Ph.D. Dissertation. Gainesville, FL: University of Florida.

Rakowski, C., 1995, "Conclusion: engendering wealth and well-being", in Blumberg, R., C. Rakowski, I. Tinker and M. Monteón, (eds), *Engendering Wealth and Well-Being: Empowerment for Global Change,* Boulder: Westview Press, pp. 285–294.

Safa, H., 1995, *The Myth of the Male Breadwinner: Women and Industrialization in the Caribbean.* Boulder: Westview Press.

Schmink, M., 1992, "Amazonian resistance movements and the international alliance", in Kosinski, L. (ed), *Ecological Disorder in Amazonia,* Rio de Janeiro: UNESCO/ISSC/Educam, pp. 149–172.

Schmink, M. and C. Wood, 1992, *Contested Frontiers in Amazonia.* New York: Columbia University Press.

Shiraishi, J., 2001, Babaçu Livre: conflito entre legislação extrativa e práticas camponesas. In Economia do Babaçu: Levantamento Preliminar de Dados, eds. A. Almeida, J. Shiraishi Neto, and B. Mesquita, pp. 47–72. Movimento Interestadual das Quebradeiras de Côco Babaçu. São Luís: Balaios Typographia.

Soares Filho, B., D. Nepstad, L. Curran, G.Cerqueira, R. Garcia, C. Ramos, E. Voll, A. McDonald, P. Lefebvre, and P. Schlesinger, 2006, Modelling conservation in the Amazon basin. *Nature* 440|23 March 2006|doi:10.1038/nature04389

Souza, O.B., 2006, Desmatamento na Amazônia e o Agronegócio. Notícias Socioambientais do ISA. http://www.socioambiental.org/nsa/detalhe?id=2357

Thomas-Slayter, B. and D. Rocheleau, 1995, "Research frontiers at the nexus of gender, environment, and development: linking household, community, and ecosystem", in Gallin, R., A. Ferguson and J. Harper, (eds), *The Women and International Development Annual.* Vol 4., Boulder: Westview Press.

Urioste, M and L. Baldomar, 2003, Bolivia Popular Participation. Seminario Latinoamericano sobre heterogeneidad agrarian y politicas diferenciadas. Nov 27–29, 2003. Cocoyoc, Morelos, Mexico. Rimisp, FAO, Sagar. http://www.rimisp.org/webpage.php?webid=142.

Wolff, Cristina, 1999, Mulheres da Floresta: uma História. Alto Juruá, Acre (1980–1945). São Paulo: Hucitec.

Wood, C.H., 2002, "Introduction: land use and deforestation in the Amazon", in Wood, C.H. and R. Porro, (eds), *Deforestation and land use in the Amazon*, University Press of Florida, Gainesville, pp. 1–38.

Gender, Kinship and Agrarian Transitions in Vietnam

STEFFANIE SCOTT, DANIÈLE BÉLANGER, NGUYEN THI VAN ANH, AND KHUAT THU HONG

Although I do not want my child to be a farmer, I have to keep my land. When parents give gold or money to their children, they can spend it. Land always remains. If I do not want to farm my own land, I can always rent it to someone and my child can live on the money I get from the rent. If I keep my land, my child cannot sell it. I must protect and keep my land even though I do not want my child to endure the hardship of a farmer's life.

Female interviewee, Can Tho Province

INTRODUCTION

Analyses of gender and development have come a long way in recent decades, yet relatively few gender-sensitive development interventions and research projects explicitly address women's property rights and, specifically, their right to land (Deere and Leon 2001). Moreover, public policy has tended to ignore differences in property rights of women as against those of men. This is due to the way development discourse has been constructed. For example, in economic theory and development policy, the household is taken as a single unit comprised of common interests, where resources are pooled and shared. Thus, conflicting interests are overlooked or downplayed (Mukhopadhyay 2001). The gendered nature of property relations can also be obscured in the context of feminist struggles that focus increasingly on issues of identity and recognition at the expense of redistribution (Agarwal 1994a).

Women's relationship to property differs from men's; it is fundamentally shaped by kinship structures and marriage practices. As Friedrich Engels (1972 [1845]) noted, a major dimension of women's historical subordination stems from their lack of control of land as an important means of production. Compared to men, women's entitlements are embedded, to a far greater degree, in family and kinship structures (Hirschon 1984; Kabeer 1989). Patrilocal residence patterns after marriage generally constrain women's prospects of accumulating assets in the form of land. Hence, the family (within and beyond the household) is a crucial element in understanding the linkages between gender and land.

Designers of land reform programmes have typically overlooked gender and kinship ties when redistributing land to landless and land-poor households (Deere and Leon 2001). Consequently, policies in socialist and capitalist countries alike have neglected women's rights to land. For communist parties, addressing the issue of access to land by gender was considered potentially divisive within the overall objective of uniting proletarian interests against large landowners. Communist parties further reproduced the notion of "peasant" as a male category, erecting blinders to an examination of how women's access to land was generally mediated by men (Agarwal 1994a), be it their husbands or leaders of work brigades, communes or other levels of administration. Both agrarian reform programmes and socialist programmes of collectivisation of agriculture have now largely ended. Socialist economies, such as Vietnam's, have witnessed a shift from social property models to systems based on individual and private rights.

This chapter offers a gender analysis of the agrarian changes that took place as Vietnam transitioned from a socialist to a market economy, a process that is referred to as *doi moi* which formally began in 1986. More specifically, it examines how the current land tenure systems, combined with the existing kinship structures, affect women's rights and access to land. It studies the relationships between policies, gender, kinship and land, based on a critical analysis of the literature and also original data that we collected in 2004. Because

Vietnam is a diverse country with different land histories, kinship systems and patterns of gender relations, we conducted our study in two localities—one in the north and another in the south. These two case studies highlight the extent to which women's relationship to land may differ within a single country, and so also the relevance of examining the issues at the local, rather than strictly national level. Some studies have documented gender differences in access to land in urban areas of Vietnam (Thai Thi Ngoc Du 1999). In contrast, our analysis focuses primarily on entitlements to agricultural land, which is often the mainstay of people's livelihoods in rural areas, where opportunities for economic diversification may be limited.

We begin the chapter with a presentation of our analytical framework and a review of the existing literature on gender implications of Vietnam's agrarian transitions. We then discuss our team's methodology for collecting and analysing the original data. This is followed by a review of how women access land, with an emphasis on the role that kinship-based institutions, such as marriage and inheritance practices, play. In light of these case studies and inspired by the work of Jackson (2003), we argue that local contexts strongly mediate the outcomes of national policies.

ANALYTICAL FRAMEWORK

This section is comprised of three aspects: globalisation and land reforms in Vietnam; gender and agrarian transitions; and gender inequalities and women's land rights.

(a) Globalisation and land reforms in Vietnam

Changes in gendered access to land worldwide are taking place within a context of accelerated economic globalisation and predominant neoliberal policy orientations among governments and international institutions. The process of rural economic restructuring and the quasi-privatisation of land in Vietnam reflect a global shift in rural governance towards private property rights and individual land titling to strengthen incentives for production, innovation, and investment (Scott 2009). These reforms emerged in response to a number of internal and external challenges facing Vietnam's agricultural sector in the 1980s, including stagnation in productivity, the breakdown of collective management structures and declining foreign aid from the Soviet Union. Such circumstances propelled policy-makers to address the question of how to develop a property rights regime and an adequate institutional structure to support the transition to, and development of, a market economy. The resulting property rights regime and quasi-privatisation of land are central elements of Vietnam's rural reforms. The ideological reorientation implicit in *doi moi* (the economic "renovation" that began in 1986) reflects changing incentive structures and a new pragmatism among policy-makers, moving away from egalitarianism, collectivism, and "the plan" to acknowledge and embrace the attributes of entrepreneurship and market competition.

The state increasingly moved towards becoming an agent to encourage market development. The stigma was lifted on individual enrichment and private sector marketing and financing—elements that were previously considered capitalistic and exploitative. Paralleling the neoliberal perspective prevalent in development discourses around the world, the principle of farmers' choices in the market economy is underlined: "rural incomes will grow more rapidly where households have *freedom* to respond to changed market or other circumstances and can *choose* input or marketing services from a *range of competitive suppliers*" (MARD and UNDP 1998: 39, emphasis added). Within the overall set of economic reforms initiated in the late 1980s in Vietnam, decollectivisation and the provision of secure land rights occupy a central place. The modernisation of Vietnam's land administration system, through clearly defining boundaries and issuing long-term land use right certificates, reflected the objectives of market-oriented land reforms that are characteristic of economic globalisation: to improve security of tenure for the landholder, increase domestic and foreign investment in land, reduce land disputes, ensure better infrastructure planning and coordination, and the establishment of a fair, equitable, and efficient taxation system, among other benefits (ADB 1997: v-vi). Yet international research has raised questions about the efficacy of land markets for small-scale and female producers. Too often, neoliberal prescriptions for land markets and land titling programmes have marginalised women

(Razavi 2007; Razavi 2003; Deere and Leon 2001)—an issue we examine through this chapter in the context of Vietnam.

(b) *Gender and agrarian transitions*

Agrarian transitions classically refer to the introduction of capitalist relations in the countryside to modernise a peasant or subsistence economy. In socialist countries, however, economic and social relations shifted from feudal and customary institutions to agricultural collectives and state farms, instead of more capitalistic relations, as in Japan, Korea and Taiwan. More recently, agrarian transitions in post-socialist countries are characterised by the dismantling of a collective system to privatise land for individual household management. China and Vietnam, with the characteristic of being mainly agricultural countries, are the paradigmatic cases of this trend in Asia.

Critical studies of agrarian transition (e.g., Hart et al. 1989) have largely focused on class differentiation, rural inequalities, and capitalist accumulation. Issues of gender within agrarian transitions have only recently attracted much scholarly attention. Around the world, women hold rights to only one per cent of land, although this varies by country. In Uganda, for example, women own 16 per cent of land, a relatively high figure (Seager 1997). In some countries, women's rights to land are legally recognised, although they may face problems in having their rights acknowledged in practice. This is the case in most Latin American countries. In many countries, the legal system, as well as inheritance and divorce laws, discriminate against women.

At times, women's access to land has been considered in the context of agrarian reform rather than as a general right. With the end of agrarian reforms in many developing countries, women's access to land now depends less on state allocation and more on markets and kinship relations (e.g., inheritance). Women's bargaining position within the rural household can depend significantly on their access to property (Deere and Leon 2001). Many post-socialist and other developing countries have recently experienced rapidly changing market conditions, an individualisation of property (i.e., a shift away from collectivisation or communal property rights) and a decline in social security networks. Many of the land reform laws in previously socialist countries, in both Eastern Europe and Central Asia, are disadvantageous to women, excluding them from entitlements to land and forcing them back into reproductive roles or subsistence production (Funk and Mueller 1993; Kandiyoti 2003).

(c) *Gender inequalities and women's land rights*

Since the first UN conference on women, held in Mexico in 1975, gender equality has been a key focus, generated by the promotion of progressive policies by the international women's movement. At the 1995 UN Beijing Conference on Women, women's rights to hold and control property, not merely through their relationship with male relatives or spouses, were emphasised (Mukhopadhyay 1998). Among the most contentious issues in the debate on women's equality were gender differences in access to and control over property. The relationship between women and property took on more relevance after the creation of the Convention on the Elimination of all forms of Discrimination Against Women (CEDAW, adopted in 1979) and through various international forums on women, population and development. These conventions can be seen as an international consensus to limit the detrimental effects that land tenure policies can have on women.

Despite having established progressive inheritance laws that acknowledge women's rights to property, many countries have experienced opposition through cultural norms based on patriarchal inheritance systems. Among the constraining factors are patrilocal post-marital residence patterns; low levels of female literacy (and legal literacy); opposition from within the household or extended families; the perception of gender needs and roles; social, economic and political power held mostly by men; and male bias among local government administrators and professionals (Agarwal 1994a, 1994b). Most countries of sub-Saharan Africa and Asia have a dualistic legal system in which modern law may contradict customary or religious law. This can impede gender equity and women's rights to property. Thus, the debate over women having their own property rights does not end with legislation, but rather is an ongoing struggle at the level of state, community and family to achieve implementation.

In addition to the gap between law and practice with respect to inheritance, issuing *joint* land use rights instead of *separate* rights for women and men has important implications in that the former could potentially lead to difficulties when the question of inheritance arises or in the event of dissolution of marriage. If women lack rights to their own land, it could restrict their options to leave a marriage even if it is ridden with conflict or violence, and might limit their control over the benefits gained from selling their produce. Moreover, women and men might have different land use priorities that could be equally pursued if they had autonomous decision-making (Agarwal 1994a; Xu 2006).

Agarwal (1994a) has elucidated three primary arguments for women's rights to land. First, the welfare argument underlines the way in which land serves as security against poverty, suggesting that a woman's direct access to land and other productive assets can significantly decrease the risk of poverty and help ensure her own as well as her children's well-being. Land can be used by women as a bargaining tool both within the family and in outside institutions. Second, the efficiency argument indicates that land can make women more economically productive by facilitating access to credit, technology and information. This rationale underscores the well-being of women and society more generally through increased production. Third, arguments over equity and empowerment emphasise that acquiring land is central not only to improving a woman's economic circumstances in absolute terms, but also in enabling her to negotiate more equitable relations with men. Thus, empowerment within the household is linked to economic equality. Having her own recognised rights to land can also stand a woman in better stead when it comes to bargaining with potential employers, given that she has a stronger fallback position.

The discourses of development agencies that rationalise individual land rights for women tend to focus on the conventional economic arguments of welfare and efficiency. These arguments are often based on the premise that women manage expenditures more appropriately or altruistically and use land and credit more productively than men (Kodoth 2001). Such reasoning emphasises the role of market forces in creating opportunities. The state features in such discourses not in a role of redistributing assets but in a narrower role of supporting investment in land and providing infrastructure within the existing economic, social and legal structures. Yet, as Kodoth (2001: 294) argues, "to ground claims to property in better productivity or more efficient use of resources is to advance a merit-based claim that is inherently inegalitarian, implying that less 'efficient' producers be denied resources." Instead, equality must be argued on its own merit.

Various types of constraints result from women's lack of individual rights to land. Women may face pressure to cede their land to their brothers if they want to maintain harmonious family relations or if they are less able to cultivate the land themselves. Bina Agarwal (1997) and Amartya Sen (1990), among other scholars, have debated the extent of women's awareness of their own self-interest in land rights. They discuss why women are frequently reluctant to demand these rights, whether out of ignorance or a conscious strategy. The interaction between individual self-interest and the collective group interests is an important and unresolved question for our analysis of Vietnam. At times, a woman's membership of a family, commune, village, class or ethnic group, more than her gender, can shape her identity and the decisions she makes.

At the same time, the composition of the household and status of the household head can have important implications on access to land. An increasing number of studies internationally have drawn attention to the circumstances of female-headed households. Yet, the very term "female-headed household" masks enormous variations that are too often not disaggregated (Scott 2003). Chant (1997) distinguishes between *de jure* and *de facto* female-headed households. The former is used to refer to cases in which the female head is widowed or legally separated, while the latter refers to instances in which husbands or male partners are away working. A further distinction is made between single mothers living with their parents or other relatives, where the latter are designated as household heads. This has been termed "hidden" female-headed households (Moser and McIlwaine 1997: 27). Given the problems of collapsing all these variations under the label "female-headed households", we instead discuss the impact of the land tenure changes on different groups of women, specifically divorced, single and widowed women, as well as second wives.

GENDER AND AGRARIAN TRANSITIONS IN VIETNAM

It is well known in Vietnam that, from the time of the Le Dynasty rule in the 15th century, the Hong Duc legal codes legislated inheritance rights for sons and daughters (Ta Van Tai 1981). While not many studies have documented women's inheritance in practice, some evidence from the colonial period indicates that women did inherit land on a regular basis. The French published numerous works in which they reported that women in Vietnam had a higher status than those in China, and women's access to property was a centerpiece of their argument (Lustéguy 1935; Protectorat du Tonkin 1930). In our study, some elderly women reported having inherited agricultural land, though their brothers inherited larger shares. This observation echoes Tran (2006) who argues that while some daughters inherited land in 18th century Vietnam—albeit a much smaller share than their brothers'—many did not. In the communities we studied, few daughters became landholders during the colonial period, partly because not many families owned land. In the colonial period, some Vietnamese women living in urban areas owned property in the form of small enterprises (factories), land and real estate (Papin 1997).

During the period 1955–75, Vietnam was split into two, with the Communist Party ruling in the north, and the French and US-backed administration in the south. Agricultural collectivisation in northern Vietnam was initiated and then accelerated in the late 1950s. By the end of the 1960s, 86 per cent of the households had joined collectives. From this time until the early 1980s, the economic functions of the family household were de-emphasised, and collectives became the principal unit around which most agricultural production tasks were organised. The household in this period was mainly a unit for distribution. Although in many ways agricultural collectives undermined family production, one should not overlook the persistence of the "family economy" during this period, particularly in relation to the "five per cent land"—that portion of collective land which was allocated to households for individual production. The "five per cent land" was often the most developed of all agricultural land in a commune, sometimes three times more productive than collectively farmed land (Bhaduri 1982). In all, 40 per cent of the cash incomes of collective members came from this land. It is said that "the co-op provides the backbone to the entire material life and security of a north Vietnamese peasant... while the family economy plays a complementary side role in improving the quality of his [sic] life" (Bhaduri 1982: 52).

Concerning gender relations and the household gender division of labour during the collective period, initial analyses of the socialist period were extremely optimistic. In a celebratory tone, Mai Thi Tu and Le Thi Nham Tuyet (1978: 214) rejoice that,

> Collectivization of agriculture meant that Vietnamese peasant women (90% of the female population) gained complete freedom both in their work and economically: when they entrusted their individual plots of land to the collective, the Vietnamese peasants became active members ... on equal footing with men and first and foremost with their husbands. Gone were the days when they did the field work, raised domestic animals, did the household chores, cared for their children and performed other activities single-handedly, while their idle husbands relaxed in the central room of the house, but were nonetheless considered the "main pillars" of their families. Work was paid separately from then on ...

While such a reading captures some of the *de jure* objectives of collectivisation policies, it pays little heed to the *de facto* on-going disproportionate contributions made by women, the elderly and children to the upkeep of family plots on the "five per cent land" during this period. Indeed, although post-revolutionary laws in Vietnam provided for formal equality between the sexes (i.e. the 1959 Law of Marriage and the Family), unequal structures persisted implicitly in a variety of forms, including uneven compensation for labour along gender lines. Work points for the collective labour contributions of women tended to be lower than those for men, reflecting the dominant discourse of what constituted appropriate feminine and masculine work (Bélanger and Barbieri 2009). "Women's work"—pulling-up and transplanting rice seedlings, weeding and fertilising, done either by hand or with simple tools such as hoes, sickles or baskets with shoulder poles—was perceived as being "light" or "simple", and therefore assigned fewer work points. One workday of fertilising or transplanting was assigned 8 or 10 points, respectively, whereas one workday of ploughing or carpentry, which was perceived as being more challenging and technical, earned 12 or 14 points respectively (Tran Thi Van Anh 1995).[1]

Following the end of the war in 1975, and particularly through the 1980s, many collectives began to dissolve. Policy reforms followed in an effort to keep up with the *de facto* changes in the organisation of land in the countryside (Kerkvliet, 2005). This so-called "de-collectivisation" process led to a change in the official status of the rural household, legitimising a shift from collective to individual (household-based) production (Scott 2009). It began with contracts and quotas for certain tasks (Contract 100 in 1981). Later, through Resolution 10 in 1988, land was allocated to each household on the basis of the number of labourers. Finally, the Land Law of 1993 issued long-term land use certificates (20 years for annual crop land and 50 years for perennial crop land), based on household size. These reforms, which shifted the basic unit of production management from the collective to the household, resulted in a fairly egalitarian allocation of land on per capita basis.[2]

Werner (1983) provides a useful analysis of the gendered effects of this policy of household contracts, noting that it was principally women's work that was de-collectivised and reverted to the household's responsibility. Three of the six main tasks previously performed by the collective and assigned to the household under Contract 100— namely transplanting, weeding and some harvesting—were all tasks performed largely by women. Ploughing, water and pest control, and some harvesting remained in the hands of collectives. Werner (1983: 49) highlights the significance of this shift as an "increase in women's work and domestic labour as a solution to the economic crisis and the decline in participation of women in social production and public life."

A final component in the process of policy reform was the 1993 Land Law provision, allowing for five rights in agricultural land: the right to lease, transfer, exchange, inherit and use as collateral.[3] It also called for the issuance of long-term land user-right certificates

(LUCs or Red Books) for periods of 20 years for annual cropland and 50 years for perennial cropland (e.g., land on which fruit trees are grown). Although the state retained formal ownership of the land, leases are expected to be extended upon expiry. The long-term allocations of agricultural land following the 1993 Land Law were generally determined on a per capita basis.[4]

If we examine land access on a *de jure* basis, the 1993 Land Law stipulated that land shall be granted to all stable land users. Hence, both men and women should be entitled to certificates. Yet, in many areas, even if both the wife and husband worked the land, certificates were issued only in the name of the head of household, the majority of whom were male. This practice was encouraged, in part, because land use certificates had space for only one name. After considerable discussions on the implications of this situation in 2003, the 1993 Land Law was amended to ensure women's title rights in land. A new article (Item 3, Article 48) stipulates that the name of both husband and wife must be recorded on the land certificate if the land is common property of the spouses. This change was to harmonise the Land Law with Article 5 of Decree 70 (in 2001) on the implementation of the Law on Marriage and Family, which specifies that all documents registering family assets (residential property and land use rights) must be in the name of both husband and wife and that consent of both parties would be required for land transfers. Over the past decade, encouragement by international donors and NGOs has made gender and land a mainstream issue, received with enthusiasm by the Women's Union and social researchers.

A World Bank (2002) document highlights the significance of joint tenure for enabling both spouses to "take advantage of the opportunities that such property rights entail for the *well-being of the rural economy*" (emphasis added). Thus, rather than emphasisng the importance of joint allocation of Land Tenure Certificates in terms of gender equity or the welfare of women, the World Bank's position has mainly underscored the significance of this for overall economic performance and productivity. The same document confounded equity and efficiency goals in stating "properly documented joint land use rights for both wives and husbands can significantly reduce gender asymmetries in access to and control of real property, *and thereby increase productivity"* (emphasis added). The findings of this study suggest that the joint titling of land goes far beyond productivity; it gives women access to a crucial asset and protects them from their husbands' unilateral decisions (i.e., selling the land without the wife's consent).

The significant reforms in the organisation of production since the 1980s have been based on a reluctant recognition of the household's effectiveness as an economic institution. The household thus re-emerged as the primary economic unit (or remained so, as the case may be), responsible for tasks such as the creation of jobs, division of labour and coordination of production. This process accordingly called for new decision-making patterns within the household, with the head of the household taking on a new role; assuming higher economic and legal powers than other members. This could potentially strengthen the authority of the household head and reinforce patriarchal structures (Tran Thi Van Anh 1995, 1997). The relationship between policy change and kinship practices is significant in this case. Kinship is not a static set of precepts but rather consists in fluid practices. When the household is reinstated as the unit of production, a mix of old and emergent household dynamics unfold. In the case we examined, kinship practices in the post-collectivisation period disadvantaged women in a number of ways, as documented below (Bélanger and Xu, 2009).

In the collective period, the agricultural collective dispensed services—although generally of quite poor quality—for health, education, child care and social security for the old and disabled. Under the current process of *doi moi*, many public services were phased out or became more costly. Women often took on some of these caregiving responsibilities in addition to maintaining their significant contributions to household economic production, for which they did not receive any compensation like they did during the collective period. In some areas, notably in the Red River Delta, the entire responsibility for agricultural production was left to women, while men migrated elsewhere in search of waged work. In some cases, however, the reverse occurred, such as when unmarried women migrated to the Mekong Delta to work as agricultural labourers. Marketing and small trading was another type of labour contributed by women that has taken on renewed significance with the opening up of the market economy.

In the recent literature on Vietnam, a debate exists with respect to the medium-term impact of de-collectivisation: some argue that the land tenure system in Vietnam is pro-poor and diminishes poverty levels (Ravallion and van de Walle 2003), while others contend that the current system is creating a land market that deepens economic inequalities, increases landlessness of the very poor and fosters the emergence of a group of rich peasants with relatively large land-holdings (Akram-Lodhi 2005). Kerkvliet's (2005) research suggests that markets alone do not determine the way land is managed in Vietnam. Rather, because peasants disapprove of land concentration and inequalities, they are in favour of some forms of periodic land redistribution. In this way, peasants' views of an acceptable land tenure system are influenced by the socialist, family and community schools of thought and this combination of influences serves to temper land markets (Kerkvliet 2005).

Sikor (2001) argues that inequalities existed prior to de-collectivisation, and varied depending on the family life-cycle: large families obtained more returns from their agricultural work because children could provide labour, whereas smaller families with younger members tended to obtain fewer returns. Sikor contends that it is wrong to question whether or not inequalities in access to land have emerged during de-collectivisation, since inequalities already existed during the collective period. These inequalities were not directly mediated by land, but rather by household size and the ability to collect work points and to secure rations. In this debate, the issue of gender in de-collectivisation has received scant attention. However, indications are that recent land policies in Vietnam fail to address gender inequalities in rights and access to agricultural land (Scott 2003). This chapter further explores this argument.

All the above processes and discussions are mostly relevant for the northern and central regions of the country. In the southern regions of Vietnam, the trajectory of agrarian reforms differed significantly, as revealed in our interviews and historical mapping exercises. There was an agrarian reform between 1955 and 1957 under the Ngo Dinh Diem regime, which aimed to redistribute land to small landless farmers. Landlords were forced to sell their land to their tenants and had the right to keep only a portion of it. Despite this land reform, the tenant system persisted and another policy in 1970 aimed to eliminate the tenant system completely. Land was, once again, taken away from landlords, and farmers received land ownership certificates, but they could not sell or lease the land for 15 years. In the late 1970s, following reunification with the north, the new Hanoi-based state administration made efforts to form agricultural collectives and re-allocate land to farmers. The success of this initiative was very patchy, and, by the 1980s, much of the recently allocated agricultural land was returned to its previous owners. In other places, agricultural collectives existed in name only. Despite all land officially belonging to the state, in practice it is viewed more like private property in the south.

In light of the review of the literature and of indications of rising gender inequalities through the de-collectivisation process, a research project focussing on the gendered dimensions of Vietnam's recent agrarian transitions seemed timely. The way women, as opposed to men, accessed land, and the situation of women who did not fit the "default" categories of the land law—particularly wife and daughter—were two questions that animated this research project. Broader debates about globalisation, agrarian transitions and gender also prompted us to examine the case of Vietnam, with its recent experience of de-collectivisation of agricultural land. The passage from collective ownership to household land-use rights was one type of agrarian transition that characterised the post-socialist era and called for examination from a gender perspective.

METHODOLOGY

To examine women's relationship to land, the team chose qualitative and ethnographic approaches. Two communities were selected based on the predominance of agriculture as an economic activity, their willingness to participate in the study, and their geographical accessibility for the research team. Given the important regional differences with respect to land and agriculture, the research was conducted in both northern and southern Vietnam. One commune in northern Vietnam was located in Ha Tay Province in the Red River Delta region and the other was in Can Tho Province, located in the Mekong River Delta region (see Figure 1). Both provinces are located in the two biggest plain areas of Vietnam and are long-established agricultural areas compared to other parts of the country.

Figure 1

During the fieldwork period, the southern community changed its administrative designation from a rural commune to become an urban ward. This change was unexpected, since our initial focus was on rural communities. Interestingly, it gave us an opportunity to observe the impacts of this new categorisation of the community on land, agriculture, livelihoods and incomes. In fact, an important impact was noted—a sudden increase in land values and household-based conflicts that followed.

Three types of data were collected. First of all, we conducted a survey which contained questions on land holdings, land transactions, livelihood strategies, the gendered division of labour and plans for the future with respect to inheritance and livelihoods. The sample was selected from the village registers. Certain types of households were purposely over-sampled: households headed by women, and households of single, divorced, separated or widowed women. The final sample included 1001 households in total—499 in Ha Tay and 502 in Can Tho. Some key characteristics of the two communities, from data supplied by local authorities and from our own survey, are shown in Table 1. Each community had over 2,000 households, for a total population of 11,600 individuals in the southern site and 9,600 individuals in the northern site. Table 2 provides information on the survey respondents and their households.

In addition to the survey, focus group and in-depth individual interviews were conducted with women belonging to different groups and those representing vulnerable groups (single, separated, divorced and widowed), and elderly women. A total of 45 individual interviews (23 in the north and 22 in the south) were conducted. Focus group discussions were largely aimed at developing a rapport with the villagers at the beginning of the fieldwork. These focus groups were assigned the responsibility of gathering data on the views of villagers and local leaders on land issues, paying special attention to gender. The team conducted a total of 10 focus group discussions (five at each study site) with leaders, young household heads, single women, and the elderly. An additional group discussion with elderly women was conducted in the northern community in order to get more information on the collectivisation process and collective agriculture, in particular, with respect to the roles of women in that

Table 1
Main characteristics of study sites

Main characteristics	*Southern community*	*Northern community*
Number of villages	11	5
Number of households	2300	2200
Population	11600	8900
Average household size	4.8	3.8
Average number of children per household	3.8	3.5
Average number of labourers (15–65)	3	2
Total land	1199 ha	502 ha
Cultivated land	Agricultural land: 292 ha garden land: 774 ha	58 ha
Main occupation	Agriculture (gardening for commercial crops and rice farming), small trading and services, mat weaving	Rice-farming; Handicrafts, small trading, carpentry, construction work
Cultivation	Mainly rice	Commercial fruits and rice
Type of house	Permanent (40%), semi permanent (32%), and temporary houses (27%)	Permanent (75%) and semi-permanent houses (23%)
Main transportation mode	Bicycle, motorbike	Motorbike, boat, bicycle
Village road	Earth road, betonized	Brick, betonized
Electricity	Available	Available

Source: Commune People's Committee reports; interviews with local authorities.

period. All scheduled interviews were audio recorded and transcribed in their entirety. The software package N-VIVO was used for thematic coding of the interviews in Vietnamese.

The interviews were aimed at understanding the dynamics of gender relations within the family and kinship structure, decision-making power within families, and the process of reshaping gender norms. In addition, we sought to understand the practices regarding land rights for women and men, and the strategies adopted by married, divorced, widowed and single women and men to negotiate

Table 2
Main characteristics of survey respondents.

	(percentages)	
	Southern community (n=502)	*Northern community (n=499)*
Sex of household head		
Male	63.7	54.1
Female	36.3	45.9
Age of respondent		
<35	5.0	16.2
35–44	22.9	28.1
45–54	33.3	25.5
55+	38.8	30.3
Education level		
Primary school or no schooling(<5th grade)	53.3	28.2
Secondary school (6–9th grade)	30.3	48.6
High school (10–12th grade)	14.6	19.0
College or university	1.8	4.2
Marital status*		
Currently married	73.2	76.6
Separated/divorced	3.2	5.0
Widowed	20.2	13.8
Single household	3.4	4.6
Main occupation**		
Farming	48.3	66.2
Cadres	3.6	12.1
Services/handicrafts	18.8	11.3
Others	29.3	10.5

* Separated, divorced and widowed households were over-sampled for the purpose of analysis. Most households of such categories in the community have been included in the sample (according to the village registration book)

** Others included retirees, housewives, etc.

these rights within and outside the family and kinship structure. The sample was purposive in that the research questions were relevant to the selected cases. We also interviewed village cadres regarding the evolution of the land tenure system in the villages, such as actual implementation of land distribution and redistribution and the adjustment of state policy based on the local customs, especially the gender norms.

Lastly, participatory research techniques were used to reconstruct the local histories of land policies. Local women were also invited to draw maps of their own communities and indicate the important locations on them. The methodology of the study was based on community involvement. The approach being feminist, participation of women from the communities was encouraged. Several women from the two communities participated in a gender mapping training (which was part of the project) and were members of the research team from the beginning.

The study was well received in both communities. Initially, approval had to be obtained from community and district leaders, who were practically all male. Once we affirmed our desire to work with women and to involve them in the research process (mostly questionnaire design and data collection), the research project was perceived locally as a women-centred one—a message we hoped to send out. By involving women and focusing on them, the project helped draw attention to the topic of land tenure and agriculture as essentially being a women's issue. Community leaders tended to construct land issues as male issues, even though women performed most of the agricultural work, particularly in the northern community. Local authorities in both communities provided support, which contributed to the success of the fieldwork and enhanced the quality of data collected. All interviewees were fully informed about the goals of the research and a verbal agreement was made prior to their participation in the project. A small compensation of cash was offered to each participant for his or her time. At the evaluation stage of the project, representatives from the two communities met in Hanoi and exchanged experiences related to gender and land.

FINDINGS: WAYS TO ACCESS AGRICULTURAL LAND IN VIETNAM— A GENDER ANALYSIS

Entitlements to land can be mediated by various institutions: (1) those that are market based, (2) those based on the formal legal system and (3) those beyond the market and the legal system, such as kin networks, customary law, social conventions and norms (Leach et al. 1999). In the current context in Vietnam these three mediating factors can be represented as (a) state land allocation and certification following the 1993 Land Law, (b) market transfers (pseudo "buying"/"selling"[5]) and leasing of land use rights—what we refer to as "land transactions" and (c) inheritance and other kinship-mediated arrangements (e.g., informal user-rights). In practice, these distinctions are not clear-cut, since kinship and other social networks may influence land market dealings and, in some cases, state land allocation as well. Based on other studies and the data generated by the team, this chapter explores how these various institutions that mediate entitlements to land are gendered. Because the primary site of observation of gender-based inequalities in this study is the kinship system, we particularly elaborate on the inheritance practices and other kin-based land transfers.

(a) State-issued land allocation

In the northern community we studied, most individuals accessed land through state-issued land allocation. In the southern community, it was more common to access land through market transfers and inheritance, since land was never collectivised as it was in the north. Thus, this section deals mostly with the processes at work in the northern community. As stated above, state-issued land allocation was done on a per capita basis in 1993. Agricultural households were allocated user-rights to paddy land for 20 years. The amount of land allocated per individual varied, depending on the commune's total land available. In the northern community, households received 1.4 *sao*[6] for each working-age adult and 1 *sao* for each child aged 15 or less and each adult 60 years or older. In addition to size, the quality and proximity of land were also taken into account in the distribution process, resulting in households receiving land of varying quality in different locations.

Although the names of both husband and wife were to be indicated on all land tenure certificates by 2005—according to Vietnam's national poverty reduction strategy (World Bank 2002)—in the two communities where this survey was conducted in 2004, we found that this objective was far from being met (see Table 3). In the focus groups with community leaders, the addition of women's names to land use certificates did not seem to pose a problem, but nor was it

Table 3
Name(s) on the Land Use Right Certificate for agriculture land (%).
Currently married individuals only.

	Southern community (N=281)	Northern community (N=372)
Husband	73.3	50.5
Wife	22.1	46.2
Both husband and wife	1.1	2.2
Others	3.6	1.1
Total	100.0	100.0

treated as a priority. In contrast, the same regulation for residential land was seen as being in complete contradiction with local practices and impossible to implement. At the time of the survey, about half of the surveyed households in the North had their certificates for agricultural land in the husband's name and the other half in the wife's name. In this community, long-term out-migration of male labour to cities and other provinces was common. Women were thus responsible for all the agricultural work, and this was reflected in the titling of certificates. In contrast, in the southern community, where men are often more involved in agriculture, it was they who were generally listed as the sole right-users (or owners). Table 4 shows the gender division of labour among married households. The findings revealed clear north-south differences. During the interviews, research participants from the northern community explained that it was easier when women had their names on the certificate, since they were the ones making decisions and transactions related to the agricultural land.

Although agricultural land was, in most cases, allocated on the basis of household size—a seemingly fair criterion—discrimination in land allocation is manifest in more subtle ways. In a number of provinces in northern Vietnam, some households received only a portion of the land that was due to be allocated to them because they owed money to the collective from unfulfilled quotas in the past. The withheld portion of land was rented out by the collective to other farmers until sufficient rent could be collected to cover the debt, at which time the land was returned to the original household. The practice of withholding land affected up to 15 per cent of households

Table 4
Main source of income of women household heads by their marital status (%)

	Southern community (%)			Northern community (%)			Total	
	Currently married	divorced/ separated/ single	widowed	Currently married	divorced/ separated/ single	widowed	Thuong thanh	Daidong
Farming only	16.9	34.4	14	13.7	31.3	22.7	17.4	16.6
Farming and other jobs	64.4	28.1	55	84.7	62.5	68.2	60.1	80.3
Not farming	18.8	37.5	31	1.6	6.3	9.1	22.5	3
Total count	100.0	100.0	100.0	100.0	100.0	100.0	100.0	100.0

in some delta villages (Tran Thi Van Anh 1995), over eight per cent of households in some villages in Hoa Binh (Smith 1997: 164), and, at times, up to 40 to 50 per cent of a household's allocation (CGFED 1996: 37). In some areas, land was reportedly withheld in cases where households failed to implement family planning (Tran Thi Van Anh 1997). In cases where land was withheld and households left with insufficient land for their own subsistence, household members were forced to seek wage labour. We also identified households in this situation in our data. In one case, a family consisting of a man who had married two women did not receive any land in 1993 because he had a debt dating back to the collective period. The family lived in great poverty. Members of this landless household all worked as agricultural day labourers and the children were forced to quit school to join their parents at work at the age of 12.

Legal provisions for state-allocated land were gendered because they failed to take into account cases of women not attached to their parents' or husband's households. Single women (living inde-pendently), divorced women and widows were often excluded from allocation. In the northern communities, a group of older single women organised a meeting with the people's committee of their village to claim land, since they had not received any during the initial distribution of 1993. Because they did not belong to any household through marriage, their status was ambiguous. The Land Law only recognised two categories of women: daughters and wives. Unmarried adult women claiming land did not fit into either of these two groups, which presented a challenge to the law. Following the discussion, these women were allocated land several years after the 1993 distribution from a small number of plots that the commune had kept for rental to particularly poor villagers.

Village "membership" was the first criterion for deciding who was entitled to land allocations and who was not. As a result, some women, who had migrated to the village for marriage, were not entitled. Consequently, some families received a smaller share of their entitlement for their household despite the fact that they had lived in the village for many years. In contrast, men who had never lived in the village could be eligible for land if, for example, they were sons of village men and had been born elsewhere. In one particular case, an elderly man with two wives in the village had a relationship and fathered a son with a woman in another province. The son had never been to his father's village of origin. He was, nonetheless, allocated agricultural land. In addition, he was the official heir of his father's residence and residential land plot. Village membership was, therefore, not established on the basis of residence, but on the principle of male patrilineage. Customary patrilineal practices, as opposed to gender-neutral criteria, were thus used to implement the new policy in some localities. Such traditions are particularly strong in the Red River Delta (Bélanger 2002).

State-issued land allocation allowed all households in the northern community to obtain user-rights to paddy land for 20 years. The system of state-issued land allocation on a per capita basis (each individual above a certain age in the household was allocated a certain amount of land) allowed all households in the northern community to obtain user-rights to paddy land for 20 years. This type distribution promoted a sense of equity among household members: when peasants in the northern community were asked how much land their household had, they listed the plots that each family member had received in 1993, as opposed to referring to the household's total acreage. For instance, upon marriage, young women were allowed to keep their share of state-allocated land, provided that they married in their village of origin (endogamous marriage). Elderly women too preferred to keep their land, even when they could no longer cultivate it themselves and had to rent it out.

(b) Market-based land transactions

Market-based transfers of land were extremely common in the Vietnamese countryside. However, many transactions were not officially recorded, so official data only accounted for a certain proportion of these (Kerkvliet 2005). Leaders of the communities that were studied acknowledged that they were not aware of all transactions that took place, since many were short-term and not officially registered. During the survey, we collected detailed information on land transactions and on women's involvement in these transactions. Land transactions began after state allocation was completed and they substantially transformed patterns of ownership or user-rights.

We focus our discussion on the implications of land transactions for women. For some, these were means by which they could redress some of the inequities they may have suffered at the time of distribution. In this respect, women's power over land transactions was extremely important when assessing gender and power relations within households and communities.

It was observed during the fieldwork that land transactions played a contradictory role. On the one hand, they contributed to a certain equilibrium in the land market. In the north, for instance, households with a surplus of land frequently leased part of their land to households that had too little land to feed their families. A frequent pattern was that young couples who had their children after the state-land distribution of 1993 leased land from families with older children who had left home. On the other hand, land transactions had also led to speculation, landlessness, and concentration of land in the hands of a few. Very poor families facing an urgent need for cash, for example, might "sell" (i.e., transfer) their user-rights, thereby increasing landlessness. Some families had sold their land because they were engaged in cash earning activities and no longer required the land for agriculture. If they failed to earn enough and went bankrupt, it would be very difficult for them to purchase land again. With Vietnam's transition to a market economy, there was a reappearance of landless peasants (mostly teenage girls and married women) who worked as day labourers for other farmers. In the north, however, most families preferred to retain their user-rights and to lease their land if they did not need the crops for survival. Land was seen as a security that families could fall back on in case of adversity. Women were often the guardians of the land when their households faced a crisis. In the north particularly, they protected it at all costs from being transferred, only giving it up when there was absolutely no other option.

The most common land transactions recorded in our survey differed for the northern and southern study sites. In the south, households were more engaged in "selling" and "buying" land, while households in the north were more likely to lease their land. For the purposes of this chapter, women's involvement in land transactions is particularly relevant. Table 5 shows that, overall, women were much

Table 5
Gendered decision making regarding land transactions
(% households)

Name on land transaction record	Southern community	Northern community
Renting land		
Husband	70	24.6
Wife	10	56.1
Both husband and wife	0	1.8
Others	20	17.5
Count	10	114
Buying land		
Husband	76	21.3
Wife	14	68.1
Both husband and wife	2	2.1
Count	43	47
Giving land in the form of inheritance		
Husband	70	63.6
Wife	25	27.3
Both husband and wife	0.4	0
Others	4	9.1
Count	231	11

more involved in land transactions in the northern community than in the southern one. Decision-making with regard to the selling or purchasing of land was male-dominated in the south. In both communities, men dominated when it came to banking transactions involving the mortgaging of agricultural land.[7] In the northern community, women did most of the agricultural work and had some decision-making power over land transactions, whereas the pattern was reversed in the southern community. In both communities, decisions pertaining to inheritance of land were more frequently made by men. Overall, these results demonstrated important regional differences and showed that the household division of labour (women's involvement in agricultural work) was important for their power over land transactions.

Rural Vietnam's growing income inequality continues despite a fairly limited degree of land concentration to date.[8] Income disparities in rural areas seem to be more attributable to increases in non-agricultural income than to the accumulation of land. Nevertheless, the number of landless agricultural households is growing. According to national statistics from the government of Vietnam, in 2002, 18.9 per cent of rural households were landless—about twice as many as five years earlier. Landless agricultural households[9] were particularly concentrated in the southeast region and Mekong Delta; 89 per cent of all landless agricultural households were located here. More striking still was the fact that landlessness among the poorest quintile grew from 26 to 39 per cent between 1998 and 2002 (Joint Donor Report 2003: 39). The main income source of these households was wage labour in agricultural production.

Also, according to national statistics, among agricultural households that were *not* landless in 2001, the vast majority (64 per cent) had less than half a hectare of agricultural land. Compared to 1994, the largest change was a five per cent decrease in households that had 0.2 to 0.5 hectares (GSO 2003). These households appeared to have either shifted downward, to below 0.2 hectares or become completely landless. Some households increased their amount of land, particularly the 1 to 3 hectare group of households, which grew by 2.5 per cent over the same period. The data revealed an increase in the number of households with landholdings of over one hectare and a concurrent decrease in those that had less than one hectare. This phenomenon was particularly marked in the southeast region, where there was an abundance of industrial and service opportunities, and the Central Highlands, where such opportunities did not exist. These diverging experiences show that while land loss is often an indicator of economic insecurity, this may not always be the case.

In this survey, we explored some of the reasons for landlessness. Findings indicate that because households tended to keep their land as security, landlessness generally only occurred as a result of chronic indebtedness and the need to repay loans. The survey also revealed that divorced and widowed women were more likely to be landless than husband-wife households.

(c) Kinship and inheritance

Besides state allocation and market transfers, the most common means of accessing land was through inheritance from parents.

Although rights to equal inheritance for men and women were guaranteed by the 1959 Marriage and Family Law, inheritance patterns in practice have not been widely documented, particularly regarding division among offspring, and inheritance for daughters, widows, divorced women and second wives (currently illegal, but implicitly tolerated). In the collective period (until the late 1980s), inheritance of agricultural land in the north was a non-issue, as land was accessed through one's status as a collective member. Since then, however, the state no longer takes responsibility for ensuring that land is accessible to *individual* household members (Smith 1997). Although the Vietnamese Land Law was based on the principle of equal ownership of land by all household members, the rights for individual household members were not spelled out. The changing status of the household brought about changes in the rules vis a vis access to land; land was now accessed at the level of the *household*, through state allocation, or at the level of the *individual* by market transactions or through inheritance. As a result, kinship-mediated land inheritance had a greater impact on individuals' well-being.

Inheritance patterns documented in this study showed that in the northern community, women almost never inherited anything from their parents. Since women were constructed as "the children of others" and were transferred to their husband's family upon marriage, inheritance was given only to sons. This was justified because the sons were considered to be responsible for the care of parents in their old age and for ancestor worship after their death. In the numerous stories we collected, it was noted that when parents wished to give land (agricultural or residential) to a daughter, male elders opposed this decision, and this sometimes created a conflict between the female heir and her male relatives. In such cases, women either gave up their inheritance or sought redress from the courts. Using the legal system to solve a conflict usually resulted in the woman having to leave the community. Women who used the justice system were often stigmatised and ignored by their kin following a court case. Most of these women were unmarried and received land as compensation for a life devoted to the care of their parents. In some cases, "late marriage" could also penalise women.

Here, we highlight the case of a woman who "inherited" her parents' debts but whose claims to a share of inheritance were refused:

> Mrs Gia married late because she took care of her younger siblings and of her grandfather following her parents' premature death. Twenty years after her parents' death, she was still struggling to pay her parents' debts. She was obligated to contribute to her husband's family, so she could not use any of her meagre income to help pay off her parents' debt. She suggested to her siblings that they use their parents' land to pay off the debt, but they disagreed. She asked them to divide a portion of this land for her but again, they disapproved, and they even erected a fence in order to prevent her from accessing the land. She had sent twenty letters of protest to various levels of government, from the commune level to the district level, but there was no resolution. She was demanding part of her parents' property to be used to pay off their debt, with the remainder of land being divided between the four siblings. Her relatives did not approve of her proposed solution, because they thought that since Mrs Gia was already married, she was not entitled to any of her parents' property. She felt it was not fair to her because she sacrificed her youth to raise her siblings and care for her grandparents. The government had not been of any help, because custom in this region dictated that women did not inherit property. The relationship between her and her younger brothers was now very tense. When she visited her parents' house, her brothers closed the doors to prevent her from entering. She had little knowledge about land and inheritance laws, and since she was so busy with family affairs, she did not participate in the activities of the Women's Union.[10]

In contrast to the northern community, women in the southern community would inherit agricultural land from their parents. In general, however, sons received larger shares than daughters. In the case of families with small plots, only sons inherited. According to this survey, 75 per cent of men received inheritance in the form of land; while in the case of women, only 19 per cent did (the remainder did not receive any inheritance most likely because their parents had no estate). Despite the more flexible system in the south, men remain substantially advantaged in comparison to women. In the past, it was not uncommon for daughters to turn down their inheritance and leave it with one of their brothers. But the increasing price of land had a significant impact on family relations and inheritance patterns, as is obvious in the increased number of conflicts over land ownership and transfer. This increase in land prices also prompted the women to keep the land they had inherited, and this sometimes triggered family conflicts.

In this survey, we tried to find out more about the attitudes and intentions regarding inheritance. There were clear differences between the two communities. When asked about the rights to inheritance in case parents had daughters only (see Table 6), the vast majority of respondents (98 per cent) in the south stated that inheritance should go to daughters if there were no sons. In contrast, one third of the sample in the north thought that inheritance should go to a male relative who would become responsible for ancestor worship, of his uncle and aunt; another third favoured splitting the inheritance between a daughter and a male relative; and only one fourth thought that it should all go to the daughter(s). Interestingly, attitudes seem more open than current practices. In the south, daughters could take on the responsibility of ancestor worship rituals for the souls of their

Table 6
Intended heir for inheritance of land in case of having no son (%)

	Residential land		Agricultural land	
	Southern community	Northern community	Southern community	Northern community
Daughter and son in-law	99.2	24.0	97.6	52.0
Heir & worshipper	0.2	35.6	0.8	31.7
Care taker	0.2	0		
Daughter & worshipper	0.2	37.8	0.4	15
Other (relative, person in need)	0.2	2.6	1.2	1.2
Total	100.0	100.0	100.0	100.0
Count	497	492	246	492

parents after the latter's death, while in the north, sons could only be replaced by male relatives, not by daughters.

Upon divorce, women had the right to an equal portion of the household's assets. Yet, in practice, they were more likely to be given monetary compensation worth less than half the value of the household's total worth. This reinforces Agarwal's call, discussed earlier, for women to have property registered in their own name so as to facilitate their bargaining power in such instances. In the case of the northern community, women who divorced generally retained their user-rights to an individual share of the land. However, residential land was almost impossible to obtain, since it was passed on from parents to sons only. Many women who found themselves in abusive relationships or with husbands with gambling or drinking problems did not leave because they had nowhere to go following a divorce. Often, women who divorced had to give up their children (especially male children) to the husband's family. In addition, in-laws often objected to a divorced woman marrying their son.

Single women often lived with their parents and took care of them until the latter passed away. Following that, they might be able to stay with their brother's family. Some single women received an inheritance from their parents in the form of a small plot of residential land, so they could build a house for themselves. Some of these women also chose to become "second wives", so they could hopefully give birth to a male child and secure support for their old age. Often the son of a second wife was raised by the first wife, but the son would be responsible for both his mothers—his father's first wife and his biological mother.

> Daughters who marry or stay single in their parents' house are the same—they are not given land. Even if the family has lots of land, it is only given to sons. For example, Ms Yen, who had a large plot of land, did not give any to her single daughter. Daughters should be conscious of their status and be prepared to save for their future. Families may lend money to daughters to buy land, but they do not give land to them. (Old woman, northern community)

One woman in a group discussion talked about securing a future for herself by becoming a second wife in the village,

If the husband is better off he would buy her a house or her parents would buy a small piece of land for her to build a house on so that her husband could visit. He would visit her sometimes because most of his time would be spent living with his first wife. When his second wife gives birth, her husband will take responsibility for the child. If she gives birth to a son, the land of the first wife will definitely belong to him in the future, whether the land is small or large. (focus group discussion with women, northern community)

Widows represented another case in point. If a woman was widowed at a young age, her identity became ambiguous. She might stay with her husband's family and inherit the household's land, assuming it was in the name of her husband, or she could return to her parents' house, generally still claiming her husband's assets, depending on her relationship with her parents-in-law. In instances where a woman was widowed at a later age, when the parents-in-law had already passed away, land might be transferred to her or her sons, following Confucian morality.[11] Indeed, even when a woman did not give up legal "ownership" (in the form of a land use certificate), in practice, she might forfeit making decisions regarding use of the land. This reflects the divergence between a legal right and its social recognition, and underscores the need to observe the processes and not merely the outcomes.

In the northern community, one old widow had only a step-son and decided to transfer two thirds of her land to him, keeping the rest for herself while she was still living. Although she also had a daughter, she planned on leaving all her land to her stepson after her death. When her step-son asked the local authorities to register all their land in his name, she approached the local administration to maintain the land use certificate in her own name to protect her portion from being taken away by her step-son. As she explained,

I would like to keep only one *sao* (360 m^2) to keep my right (to the land) because when I die the land will belong to him (step-son). If I kept the land for selling purposes, I would have sold it long ago when I had a big debt. Now that I am close to the end of life I do not need to sell the land, but I should keep my rights to it. I will not give him all land. (74 year old woman, northern community)

In another discussion, local authorities explained the attitudes of parents with respect to transferring land to their children:

> Parents normally retain the (rights to) land. Only after a son marries and has children do parents give land to their son at which time he holds ownership of it. Even when families own four or five pieces of land, they do not transfer ownership of it to their sons because they fear that the sons may sell the land if they need money. Therefore, parents often give (transfer) land ownership by dividing the land between their children when they (parents) are close to the end of their lives. Nowadays, things have changed slightly—parents can buy land for their sons after they (the sons) marry. (Focus group discussion with local authorities, northern community)

Although the Land Law was based on the principle of equal ownership by all household members, rights were not clearly spelled out. Land allocation was only formalised with the issuing of land use certificates following the 1993 Land Law. Hence, in practice, clear inheritance patterns are difficult to discern. While the Family and Marriage Law provided for equal sharing of assets upon divorce and the division of inheritance among siblings, other cases were worked out on a family-by-family basis.

There were also many legal gaps by way of which women could be denied their rights, particularly since the Land Law and the Law on Marriage and Family were only linked in 2003. As mentioned earlier, in the event of divorce, land was generally not split, so the husband's family often paid compensation to the wife for agricultural land (and the house), but the amount paid was generally considerably less than the market value. Following divorce, the wife often returned to live with her parents. She often also ended up owning much less land than her husband. Yet, typically, she took on the responsibility of the children (especially female children). Some parents-in-law have gone to court to reclaim a wife's land after divorce, but generally the courts have upheld the wife's rights (Oxfam 1997).

The situation of non-married women (divorced, single, widows) was particularly vulnerable with respect to access to a residence, as explained above. While the focus of this chapter is on agricultural land, women's vulnerability to expulsion from their residence is

Table 7
Name on the land use certificate (residential land) of
non-married women

	Southern community		Northern community	
	Divorced/ separated/single household heads	*Widowed*	*Divorced/ separated/single household heads*	*Widowed*
Male	13.0	24.2	10.3	9.0
Female	43.5	55.8	41.4	64.2
Other*	43.5	20.0	48.3	26.9
Count	23	95	29	67

* Other included parents, siblings, relatives. Some did not even have a Land Use Certificate.

worth mentioning since it is tied to their access to agricultural land. Without residence, women did not qualify for "village membership" and their access to agricultural land was thus threatened. Table 7 shows that at the time of the survey a large proportion of women did not have legal ownership of their residential land. Hence they lived in fear of expulsion at any time by relatives looking for a place to live.

As we have seen, women's access to land was in large part determined by the patrilineal kinship system. Customary practices and notions of "village membership" generally put women at a disadvantage over men, even with a seemingly egalitarian system of state-allocation. Women's roles in land transactions, however, revealed their agency in their efforts to circumvent customary patrilineal practices.

The above discussion, however, should not suggest that kinship practices alone mediated gendered access to land. In fact, socio-economic changes had a direct influence on kinship practices in ways that could either reduce or exacerbate inequalities. A case in point was in the southern community, where land values increased dramatically around the time of the fieldwork. In some families we studied, the practice of giving inheritance to both sons and daughters led to family conflict. In both cases, men and women were using "tradition" to claim their rights, given the new socio-economic context. On the one hand, the old practice of daughters "giving up" their right to inheritance so their brothers could support their new families was still being demanded of women. On the other, daughters desiring to benefit from the increasing wealth flowing into their community were demanding the "traditional" inheritance rights of women. In this case, the impacts on gender relations of socio-economic changes arising from increased land values were too recent to be fully assessed. To be sure, they led to a higher incidence of family conflicts and the increased risk of landlessness for many.

In the northern community too, the socio-economic context mediated gender differences in access to land through inheritance. Given the scarcity and shrinking sizes of land holdings, families wishing to give an inheritance to each of their children were faced with the problem of land fragmentation. As a result, it was often only the eldest son who inherited all the family's holdings. The younger sons found themselves in the difficult position of having to settle elsewhere, sometimes with rather limited support from their parents or the eldest son in the family. Class differences were emerging among sons by birth order in an unprecedented way.

CONCLUSION: WOMEN'S ATTACHMENT TO LAND

All the women we interviewed and surveyed, including those with salaried employment such as teachers or nurses, wished to protect their agricultural land at any cost. This fact led us to carry out a secondary analysis of our narratives and to examine in this concluding section what we called the meaning of land. What were the reasons, besides socio-economic considerations, for this strong attachment to agricultural land in the current context of rural Vietnam? Three factors emerged powerfully and we briefly describe them here.

For most women, "land means survival". It was difficult to rely on subsistence agriculture alone, and households worked hard at developing diverse livelihood activities. In the midst of these transformations, women were the guardians of land. In our study, for most women who did not rely on land alone to feed their families, land was seen as something to fall back on in case of a financial or family crisis. Women also hoped that their land would some day become more valuable and that, perhaps, they would be able to invest in a cash crop. For women without any source of income except agriculture, land was needed for daily survival, although they were systematically plagued by chronic indebtedness. Needing land to survive was a recurrent theme in our interviews.

Beyond economic survival, "land means belonging." Landless female peasants had lost their sense of belonging to their community. Owning land (or having user-rights) was particularly important to women, since they acquired status and legitimacy through belonging to a male lineage. In this male-centred kinship system, women's involvement in agriculture and land transactions was very significant. Through their material connections to the community, they could claim their autonomy from the male lineage they joined after marriage. In addition, by protecting their access and right to land, they were protecting their fallback position in the event of divorce or widowhood and in their old age. Having land gave them the bargaining power.

Finally, "land holds significant symbolic value". Attachment to land was enhanced because of the importance of ancestor worship. In both the north and the south, family members who passed away were buried on family land. In the southern community, in general, family members were buried behind the house, in the family garden. In the northern community, they were buried on the rice land. In addition to the physical "presence" of the deceased relatives on family land, it was believed that the spirits of ancestors lived in the family house. People had a responsibility to care for the ancestors by making them offerings and celebrating death anniversaries. Performing these rituals brought luck to the living; neglecting the care of the souls of dead relatives would result in future misfortunes. The rituals were also the main symbol of patrilineal continuity. They were ideally meant to be performed in the space where the dead people used to live, a belief which sometimes made the sale of land very problematic in the emerging land markets. Also, in an increasingly mobile society, land was a symbol of stability and a place most people wished to return to in their old age.

These findings confirm that land is a special form of property, linking economic, cultural, political, and legal dimensions of social life. The bases for land access, and more broadly for livelihood vulnerability, are in a flux in the new economic and institutional context of contemporary Vietnam. De-collectivisation has involved shifts in formal and informal social institutions, which in turn shaped new patterns of access to, and exchange of land. This chapter has discussed how land tenure changes in Vietnam transformed women's relationship to land. In the north, de-collectivisation resulted in the resurgence of patrilineal inheritance practices and in the demise of women's status as full members of families and households. On the other hand, the emergence of individual and household land transactions provided new opportunities for women to participate in the land markets. However, they faced many disadvantages compared to their male counterparts. In the southern community, land speculation, concentration of land in the hands of a few, and landlessness made women vulnerable to poverty. Nonetheless, some women were taking advantage of the new opportunities arising from economic development and increasing land values in the region.

Given Vietnam's push to increase agricultural productivity in the current global economic context, small farmers have remained highly vulnerable and female farmers more particularly so. Future policies should address the gaps and vulnerabilities identified in this chapter and promote the well-being of all those working the land—men and women, young and old.

NOTES

1. Recognising the discrimination women faced in the work point system under collective agriculture and the important control that women had over marketing activities prior to collectivisation, a significant avenue for future research could involve an exploration of the role that women played in bringing down the cooperatives and calling for a new organisation of agricultural production. This line of reasoning might lead one to posit that the control women wielded in the sphere of marketing prior to collectivisation gave them a degree of autonomy that was taken from them under collective agriculture, thus explaining a possible motivation for their opposition to the latter. An alternative reading, however, in a CGFED (1996:42) study in the Red River Delta, documents women's complaints regarding the greater workload they faced with marketing responsibilities in addition to all of their usual tasks. Perhaps, more than anything, this underscores the ambiguity in interpretation (or co-existence of multiple benefits and constraints) in women's relationship to markets, which varies significantly among and within groups of women from place to place.

2. This was somewhat less true in parts of southern Vietnam, where a form of restitution to pre-1975 owners took place. [see footnote 8]

3. A significant amount of "forestry land" has also been allocated to households for production, as well as for reforestation and forest protection objectives. This includes forested land (although not virgin land), bare land (to be reforested) and land which is not forested at all but planted for personal use and industrial crops on hilly slopes.

4. However, farmers in some areas (e.g., Thai Nguyen province) have suggested that there were no adjustments in the allocations in 1993, compared to those following the 1988 reforms, which were to be based on number of labourers in a household. Moreover, in much of south Vietnam, where collectivisation efforts were much shorter-lived and less successful, lands have been largely re-allocated on the basis of land distribution in 1975 (i.e., prior to collectivisation efforts in this region), with some exceptions for very large land holdings.

5. We say "pseudo" because it is not legally possible to sell or purchase user-rights. In reality, peasants transfer their user-rights to another household for a sum of money, but do talk about "having sold" or "purchased" agricultural land. At the end of the contract (2013) the user-rights will have to be re-transferred to the original household. Households desperate for cash sell their user-rights, although the returns of these transactions are generally very low since sellers tend to be in an extremely weak position.

6. One *sao* in northern Vietnam equals 360 square metres of land.

7. This information is not shown in the tables.

8. The allocation of agricultural land through de-collectivisation appeared to have been most equitable in the lowlands and in northern Vietnam. Parts of the south followed a process of restitution along the lines of pre-1975 ownership patterns, while some areas of the northern mountains inhabited by ethnic minorities developed their own local rules for allocation based on ancestral land claims (Scott 2000). [see footnote 3]

9. By definition, households not using agricultural land were mainly landless households whose members worked as hired labours. In addition, there was small number of households that did not need land, such as households specialising in livestock raising or agricultural services.

10. The Vietnam Women's Union is a "mass organisation" originally established to mobilise women for national liberation. It helps to identify and address emerging socio-economic, health, cultural and political issues that have important implications for women. The organisation has millions of members, and has representation in all communes and districts around the country.

11. The "three obediences" (*tam tong*) dictate that a woman will follow the orders of her father before marriage, her husband after marriage, and her son upon the death of her husband.

REFERENCES ▓▓

Akram-Lodhi, A. Haroon, 2005, "Vietnam's Agriculture: Processes of Rich Peasant Accumulation and Mechanisms of Social Differentiation", *Journal of Agrarian Change* 5(1): 73–116.

Agarwal, Bina, 1997, ""Bargaining" and Gender Relations: Within and Beyond the Household", *Feminist Economics*, 3(1): 1–51.

————, 1994a, *A Field of One's Own: Gender and Land Rights in South Asia.* Cambridge: Cambridge University Press.

————, 1994b, "Gender and command over property: A critical gap in economic analysis and policy in South Asia", *World Development* 22(10): 1455–1478.

Asian Development Bank (ADB), 1997, *Socio-Economic Review: Final Report, Vietnam Land Information System and Agricultural Taxation Study.* TA no. 2225–VIE, Hanoi, Vietnam.

Bélanger, Danièle, 2002, "Son Preference in North Rural Vietnam", *Studies in Family Planning* 33(4): 321–334.

Bélanger, Danièle and Barbieri, Magali, 2009, Introduction: The State and families in the making of transitions. In Danièle Bélanger and Magali Barbieri (eds), *Reconfiguring Families in Contemporary Vietnam.* Stanford: Stanford University Press, pp. 1–46.

Bélanger, Danièle and Xu, Li, 2009, "Agricultural Land, Gender and Kinship in Rural China and Vietnam: A Comparison of Two Villages", *Journal of Agrarian Change* 9(2): 204–230.

Bhaduri, Amit, 1982, "Agricultural Cooperatives and Peasant Participation in the Socialist Republic of Viet Nam." In Amit Bhaduri and M.D. Anisur Rahman (eds), *Studies in Rural Participation.* New Delhi: Oxford and IBH Publishing, pp. 34–57.

Centre for Gender, Family and Environment in Development (CGFED), 1996, *Rural Women in the Red River Delta: Gender, Water Management and Economic Transformation: A Study in Three Districts and Nine Communes.* Hanoi: CGFED.

Chant, Sylvia, 1997, "Women-Headed Households: Poorest of the Poor? Perspectives from Mexico, Costa Rica and the Philippines", *IDS Bulletin* 28(3): 26–48.

Deere, Carmen Diana, and Magdalena Leon, 2001, *Empowering Women: Land and Property Rights in Latin America.* Pittsburgh, PA: University of Pittsburgh Press.

Engels, Frederick, 1845, *The Origin of the Family, Private Property, and the State.* Reprinted, 1972. New York: International Publishers.

Funk, Nanette and Magda Mueller (eds.), 1993, *Gender Politics and Post-Communism.* London: Routledge.

General Statistics Office, 2003, *Structure of Land Use, Population, and National Accounts: Agriculture, Forestry and Fisheries Land Census.* Hanoi: General Statistics Office.

Hart, Gillian, Andrew Turton, and Benjamin White (eds.), 1989, *Agrarian Transformations: Local Processes and the State in Southeast Asia*. Berkeley and Los Angeles: University of California Press.

Hirschon, Renee (ed.), 1984, *Women and Property—Women As Property*. London: Croom Helm.

Jackson, Cecile, 2003, "Gender Analysis of Land: Beyond Land Rights for Women", *Journal of Agrarian Change* 3(4): 453–480.

Joint Donor Report, 2003, *Vietnam Development Report 2004: Poverty*. Joint Donor Report to the Vietnam Consultative Group Meeting. Hanoi, Vietnam: ADB, AusAID, DFID, GTZ, JICA, Save the Children UK, UNDP and the World Bank.

Kabeer, Naila, 1989, Monitoring Poverty As If Gender Mattered: A Methodology for Rural Bangladesh, Discussion Paper 255. Institute of Development Studies. Brighton, Sussex.

Kerkvliet, Benedict J. Tria, 2005, *The Power of Everyday Politics: How Vietnamese Peasants Transformed National Policy*. Ithaca: Cornell University Press.

Kodoth, Praveena, 2001, "Gender, Family and Property Rights: Questions from Kerala's Land Reforms", *Indian Journal of Gender Studies* 8(2): 291–306.

Kandiyoti, Deniz, 2003, "The Cry for Land: Agrarian Reform, Gender and Land Rights in Uzbekistan", in Shahra Razavi (ed), *Agrarian Change, Gender and Land Rights*. Oxford: Blackwell.

Leach, Melissa, Robin Mearns and Ian Scoones, 1999, "Environmental Entitlements: Dynamics and Institutions in Community-Based Natural Resource Management", *World Development* 27(2): 225–247.

Lustéguy, Pierre, 1935, *La femme Annamite du Tonkin dans l'Institution des Biens Cultuels. Études sur une enquête récente*. Paris: Librairie Nizet et Bastard.

Mai Thi Tu and Le Thi Nham Tuyet, 1978, *Women in Vietnam*. Hanoi: Foreign Language Publishing House.

Ministry of Agriculture and Rural Development (MARD) and United Nations Development Program (UNDP), 1998, *Rural Development Strategy Framework*. Agricultural Publishing House.

Moser, Caroline and Cathy McIlwaine, 1997, *Household Responses to Poverty and Vulnerability: Confronting Crisis in Commonwealth, Metro Manila, the Philippines*. Washington, DC: World Bank.

Mukhopadhyay, Maitrayee, 1998, *Legally dispossessed: Gender, identity and the process of law*. Calcutta: Stree.

———, 2001. "Introduction: Women and property, women as property", in Sarah Cummings, Henk van Dam, Angela Khadar, and Minke Valk (eds), *Gender perspectives on Property and Inheritance: A Global Source Book*. Amsterdam: KIT (Royal Tropical Institute) The Netherlands and Oxfam Great Britain, pp. 13–18.

Oxfam UK/Ireland, 1997, A Brief Inquiry into Gender and Participation Issues in the Process of Land Allocation. Unpublished report. Hanoi: Oxfam UK/Ireland Viet Nam Programme, June.

Papin, P., 1997, Des "villages dans la ville" aux "villages urbains': L'espace et les formes de pouvoir à Hanoi de 1805 à 1940. Paris, University de Paris VII. Ph.D.

Protectorat du Tonkin, 1930, *Recueil des Avis du comité consultatif de jurisprudence annamite sur les coutumes des Annamites du Tonkin en matière de droit de famille, de succession et de biens cultuels.* Hanoi: Imprimerie Trung-Bac Tan-Van, 9(2): 259–278.

Ravallion, Martin and Dominique van de Walle, 2003, *Land Allocation in Vietnam's Agrarian Transition.* World Bank Policy Research Paper 2951. Washington, DC: World Bank.

Razavi, Shahra, 2007, "Liberalisation and the debates on women's access to land", *Third World Quarterly* 28(8): 1479–1500.

Razavi, Shahra (ed.), 2003, *Agrarian Change, Gender and Land Rights.* Oxford: Blackwell.

Scott, Steffanie, 2009, "Agrarian Transitions in Vietnam: Linking Land, Livelihoods, and Poverty", in Max Spoor (ed.), *The Political Economy of Rural Livelihoods in Transition Economies: Land, Peasants and Rural Poverty in Transition.* London: Routledge, pp. 175–200.

———, 2003, "Gender, Household Headship and Entitlements to Land: New Vulnerabilities in Vietnam's Decollectivization", *Gender, Technology and Development* 7(2): 233–263.

———, 2000, "Changing Rules of the Game: Local Responses to Decollectivisation in Thai Nguyen, Vietnam", *Asia Pacific Viewpoint* 41(1): 69–84.

Seager, Joan, 1997, *The State of Women in the World: Atlas.* New edition. New York: Penguin.

Sen, Amartya, 1990, "Gender and cooperative conflicts", in Irene Tinker (ed), *Persistent Inequalities.* Oxford: Oxford University Press, pp.123–149.

Sikor, T., 2001, "Agrarian Differentiation in Post-Socialist Societies: Evidence from Three Upland Villages in North-Western Vietnam", *Development and Change* 32: 923–949.

Smith, William, 1997, "Land and the Poor: A Survey of Land Use Rights in Ha Tinh and Son La Provinces", *Proceedings of the National Workshop on Participatory Land Use Planning and Forest Land Allocation.* December 4–6. Hanoi: Agriculture Publishing House.

Ta Van Tai, 1981, "The Status of Women in Traditional Vietnam: A Comparison of the Code of the Le Dynasty (1428–1788) with the Chinese Codes", *Journal of Asian History* 15(2): 97–145.

Thai Thi Ngoc Du, 1999, "Women Influencing Housing in Ho Chi Minh City", in Irene Tinker and Gale Summerfield (eds), *Women's Rights to House and Land: China, Laos, Vietnam.* Boulder and London: Lynne Rienner, pp. 55–76.

Tran, Nhung Tuyet, 2006, "Beyond the Myth of Equality: Daughters' Inheritance Rights in the Lê Dynasty", in Nhung Tuyet Tran and Anthony Reid (eds), *Vietnam: Borderless Histories.* Madison: University of Wisconsin Press, pp. 125–49.

Tran Thi Van Anh, 1999, "Women and Rural Land in Vietnam", in Irene Tinker and Gale Summerfield (eds), *Women's Rights to House and Land: China, Laos, Vietnam.* Boulder and London: Lynne Rienner Publishers, pp. 95–114.

————. 1995, "Household Economy and Gender Relationship." *Vietnam Social Sciences* (Hanoi), 1(45): 53–59.

Werner, Jayne, 1983, "Socialist Development: The Political Economy of Agrarian Reform in Vietnam", *Bulletin of Concerned Asian Scholars* 48–55.

World Bank, 2002, "Land Use Rights and Gender Equality in Vietnam." *Promising Approaches to Engendering Development,* (Sept.) no. 1. Accessed at www.worldbank.org/gender/promising/.

Xu, Li, 2006, *Intra-family gender relations, women's well-being, and access to resources: the case of a northern Chinese village.* PhD thesis, Department of Sociology, University of Western Ontario.

8 Conclusion
For a Politics of Difference

NOEMI MIYASAKA PORRO

Difference was a remarkable presence from the very beginning of the project that gave birth to this book. The call launched by IDRC, in 2001 for research on gender, land and globalisation, brought together grantee researchers and supporting scholars from five continents, presenting diverse interests, backgrounds, institutions and perspectives. Difference emerged also from the awarded proposals, not only in terms of sites and focuses, but in proposed ways of perceiving and working on gender, land and globalisation. And yet, recognising differences, this project was about a shared openness for dialogue; a dialogue between men and women, north and south, structuralist and post-structuralist, activist and academic, senior and junior researchers.

Difference was even more blatant in the field; here, all the researchers registered the sameness of the neo-liberal policies and structural adjustments imposed by IMF and the World Bank. However, although immersed in these apparently homogenising impositions, in and within each site, everyday practices by local people working the global, the land and their own gender were as different as the diverse expressions of economic liberalisation (de-collectivisation in Vietnam, new market drives for Amazonian resources, increased competition over natural resources in Ghana and trans-national development projects in Cameroon).

This concluding chapter will be, above all, a call for a politics of difference, or a "politics of the otherwise", as proposed by Gibson-Graham (2003: 53–54, cited in Mackenzie's chapter) to contradict homogenising discourses of globalisation. To argue for such a politics, in these closing pages, we will recall some of the political possibilities suggested in Mackenzie's conceptual chapter, reviewing them in the light of the main findings presented in the case studies.

EVERYDAY PRACTICES FOR A PLACE OF THEIR OWN: WINDOWS TO UNDERSTAND THE LOCAL AND THE GLOBAL

In our journeys through villages, forests and fields, we strove to approach issues on gender and land through the windows offered by the daily practices and livelihoods of people we met on the way. We departed from our NGOs, universities, offices and homes, aiming to engage ourselves in critical research on the interactions between gender and land, in contexts impacted by globalisation. In the field, we soon found ourselves adjusting our methodologies and concepts to approach both the many faces of globalisation, and the daily practices constituting the local, dealing with their entangled issues of location and power.

In all cases and in each case distinctly, we intended to identify, at local, regional and trans-national scales and intersections, the pervasive workings of global capital on the interactions between gender and land. Listening to and presenting our research project to the subjects, observing and discussing with interviewees, we interacted with the research subjects through diverse methods of data collection. And, in one way or another, they allowed us to envision their negotiations and, sometimes, conflicts and resistance strategies that emerged from unique social relations between men and women, in defence of their livelihoods and lands made into territories in specific places.

Place became, indeed, a major foundation to understand the particularities of each experience. Specific places—paddy fields, gold mines, mangrove stands, babaçu forests and farms along the oil pipeline—were grounds where difference could be precisely detected and examined as driver of power relations, including negotiations on gender and rights to land. It was from these places, understood as political spaces constructed by everyday practices, that we positioned our questions: How has gender been negotiated in these situations of change in land tenure and use? How have traditional practices and customary rules affected these changes? How were these negotiations inter-related to global processes imposed through structural adjustments implemented by neo-liberal policies?

In each place examined along our tortuous paths, we were able to observe how people—so diverse in their positions in respect of gender, age, marital status, class and ethnicity—were negotiating, contesting, reconsidering, and redefining notions of household, kinship, community and rights to land. As discussed in Mackenzie's chapter, we indeed confirmed in the field that none of these "institutions" delineating the local were given and fixed. Therefore, not even the most isolated village among our sites was autonomous and exempt from the workings of global capital, nor was globalisation itself above the reach of the transformations carried out by these local negotiations. They were continuously and interactively reformulated in the practice of negotiating interests, either convergent or antagonistic, between men and women, young and old, rich and poor, landless and landlords. These negotiations showed us that globalisation is not as self-sufficient and dominant as its promoters have tried to make us believe.

THE MUTUAL CONSTITUTION OF THE GLOBAL AND THE LOCAL

Our findings were, first of all, definitive negations of the dichotomy between the local and the global. What would be less dichotomous than a huge trans-national pipeline penetrating the insides of Cameroonian lands made so local by women's farms, already pregnant of roots and seeds? Symbolic reminders of the intrinsic connection and mutual constitution of the local and the global emerged during fieldwork in each site. Little pieces of gold, trespassing so familiarly in-between the soiled fingers of exhausted shanking ladies, were extracted from local lands to become an integral part of the virtual world of the precious metals' stock markets affecting global economies. Politically correct "ecological" nuts peeled by Amazonian children had to "pass" imposed European standards of quality to grace Christmas tables in Europe and the USA. The babaçu "mother-of-people" palms (*Attalea speciosa*) were slashed from local lands to make room for pastures and consummate the so-called "hamburger-global connection".

Global texts translated into structural adjustments dictated by economic liberalisation tended to be legible in every local context. Under the direction of the World Bank and the IMF, adjustments restructured national economies in general and had specific effects on African, Asian and Latino markets, lands and resources—both natural and social.

After years of IMF-sponsored structural adjustment programmes, by the turn of the Millennium, Cameroon was then once again pressed for further reforms; privatisation was a major goal. Debt relief totalling to more than one billion US dollars did not assure sustainable development and poverty reduction, and Cameroon's economy is still vulnerable to changes in the international oil and cocoa prices. In Ghana, debt relief through the Heavily Indebted Poor Country (HIPC) programme in 2002, and the Multilateral Debt Relief Initiative in 2006 were part of the adjustments, but debt relief had little effective impacts in poverty relief . High prices for gold and cocoa helped sustained GDP growth in 2007; however, sustainable development and wealth distribution is still far from reach. The Millennium Challenge Corporation Compact was signed in 2006, but poverty still haunts Ghanaian local people.

An emblematic example of the interactive proximity between the global and the local can be illustrated by CASM—Community and Artisanal and Small-scale Mining, "*a global networking and coordination facility with a stated mission 'to reduce poverty by improving the environmental, social and economic performance of artisanal and small-scale mining in developing countries*'" (CASM 2008). In spite of its name, CASM is currently chaired by the UK's Department for International Development and is housed at the World Bank headquarters in Washington, D.C. Among donors such as the World Bank, G7 members and trade associations, Tiffany and Company Foundation is a symbolic reminder of how the privatisation of wealth is dependent and constituted by the socialisation of poverty and vice versa. Private enterprises surviving on extraction of natural resources at the expense of exploitation of local people's labour are increasingly creating foundations to deal with the resulting problems. However, as the privatisation of wealth is the cause of poverty, its consequent problems will hardly be solved by these means.

Evidence throughout the chapters confirm Slater's (2003, cited in Mackenzie's chapter) association between poverty and the imposed macro-economic neo-liberal policies. Field observations confirm that the global has been sustained and mutually constituted by the local.

Neo-liberal policies allowed new readings on land as a commodity and reinforced the expansion of land markets through privatisation. Privatisation of land and its extensions—forests, mineral and water resources—made profound alterations in local contexts. Searching for alternative readings of global texts, we examined local contexts through case studies, in the hope of grasping which precise relations had been constructed by men and women facing changes in rights to land and resources. By doing that, we expected to understand how negotiating gender had constituted their rights to land and resources, not only between men and women within communities, but also between them and other social groups, under global processes.

As clearly observed in the case study in Ghana, but also in Brazil, Bolivia, Peru, Vietnam and Cameroon, these processes have been intertwined by contradictory movements of resource concentration and fragmentation. On the one hand, specific resources—gold, timber, cocoa, soy, oil, rice—commodities already consolidated in the global markets, were concentrated in the hands of specific economic stake-holders considered fit to respond to global demands. On the other, marginal resources such as mangroves and babaçu palms, marginal paddy fields, food crops not considered for compensation—mostly managed by women—have endured increasing competition among local stakeholders, tending to cause fragmentation of the natural resources (land and forest) and further disruption of social resources (customary rules and traditional territorial or inheritance rights).

As seen throughout the chapters, neo-liberal policies deployed by structural adjustments were a common presence, introducing the ethos of privatiation in each crevice of local contexts. Either fomenting privatisation of farming land in Vietnam or reinforcing competition in the Brazilian oil market, global processes were an integral part of policy changes affecting local contexts. These policies are conceived to rule and discipline local contexts. However, the very diversity of responses turns the local, in certain ways, illegible to authorities implementing neo-liberal policies. By not understanding the local, control by authorities is rendered incomplete. Difference becomes the dust impeding the smooth running of the allegedly powerful and well-oiled globalisation machine.

GENDER RELATIONS AS PART OF A POLITICS OF DIFFERENCE

Assessment of the impact of globalisation on gender and land was not our final goal. However, as a step of our research, we did assess, at some point, the impact of global processes on gender relations and land rights, registering greater challenges for women, especially poor women. At Cameroonian sites, Endeley found that the pipeline project led women to get less compensation for their losses in land rights. As a result of de-collectivisation efforts, Scott et al. learned that women in Vietnamese sites were losing rights achieved during the socialist regime, due to the return of male household headship under reinstated patriarchal kinship rules. Competition with oil palm (*Elaeis guineensis*) from Malaysian plantations provoked new burdens for women living from the extraction of babaçu palm (*Attalea speciosa*) in Amazonian forest sites visited by Porro. In both mangrove and gold mining areas of Ghana, Awumbila and Tsikata registered how labour relations were heavily marked by gender issues, demanding greater efforts by women to access the same or even less benefits from land and natural resources.

At a first glance in this assessment step, a linear cause-effect process could be read related to global rules and demands determining local contexts, with gender inequalities discriminating against women. However, soon we learned that globalisation was not a sole and main cause impinging linear top-down effects on gender and rights to land. Researching local contexts, Porro realised that structural adjustment and its effects were themselves submitted to diverse readings and adjustments by local people, and gender relations could operate a politics of difference. As warned by Mackenzie, gender, land and globalisation are inter-related and mutually transformed. Although currently this is not a major trend affecting rural social movements as a whole, in particular situations, such as those of the movements of the Babaçu Breaker Women and the Brazil-nut and Rubber Tappers, globalisation has been challenged relevantly by foci of resistance— not always so clearly visible, but of special importance at family and community levels. Gender issues were an integral part of a number of ways in which difference leads to contestation. Also, as pointed out by Tsikata's introduction, from everyday livelihoods (Ghana and Vietnam), through temporary revolts (Cameroon) to resistance grassroots organisations (Brazil), contestation was at the table. The lack of visible and recognised movements of resistance should not make us believe that globalisation has fully dictated the economic and social aspects of local contexts. Likewise, although we have not observed massive contestation by women against gender inequalities, field observations showed that resistance was driving negotiations on gender issues.

In most situations observed, resistance by men, women or both was in fact not a blatant reaction against global forces. Throughout the chapters, we have not read about massive peasant or indigenous movements fighting against ruling classes, and there were no clear manifests crying out loud against global tyranny. Instead, as Tsing (2005) has discussed, just like a wheel on the road needs an opposing force to move forward, it seems that on the road of globalisation, through which apparently we are all impelled to be contained and moved, the wheel of social movements seems indeed to be moving forward in the direction established by neo-liberal paths. However, the differences we observed in the field make the interactions with the road a struggle of rough chafing friction.

The road of globalisation demands homogeneous vehicles, but diversity and inequality were unconcealed presences at all sites. Alternative roads are still utopias, but one can realise that local men and women were not inert to the workings of global capital—be it new standards of quality, forms of land distribution or compensation for land encroachment. Neither autonomous protagonists nor lifeless subordinates, but facing encounters with global forces, men and women have experienced, in all their differences, the interactions evoking "friction", as conceptualised by Tsing (2005):

As a metaphorical image, friction reminds us that heterogeneous and unequal encounters can lead to new arrangements of culture and power. … Speaking of friction is a reminder of the importance of interactions in defining movement, cultural form, and agency. Friction is not just about slowing things down. Friction is required to keep global power in motion. … Friction inflects historical trajectories, enabling, excluding and particularizing. The effects of encounters across difference can be compromising or empowering. Friction is not a synonym of resistance. Hegemony is made as well as unmade with friction. … Friction makes global connection powerful and effective. Meanwhile, without even trying, friction gets in the way of the smooth operation of global power. Difference can disrupt, causing everyday malfunctions as well as unexpected cataclysms. Friction refuses the lie that global power operates as a well-oiled machine. Furthermore, difference sometimes inspires insurrection. Friction can be the fly in the elephant's nose (2005: 5–6).

Insurrection was not an evident trend in our sites yet, in spite of some insightful foci of resistance in the case study from Brazil and strikes by youth in Cameroon against the pipeline's agents. At our sites, there were no massive insurrections or open resistance as well-known movements in certain regions of the country such as the Landless Movement in Brazil (Deere 2001), the Ogoni in the Niger Delta (Awumbila and Tsikata's chapter) or the Asafo in Ghana in past periods (Amanor 2005). In the sites studied, the fly may still be rearranging its wings. Nonetheless, the point here is that, under friction, globalisation does not reign absolute. Friction comes from men and women living ways of life that, day after day, contradict the dictation of global workings in an everyday politics of difference.

Some grassroots organisations such as the Women Babaçu Breakers' Movement are occupying juridical grounds, where laws and rights are created, interpreted, and implemented, to fight for their differences. They occupy, as women, the juridical field as a "place of concurrence for the monopoly of the right to spell the right" (Bourdieu 1989: 212). In most cases, formalised grassroots organisations were not major actors, but women played the politics of difference in everyday livelihoods. This was the case of dona Mariana

Lino in Porro's chapter, whose mobilisation related to everyday religious practices that sustained her stake in the land disputed with the cattle rancher favoured by development policies. Gender relations between women babaçu breakers and male cattle ranchers brought out differences in the power relations in homogenising contexts of globalisation.

DIFFERENCE CALLING FOR DIALOGUES BETWEEN CUSTOMARY RIGHTS AND LAWS

Globalisation has been presented as the ideal materialisation of reliable and independent "all-equal" genderless individuals enjoying free market economies enabled by structural adjustments. Gender inequality in accessing land, especially through land markets, is an example to the contrary (Razavi 2003, Deere 2003). As a consequence, customary rights dictating specific roles and rules for each member of community would fade. However, years of adjustments and other neo-liberal expressions have not been able to eliminate either kinship relations and customary rights, or forms of labour relations diverging from "work for a boss", much less gender differences towards land rights. Although an intrusive presence at each site, globalisation was also affected by these labour relations and rights, and by the people's agency in living them. The perceived outcomes of this mutual constitution were diverse in terms of how gender equity is associated with customary rules and tradition, under current laws.

In Cameroon, women affected by the pipeline perceived themselves as having greater access to land under customary rights than under rules promoted by the promoters of the pipeline. In Vietnam, women alleged decreased control of land benefits due to reinstated traditional kinship rules under the de-collectivisation processes. As we have seen throughout the chapters, varied combinations of laws, rights and practices were part of gender negotiations, but current laws have not been able to effectively protect women in particular, and local people in general.

Formally, a trend towards greater attention to women was observed in recent national laws regulating rights to land in the studied sites. Either based on rationales of greater attention to women positively influencing efficiency for development, or gender equity as a matter of justice, these laws—now no longer new—are fine-tuned to the modernity suggested by neo-liberal policies. At least on paper, they have contradicted conventions of institutional and cultural practices, as well as customary norms, which discriminate against women's rights to land. What has been observed in practice, however, is far from what these laws are allegedly intending to assure.

For example, although women are the vast majority of farmers in Cameroon, customary systems of the studied ethnic groups deny women's rights to land tenure and control. More than 30 years after Cameroonian official laws were issued to formally confront these customary rules and practices on land tenure, people continue to live under traditions that maintain men's primacy over land ownership, while women continue to be referred to as "assets or chattels". This customary tenure is the prevalent *de facto* system ruling the majority of communities affected by the pipeline. And yet, till date, women's access to land was perceived by the interviewees as more secure under traditional systems than in situations under the rules of the trans-national project, far from the modernity alleged by the pipeline agents.

Similar to other sites, at least formally, gender equality as a goal has been a mandatory item, almost a "stamp" for political correctness, in World Bank and related development agency projects. In practice, however, the matter of gender equality was never effectively addressed. As well illustrated by the narratives of women in the Leboudi community in Cameroon, pipeline promoters did ask women about their worries regarding the pipeline, but the gathered information was just overlooked, and women were kept uninformed about the relevant matters of the project.

Likewise in Ghana sites, regardless of its productive form either for farming or mining activities, women had use rights, but usually did not own land or control its use. Awumbila and Tsikata found that access to the mangroves and mines and to the obtained benefits were gendered. Both women and men's labour were intrinsically connected to gender inequalities in land tenure in their communities, even before they started to deal with these resources. As customary tenure norms privilege men against women, women had greater difficulties negotiating their access claims in contexts affected by globalisation, resulting in increased inequalities in access to land and its resources. Although in Ghana male migration has allowed women greater access to land, male absence has also brought further difficulties, and instead of decreasing inequalities of customary tenure systems, new rules seem to intensify the burden on women. Moreover, placing land as a commodity in the land market brought women face to face with new challenges. They had to deal with unfamiliar transaction costs in addition to already established discrimination in customary forms of land tenure and access.

In Vietnam, under collectivisation, women indeed had greater formal rights to access land. However, in addition to their work in the cooperatives, women had to struggle to sustain their families from the so called 5 per cent family farms. Under de-collectivisation, post-revolutionary laws stated greater gender equality, but reinstated kinship-based norms ruling access and control of land and maintained traditional discrimination against women. In addition, de-collectivisation did not seem to eliminate the effects of patri-local post-marital residence patterns, low female literacy and family opposition to women's ownership of land. Rather, it brought new dynamics challenging women's emancipation.

Similarly, in Brazil, Bolivia and Peru, most recent land laws have been amended to ensure women's rights to land titling. In Brazil, programmes related to land redistribution have promoted changes at executive governmental agency levels, such as normative instructions assuring equal rights in cases of separation or divorce of couples to whom reformed lands had been granted. However, in practice, these advances have not been able to keep up with the current state of discrimination against women in regard to land ownership. In spite of legal and formal advances, practices and realities have not progressed as expected. Privatisation and increasing expansion of land markets have furthered women's difficulties in attaining and maintaining land ownership, which would increase their bargaining power in the diverse struggles they face within the household, community and society.

Laws formally stating women's rights to land are necessary but not sufficient to assure the grasp of these rights. Understanding local differences and particularities of women's lives in their relationship to land is essential for adequate laws and programmes.

KINSHIP AND CUSTOMARY RIGHTS IN CONTEXTS OF GLOBALISATION: CHALLENGES FOR LOCAL CAPACITY BUILDING

Certainly, kinship and customary systems, as well as other social relations based on tradition, are not static over time and place, nor free from intersections with other systems. Rather, as we have discussed in Mackenzie's chapter, global trends reflected in law and policy changes are inter-connected with the dynamics based on local realities.

De-collectivisation in Vietnam, for example, as an early expression of powerful global trends of privatisation, decreased the dominance of cooperatives, and renewed the importance of households as a very local scenario of patriarchal kinship relations. Certainly, today's patriarchal relations are not exactly the same as before collectivisation, and will face current dynamics on different grounds. As the patriarchal household regains a central role as the unit in control of the production and access to land, thus displacing the cooperatives, new dynamics and configurations are expected. Disadvantages for women in negotiating their rights were already observed in the field. Although definitive answers to the outcomes of these negotiations are not yet possible, the woman who lived practices and rights under collective schemes will certainly face these disadvantages from decollectivisation with renewed perspectives on the new laws and rules.

Some answers are possible, though. As Endeley suggests in the case of Cameroon, knowledge may be key to defining the outcomes of negotiating gender. The power of knowledge, nonetheless, is not simply access to information about new laws, but is related to how one appropriates the accessed information and builds it up in the construction of the local, individually and collectively.

This capacity can challenge the manner in which knowledge about the global has been produced, and as a consequence, the manner in which local people have been submitted to its power. The idea is to bring about a "counter-narrative whose principles and practices '*recognize particularity and contingency, honor difference and otherness, and cultivate local capacity*'' (Gibson-Graham 2003: 54, 51, emphasis in original, cited by Mackenzie).

According to the Cameroon study, on the one hand, ignorance of rights assured by the new laws allows for the maintenance of discrimination against women promoted by customary systems and kinship rules. On the other hand, disregarding social cohesion associated with these same customary systems may also result in not accessing the benefits of new laws. At the Cameroon sites, especially because women's rights to land and the benefits thereof are mediated by men, complex negotiations take place, involving individual and collective endeavours. Therefore, local capacity building must necessarily include both men and women.

As mentioned in the Mackenzie chapter, Walker (2003:143) argues that "*the focus on individual rights for women needs to be tempered by a deeper appreciation of the importance of household membership in poor women's lives*" as local women themselves often deal with their specific problems without separating their own interests from those of their husbands or families (either because of ignorance of their individual rights or as a conscious strategy as recalled in the Vietnam case study). Although women continue to face unfavourable gender relations within their households and customary systems, family and community are still the sites where they manage to mobilise support through networking. Therefore, considering the actual range of available options, a joint effort is needed to define practices that combine promotion of women's individual rights and of "*a more gender-equitable reconfiguration of household and community ties*" (Mackenzie).

Within this new reconfiguration, as the study in Brazil suggests, not only knowledge about new laws and rights, but also of the self, of who is the subject in charge of the negotiations, define the outcomes of negotiating gender.

For each case study, one can ask "*how is a subject position such as that of 'woman' or 'man' brought into being through the negotiation of rights to the land?*" (Mackenzie). As the Brazilian babaçu nut breaker woman affirmed in Porro's chapter, her position as a woman itself came into being through the process of fighting for her traditionally occupied lands:

> I believe it was my participation [in the social movements] that began through the [land] conflict. Sometimes, I say that until 1985 [the year when she and other villagers fought for their traditional land], I was another person. I was a person of the female sex, but I was not really a woman, and now I am. (Maria Adelina Chagas, quoted in Porro chapter)

In her view, therefore, the construction of her own gender, which was intertwined with the construction of land, was a consequence of the process of local capacity. Meanings of land may change just as the meaning of gender itself has undergone transformations. Otherwise, using women and men as fixed and undifferentiated analytical categories would not provide the questions necessary to reach answers in such a complex intersection between kinship, customary rights and official laws. The achievement of rights, translated into actual practices, emanating either from attained laws or transformation of cultural norms, is undoubtedly a time-and-place specific process.

As seen in the case of the Vietnamese southern community, where land value had increased, frictions were mediated by kinship norms in varied directions. Once land markets imposed new situations, men wanted to revert to the tradition of daughters forfeiting their inheritance rights for the sake of their brothers, aiming to retain male ownership. Meanwhile, women reclaimed retention of their rights, also alleging traditional kinship norms. Friction between tradition and new market rules led to increased questioning of family as a monolithic unit, outlining conflicts and the risks of landlessness. Similarly, in Ghana, increasing commoditisation of mangroves resulted in more structured and formal mangrove tenure. These processes of change were plagued with contestations and conflicts.

As said in the Mackenzie chapter, a critical point in our research was to understand these processes—both material and discursive— through which women and men negotiate the meaning of being a "wife" or a "husband", a "daughter" or a "brother", a "landowner" or a "tenant" on the land. As these are not fixed positions, but are in continuous transformation through either friction or resistance in the ever changing local contexts, they are the subject of contestation and negotiation at household, community and global levels. Also, because these are not fixed positions, continuous research is needed to envision other possible forms of gender relations and rights to land.

ANOTHER WORLD (IN THE SAME LANDS) IS POSSIBLE: REVISING THE ROLE OF THE NATION STATE

In no other chapter than the one on Cameroon, was the sense of inevitability of globalisation so pervasive and final. The 1000 kilometer pipeline was already there, buried forever. Friction and eventual resistance, such as the Meyang strike, were not against the trans-national development project itself, but against the modes of compensation for the consummated violation of traditional lands. Contestation was not against the already installed pipeline, allegedly a public project to eradicate poverty through compensation. Instead, struggles were about whom, how much, when, these returns would compensate this unavoidable co-existence.

The catalogue prepared by COTCO, from which people had to pick what they wanted as compensation, was the ultimate symbol of settled matters and the ironic freedom of "choice" offered by global capital, and the "choices" made would apparently signal consent. Women expressed their lack of knowledge on how the matters of compensation were decided, and much less how the whole project of the pipeline was settled. The global was already there, inevitable. This freedom of choice made within a previously demarcated containment was also pointed out by the Vietnam researchers, as they quoted the promoters of globalisation: "rural incomes will grow more rapidly where households have *freedom* to respond to changed market or other circumstances and can *choose* input or marketing services from a *range of competitive suppliers*" (MARD and UNDP 1998: 39, emphasis added, cited in Scott et al.'s chapter).

Privatisation, competition and entrepreneurship, understood as prioritising individual choices and gains, even at the expense of collective well-being, were aspects imbued with the imposed logic of globalisation. In this sense, neo-liberal policies have been assumed mostly as a neutral technology adapted to fix the old-fashioned maladies of collectivisation, customary and other traditional norms, to implement efficient adjustments, completely detached from the political arena. As seen in our case studies, globalisation has presented itself as unavoidable, a universal truth supposedly independent from, and above, all the disputes between groups with differentiated power.

In Brazil, local leaders discussing economic alternatives to protect babaçu as the foundation for their traditional communities' livelihoods, felt globalisation *"just like a completed spider web uniting all possibilities, without alternative exits," "all done and ready"*. Impacting natural resources, including babaçu, the Brazilian government is now pushing for bio-fuel production—deemed as the main response, economic and ecological, to climate change—but only from those sources deemed competitive in the international market. Babaçu is not being considered among them; rather, "the mother of the people" was assumed to be a plague damaging pasture expansion. Today the news portrays the debate over bio-fuels vs. food for local people as settled matters, describing the global web as follows: the US government gives subsidies for thousands of US farmers for bio-fuel production. The maize to produce ethanol takes the place of soy production. The world's soy price goes up and encourages Brazilian farmers to clear Amazonian forests for new soy fields, and to buy up large expanses of established cattle pasture. Cattle ranchers move further into the Amazon, and cattle feed becomes more costly, promoting further forest conversion to pasture. Much of the Brazilian soy is shipped to feed cattle in Europe (Phillips 2008.) There is no definite research to explain these webs, but higher consumption patterns of beef, fuel and soy by emergent countries are deemed as unavoidable as the workings of global capital.

This unavoidability has been conceptually unmasked (Mackenzie's chapter, Bourdieu 1998) and, in practice, is under constant friction and acts of resistance. Part of this sense of inevitability comes from a characteristic of globalisation, the lack of a personified and recognisable entity mentoring and driving its expressions. Although IMF and the World Bank have been charged responsible, the dominance of market forces tends to make it difficult to hold anyone responsible.

. In terms of land, in past attempts for agrarian reforms, it was clear that large estate owners and land grabbers were the adversaries against small farmers and traditional communities. The responsibility to solve land rights and allocation were clearly attributed to the state. In the transition from allocation by the state to greater prominence of land markets and the private sector defining agrarian issues, it became difficult to clearly identify opponents and easier to spread divergence within communities.

While frictions and resistance observed at local contexts do not evaporate in an ethereal global space, the nation-state is still the scenario to look at for answers to struggles by local people. Interviewees have indicated the responsibility of the nation-state, and the responsibility of national governments in an era of globalisation. As the Chief of Akongo in Cameroon said, *"there was a lot of disdain from COTCO towards the local population and this seemed to be encouraged by our own government. Each time the population came up to defend their rights it was the Sub-Divisional Officer who sent policemen to disperse the population. As a result, the human factor was not taken into consideration in this project."*

Surely, conflicts and alliances between chiefs and government in Cameroon and Ghana, and local authorities and central governments in Vietnam and Bolivia, Brazil and Peru, are also integral parts of the nation-state. Therefore, the contradictions resulting from relations between national governments and global institutions promoting structural adjustments are deeply impregnated with these kinds of frictions, and provoke fractures and crevices in the allegedly solid workings of global capital.

Although Brazil has followed directions for structural adjustments, managing to entirely pay its external debt, and "pass" many global ordeals, the neo-liberal project was not fully accomplished. In Latin American countries, *"neoliberalism is not a coherent, homogeneous and totalizing project, [that] the prevailing logic of structural adjustment is far from inevitable, and it is precisely at the interstices generated by these contradictions that social movements sometimes articulate their politics"* (Paoli and Telles 1998). An emblematic illustration is that of Brazil, which in April 2008 earned its investment-grade credit rating by Standard and Poor, after undergoing structural adjustments, just before the 2008 food crisis came about. A babaçu breaker woman ironically comments on this achievement in the neo-liberal project: *"[Brazil] paid its debts? Good! Has put on a good face for foreign creditors? Good too! Bad is for me who has to pay R$ 5.50 to eat beans. Who is the one to assure my beans on the table? The bank? Babaçu is who puts beans on my plate. That is why we fight for it."* (Pedreiras, July 2008).

Guardians of marginal resources are overlooked by global markets focused on commodities such as timber, soy and beef. Social movements among the babaçu breaker women and other traditional communities channel friction and local resistance to articulate their politics in the national scenario. In Brazil for example, in a national scenario structurally adjusted by and for neo-liberal policies, it is not a surprise that although the number of land conflicts in general have decreased, the majority of families involved in land conflicts were traditional farmers, especially women, struggling against agri-business (CPT 2008). Resistance has come from where difference poses a challenge to globalisation. In the interstices lived by babaçu breaker, rubber tapper, riverine, and black communities, gender justice and respect for their identities and territories are the main stakes against a national government privileging international agri-business interests.

Similarly, after five years, the Ghana government's Land Administration Project (LAP), shows no signs of a potential to reduce poverty and enhance economic/social growth by improving security of tenure and developing the land markets. This programme, funded by multi-donor supporters, was to establish an efficient system of land administration—both state and customary—based on clear, coherent polices and laws supported by appropriate institutional structures. However, friction between local realities and global discourses has led to critiques of the governmental capacity to promote tenure security and organise land markets through title registration, adjudication of boundary disputes, consolidation and conciliation of land laws and the institutional reform of land tenure agencies. Addressing gender inequality in customary land and resource rights is another unaccomplished challenge faced by the nation-state. In this situation, national societies and social movements promoting women's rights to land may find support in global connections, embracing them in other forms of globalisation, not in just its strict economic aspect.

TRANSFORMING GLOBAL ENGAGEMENTS INTO A POLITICS OF DIFFERENCE: A CALL FOR FURTHER RESEARCH

Although the variables examined in each chapter were mostly related to globalisation in its economic aspect, the results in terms of effective access to and use of land, and gender equity were often associated with the realm of rights. At the end of this book, we call for further research on rights, to better understand these connections. Like the Women's Union and social researchers in Vietnam, social organisations, movements and institutions around the world found hope in another face of global connections: concerted efforts for women's rights to land at international arenas, as related to human rights. As recalled by Scott et al., these global engagements resulted in relevant achievements, especially the CEDAW—Convention on the Elimination of all forms of Discrimination against Women—in 1979. The contributions of this convention to women and feminist movements in each nation were felt and expressed in advances in national constitutions and laws of their countries.

These global engagements also have close interactions with processes of mainstreaming gender in major international agencies of development, which in turn influenced women's rights to land. As most of these agencies are simultaneously enforcing neo-liberal policies on African, Asian and Latin American countries, scepticism and close watching for effective changes are an integral part of these interactions (Kurian 2000). Nonetheless, it is also true that many relevant notions and concepts on gender equity emerged from these domains of development and had concrete effects at local level. These contradictions and eventual achievements lead us to examine the economic aspects of globalisation under other perspectives.

These achievements were associated with global engagements in favour of human rights as universal rights (UN 1948), including women's equal rights to land and related issues of access to natural resources and identity: "[*W]ithin the past half century notions of human rights, environmental conservation and pluricultural autonomy developed along with and in response to the changes brought about by global integration"* (Deere 2005). These interactions between the realm of rights and global connections demand a closer examination of the actors involved, and a better understanding of this object of inquiry.

The last decades saw renewed worldwide manifestations of what has been called "new social movements". Well known social movements of the 20th century, human and indigenous rights, black movements and feminism, were joined in their last decades by those for gay rights, formal recognition of ethnic identities and environmentalism. These social movements labelled as "new," are connected into global engagements, pressuring for changes in specific domains. Scholars analysing them found their emergence not in class conflicts, pointing out that their opponent target was not the dominant class, nor was the state the main arena of contestation. Such movements do not act in open confrontation against the government, but instead challenge dominant codes driving society, proposing new symbols and values (Cohen 1985, Meluci 1989).

Mobilisation in these cases aims against oppression seen as universals: women's discrimination, homophobia, environmental destruction, ethnic erosion, genocides and so on. The universalising character of these global engagements gives momentum capable of opening relevant channels of negotiation with specific agencies and institutions in global domains. However, this universalising character also demands careful consideration by those who want to understand local situations such as our case studies.

Rabinow (2002) discusses how efforts founded on human rights conceptualised in a universalising logic find a common language with liberal sovereignty discourses. Considered exclusively through a universalising logic, rights of local women struggling for land lose their political grip on locality, understood within a politics of place as theorised by Gibson-Graham (Mackenzie's chapter). Once detached from the locality as a political place, they become vulnerable in domains of truth that inform neo-liberal policies. In the absence of counter-discourses, the dialogue between globally engaged social movements and the promoters of globalisation may imply new forms of subordination and disciplinary power exerted by the latter over the former.

Therefore, in the realm of rights, women may indeed find support from achieved human rights, to better negotiate gender in situations of change in land tenure under globalisation. Nonetheless, such rights achieved through global engagements should not reduce identities, suppress life histories, and preconceive places. Rather, rights must recognise and include values that have emerged from each place. By transforming global engagements towards human rights into a politics of difference, local subjects' values and the political trajectories that construct them will be precisely understood. Only then will the inevitable conflicts between classes, gender, and race effectively enter negotiation.

> Human rights are misconceived if it is understood as a breviary of values: Rights talk can do no more than formalize the terms in which conflicts of values are made precise and therefore rendered amenable to compromise and solution. This is their dynamic: They do not, in themselves, resolve arguments; they create the steadily burgeoning case law, which in turn expands the ambit of human rights claims (Ignatieff 1999:321, cited in Rabinow 2002).

The discussion above finds echoes from our case studies. Different from those "peasant wars of the twentieth century" with well-defined contestants studied by Wolf (1969), the peasantry of the 21st century analysed in this book was not involved in clear, open rebellions against the state, at least not during our research in the field. Strikes by young men in the pipeline case were for employment and compensation within the given structure. Even when their form of oppression was associated with a specific class, like in the case of Mariana Lino against the cattle rancher in Chapter 5, there were no clear attempts to dethrone the ruling class. Struggles for women's access and ownership of land, as observed at our sites in several situations, seemed in a mode of action similar to those conceptualised as the "new social movements".

Struggles were apparently restricted to everyday obstacles, without moves against structural social changes. And yet, as Ong (1987: 180) learned while studying peasant women in contexts of

292 Noemi Miyasaka Porro

globalisation in Malaysia, the "*Marxist notion of false consciousness no longer suffices*" to explain their social relations under global capital. Although friction is not the same as resistance, neither is it a passive, unproductive motion moved by false consciousness. "*Even the most utopian initiatives—say, human rights for women of the global south— are contaminated by the logics of power, and, yet, too, they carry our dreams for justice*" (Cheah 1997, cited by Tsing 2005:269)

The very search for an explanation for the lack of recognisable acts of resistance and unifying models of collective action may be misplaced, and this too carries intentions of containment, a disciplining power intending to dictate ways of resisting. The explanation of a politics of difference, in interaction with global forces, will come from a better understanding of how people are living their very human right of being themselves, in their own places.

> If the predominant theme in the twentieth century was to select a unifying model for action, predicated on dichotomized interests that minimized the expression of difference, the theme running through social movements of the twenty first century is the right of participants to be themselves (Nash 2005:22).

FINAL WORDS

We went to the field aiming to answer the questions of "*how has gender been negotiated in contexts of globalisation? How have the workings of global capital interacted with the construction of land and women's rights to it?*"

As diverse as our backgrounds as researchers, we found a diversity of answers for these questions. In all four countries, we found the sameness of structural adjustment favouring privatisation, competition for resources, and commoditisation of essential aspects of life, including land. And yet, in places submitted to decades of these apparently homogenising efforts, we have found neither a common pattern of subordinated responses nor unifying modes of resistance. In contexts of globalisation, we have found men and women negotiating diverse forms of living their gender. In each place, negotiations on gender were strongly affected by their relations to land. In some places, the construction of gender was inseparable from the construction of land as a territory. The workings of global capital were indeed transforming livelihoods, shaking the foundations of their modes of production and reproduction, in the forms of pipelines, displacement to marginal lands and resources, imposition of new quality standards, subordination to market competition, or new forms of land use. Nonetheless, by constructing land and struggling for equal rights to it, men and women have also shaped the workings of global capital through local ways of living.

In this mutual constitution of the global and the local, we argue for a politics of difference where the local can be respected as a space of negotiations in which men and women can participate with rights to be themselves, in lands as places of their own.

REFERENCES

Alvarez, S., E. Dagnino, and A. Escobar, 1998, "Introduction: the Cultural and the Political in Latin American Social Movements", in Alvarez, S., E. Dagnino, and A. Escobar, (eds), *Cultures of Politics and Politics of Cultures: Re-visioning Latin American Social Movements.* Boulder: Westview Press.

Amanor, K.S., 2005, "Night Harvesters, Forest Hoods and Saboteurs: Struggles over Land Expropriation in Ghana", in Moyo, S., and P.Yeros, (eds), *Reclaiming the Land: the Resurgence of Rural Movements in Africa, Asia and Latin America.* New York: Zed Books, pp. 102–117.

Bourdieu, P., 1989, A Força do Direito: Elementos para uma Sociologia do Campo Jurídico", in O Poder Simbólico. São Paulo: Difel, pp. 209–254.

———, 1998, *Acts of Resistance against the Tyranny of the Market.* New York: The New Press and Polity Press.

CASM, 2008, Community and Artisanal Small Scale Mining: Who we are. http://www.artisanalmining.org.

Cohen, J.L., 1985, "Strategy or Identity: New Theoretical Paradigms and Contemporary Social Movements", *Social Research* 52: 663–716.

CPT. 2008. Comissão Pastoral da Terra. Revista Pastoral da Terra jan-mar 2008, ano 33, número 191. http://www.cptnac.com.br/pub/publicacoes/8ef053e5f0195a24650bcb0922 ce5a71.pdf

Deere, C.D., 2003, "Women's Land Rights and Rural Social Movements in the Brazilian Agrarian Reform", in Razavi, S. (ed), *Agrarian Change, Gender and Land Rights.* Oxford: Blackwell Publishing Ltd, pp. 257–288.

———, 2005. The Feminization of Agriculture? Economic Restructuring in Rural Latin America. Occasional Paper written for the preparation of the report "Gender Equality: Striving for Justice in an Unequal World." Geneva: UNRISD.

Escobar, A., 1992, "Culture, Economics, and Politics in Latin American Social Movements Theory and research", in Escobar, A., and S.E. Alvarez, (eds), *The Making of Social Movements in Latin America: Identity, Strategy, and Democracy.* Boulder: Westview Press, pp. 62–85.

——, 2001, "Place, Economy, and Culture in a Post-Development Era", in Prazniak, R., and A. Dirlik, (eds), *Places and Politics in an Age of Globalization.* Boulder: Rowman & Littlefield Publishers, Inc, pp. 193–218.

Hilson, G., 2001, A Contextual Review of the Ghanaian Small-scale Mining Industry. Report commissioned by the MMSD (Mining, Minerals and Sustainable Development) project of IIED—International Institute for Environment and Development. London: IIED.

Ignatieff, M., 1999, "Human Rights", in Carla Hesse and Robert Post, (eds), *Human Rights in Political Transition: From Gettysburg to Bosnia.* New York: Zone Books, pp. 313–324.

Kurian, P., 2000, *Engendering the Environment? Gender in the World Bank's Environmental Policy.* Burlington, VT: Ashgate Publishing Company.

Melucci, A., 1989, *Nomads of the Present: Social Movements and Individual Needs in Contemporary Society.* Philadelphia: Temple University Press.

Nash, J., 2005, "Social Movements and Global Processes in Nash, J. (ed), *Social Movements: an Anthropological Reader.* Malden, MA: Blackwell Publishing Ltd, pp. 1–26.

Paoli, M.C. and Telles, V.S., 1998, Social Rights: Conflicts and Negotiations in Contemporary Brazil. pp. 64–92. In Alvarez, S., E. Dagnino, and A. Escobar, (eds), *Cultures of Politics and Politics of Cultures: Re-visioning Latin American Social Movements.* Boulder: Westview Press, pp. 64–94.

Phillips, T., 2008, Space imaging gives the lie to Brazil's recent "great achievement" of halting rainforest destruction. Correspondent in Rio de Janeiro. The Guardian, January 25, 2008.

Razavi, S., 2003, "Introduction: Agrarian Change, Gender and Land Rights", in Razavi, S., (ed), *Agrarian Change, Gender and Land Rights.* Oxford: Blackwell Publishing Ltd, pp. 2–32.

UN, 1948, Universal Declaration of Human Rights. http://www.un.org/overview/rights.html

Wolf, E., 1969, *Peasant Wars of the Twentieth Century.* New York: Harper Torchbooks.

Notes on Contributors

Dzodzi Tsikata is a Senior Research Fellow at Institute of Statistical, Social and Economic Research (ISSER) and Deputy Head of the Centre for Gender Studies and Advocacy (CEGENSA) at the University of Ghana. Her research interests are the areas of gender and livelihoods, gender and development policy and practice, land and resource tenures and the politics of land tenure reforms. She has several publications on these subjects including a book, *Living in the Shadow of the Large Dams: Long Term Responses of Lakeside and Downstream Communities of Ghana's Volta River Project* (2006).

Pamela Golah worked as a Program Officer with the Women's Rights and Citizenship Program at the International Development Research Centre, Canada. In 2009, she joined the Research and Evaluation Branch at Citizenship and Immigration Canada as a Policy and Research Analyst.

Ann Whitehead is Emeritus Professor of Anthropology at the University of Sussex, where for many years she has also researched and taught on gender and development issues. A contributor to foundational debates on feminist engagement with development and on theorising gender, she has had a wide engagement with national and international feminist politics and has written extensively on economic change and changing gender relations in rural Africa. She has co-authored (with Andrea Cornwall and Buzz Harrison) two recent books: *Feminisms and Development: Contradictions, Contestations and Challenges* and *Gender Myths and Feminist Fables: The Struggle for Interpretive Power in Development.*

A. Fiona D. Mackenzie is Professor, Department of Geography and Environmental Studies at Carleton University, Ottawa. In addition to journal articles, she is author of *Land, Ecology and Resistance in Kenya, 1880-1952* (1998). Her present research focuses on community-centred land reform in Scotland.

Allison Goebel has a PhD from the Department of Sociology at the University of Alberta. She is currently Associate Professor of Environmental Studies and Gender Studies at Queen's University in Canada. She is the author of *Gender and Land Reform. The Zimbabwean Experience* (2005), and numerous scholarly articles relating to land, gender, livelihoods, urban housing issues and environments in southern Africa

Mariama Awumbila is Head, Centre for Migration Studies and also Senior Lecturer, Department of Geography and Resource Development at the University of Ghana. She holds a Post Graduate Diploma (Population Studies) from the University of Ghana and a PhD (Geography) from the University of Newcastle Upon Tyne, UK. She has undertaken extensive research and published in the areas of migration, livelihoods and development, land and natural resource tenure and management, gender and development in Africa.

Joyce B. M. Endeley is Professor and Head, Department of Women and Gender Studies, and Director of Academic Affairs at the University of Buea. Her research interests include gender and agricultural development, gender and development policy, programme and project analysis and evaluation, women's empowerment and livelihoods concerns, gender and access to and control over credit schemes, land resources and higher education. She has several publications and has edited as well as co-authored a book, *The Social Impact of the Chad-Cameroon Oil Pipeline: How Industrial Development Affects Gender Relations, Land Tenure, and Local Culture* (2007).

Noemi Miyasaka Porro is a Brazilian agricultural engineer from the University of São Paulo, with a Masters in Tropical Conservation and Development and a Ph.D. in Anthropology (University of Florida). She worked as a social practitioner for grassroots organisations in the Amazon for over two decades, and since 2008, has been a researcher and professor in the Family Agriculture graduate programme at the Federal University of Pará, Brazil.

Luciene Dias Figueiredo holds a BA in Education and a Masters in Family Agriculture. She is currently a doctoral student in Anthropology at the Federal University of Pará. Since 1989, she has worked for rural grassroots organizations in the State of Maranhâo, Amazon, Brazil, where she remains as a social practitioner and researcher at the Inter State Movement of the Babaçu Breaker Women.

Elda Vera Gonzalez is a leader at RONAP—Organic Collectors of Amazonian nuts of Peru. She holds and runs a concession of Brazil-nut groves in the Peruvian Amazonian forests, and has participated in research and initiatives for sustainable development.

Sissy Nakashima Bello, a biologist, works as a researcher on environmental conservation projects in the Amazon, with a non-governmental organisation: Herencia—Interdisciplinaria para el Desarollo Sustenible, Cobija, Pando, Bolivia.

Alfredo Wagner Berno de Almeida is an anthropologist, senior researcher and professor at the University of the State of the Amazonas, Brazil. He has researched and supported social movements of traditional people and communities in the Amazon for over three decades, and is currently coordinating the project New Social Cartography of the Amazon.

Steffanie Scott is Associate Professor in the Department of Geography and Environmental Management and Director of the Local Economic Development Master's program at the University of Waterloo in Waterloo, Canada. Her current research addresses local food systems, agro-food system sustainability, and agrarian transition in Vietnam and China. Her past work examined livelihood vulnerability and access to land among small farmers and female-headed households through Vietnam's decollectivisation and land allocation process. Her work has been published in *Women's Studies International Forum*; *Agriculture and Human Values*; *Urban Geography*; *International Development Planning Review*; *Regional Studies*, and other journals. She is also co-chair of the Waterloo Region Food System Roundtable.

Danièle Bélanger is Associate Professor at the University of Western Ontario, Canada, and holds the Canada Research Chair in Population, Gender and Development. Her research focuses on issues of gender, families and migration in Asia. She has been working on Vietnam since the early 1990s. She is the co-editor of the recent collection *Reconfiguring Families in Contemporary Vietnam* (2009). Her most recent articles appeared or are forthcoming in *Ethnic and Racial Studies, Citizenship Studies* and *Current Sociology*.

Nguyen Thi Van Anh is Head of Research Division at the Institute for Social Development Studies, a non-governmental, non-profit organisation based in Hanoi. Van Anh obtained her BA in psychology from University of Rostov on Don (Russia) in 1986 and an MA in Demography at the Australian National University in 1997. She worked for a government research institution for 18 years and for FAO on gender for one year. Van Anh's major fields of study are gender, reproductive health and HIV/AIDS.

Khuat Thu Hong, is Co-Director of the Institute for Social Development Studies (ISDS), a non-governmental, non-profit organisation located in Hanoi. She has a BA in Psychology from the Moscow State University (in former USSR) in 1984 and a PhD in Sociology from the Institute of Sociology, Hanoi in 1997. Hong worked for the main Vietnam Government research institution for sixteen years before she moved to UNDP - Vietnam in 2000-2001 as a gender specialist. In 2002 Hong helped to found ISDS and became its Co-Director. Hong's major fields of studies include gender, sexuality, reproductive and sexual health and HIV/AIDS.